The

English-Only

Question

The
English-Only
Question

An Official Language

for Americans?

DENNIS BARON

Yale University Press   New Haven and London

Designed by Sonia L. Scanlon. Set in Trump with
Gill Sans display type by The Composing Room of
Michigan, Inc., Grand Rapids, Michigan. Printed in the
United States of America by Vail-Ballou Press, Bingham-
ton, New York.

The paper in this book meets the guidelines for
permanence and durability of the Committee on
Production Guidelines for Book Longevity of the
Council on Library Resources.

Library of Congress Cataloging-in-Publication Data
Baron, Dennis E.
    The English-only question : an official language for
Americans? / Dennis Baron.
    p. cm.
    Includes bibliographical references.
    ISBN 0–300–04852–1 (cloth)
         0–300–05660–5 (pbk.)
    1. Language policy—United States. 2. English
language—Political aspects. I. Title.
P119.32.U6B37   1991
306.4'4973–dc20   90–32041
                        CIP

A catalogue record for this book is
available from the British Library.

10   9   8   7   6   5   4   3

For Jonathan

Contents

Preface

The protection of the Constitution extends to all,—to those who speak other languages as well as to those born with English on the tongue. Perhaps it would be highly advantageous if all had ready understanding of our ordinary speech, but this cannot be coerced by methods which conflict with the Constitution,—a desirable end cannot be promoted by prohibited means.
—*Meyer v. Nebraska*, 1923

My first encounter with English as an official language occurred when I was younger and living in New York City and I went to exercise my civic duty by registering to vote. Things are different in the Big Apple now, but at the time registration was not an easy process: mine involved a circuitous trip to the Board of Elections in lower Manhattan and the presentation of my freshly minted Ivy League master's degree in English literature.

In those days in New York it was necessary to present a diploma indicating completion of the eighth grade in a school where English was the language of instruction. Otherwise, I would have had to prove to the registrars then and there that I could read and write English. My brand-new license to teach English in New York City high schools, which I also brought with me, did *not* satisfy New York's stringent voting test. Indeed, although they accepted my credentials, the registrars had the legal authority to disregard my graduate school diploma if they so desired and make me take the English literacy test anyway. There were no bilingual ballots; legislators found the very idea laughable. When the English literacy test was first proposed at the New York State constitutional convention in 1915, one delegate supporting the measure assumed that bilingual ballots were unthinkable: "Until we are ready to print the ballot in the language of the voter I favor requiring the voter to read the language of the ballot" (New York State 1916, 3:3161).

In 1965, when I was registering, I did not pay much attention to the English-only language requirement. I had just gotten my first teaching job (having passed the FBI fingerprint check required of all the city's teachers) and I was simply happy to be allowed to vote. The literacy test was, for me, a minor nuisance. I did not then appreciate that such tests frequently served as vehicles for discriminating on the basis of religion, gender, and national origin. According to the legal expert Arnold Leibowitz (1976, 455–56), American literacy tests have all been intentionally discriminatory. The first such statutes in Connecticut and Massachusetts were instigated by the Native American, or Know Nothing, party in the 1850s and aimed at the Irish population of those states. Southern literacy tests instituted after the Civil War were anti-black. California's test (1892) was aimed at Hispanics and Asians. Alaska's, in 1926, sought to disenfranchise its Native Americans. Wyoming's was anti-Finn (1897) and Washington state's (1889), anti-Chinese. In 1894 the Immigration Restriction League supported an English literacy test for immigrants rather than more blatant racial and ethnic restrictions (Leibowitz 1984, 35).

I did not know when I registered to vote that the New York literacy test had been seen in 1915 both as a calculated attempt to prevent the state's one million Yiddish speakers from voting and as a means of stopping New York's German Americans from furthering their nefarious war aims. Nor did I know that when it was finally enacted, in 1921, the literacy test was widely regarded as a tool to keep large numbers of the state's immigrant women off the voting rolls (see chapter 2). I did not even realize that the law, as it functioned in 1965, effectively disenfranchised New York's Puerto Rican community, though later that year the federal Voting Rights Act suspended English literacy requirements for voters completing the sixth grade in an American flag school (that is, a public school in any U.S. commonwealth or territory) where the language of instruction was other than English, smoothing the way for Puerto Ricans to vote in New York (the provision was upheld by the U.S. Supreme Court in *Katzenbach v. Morgan* 384 U.S. 641 [1966]).

Eventually, though, I did learn from experience. I finally became interested in questions of official languages on a professional level more than a decade later, and in another country, during a year I spent with my family on fellowship at a provincial French university. Perhaps the most difficult aspect of that year abroad was enrolling my twelve-year-old daughter, who knew no French, in a French school. I am not a sadist, there just were no English schools in Poitiers. My daughter was ready for the sixth grade, but since she was not a francophone, the school authorities wanted to put her in the first grade. If you don't know the national language in France, you start at the bottom. They were making a huge concession by not starting her in kindergarten.

When I protested the wisdom of the decision to place my daughter in a class with children half her age, the headmistress of the school was surprised. "But M'sieu," she pointed out, they had done exactly the same with a fifteen-year-old Portuguese boy, and the only problem had been getting him to shave off his moustache. Then she suggested that my daughter might do just as well not going to school at all.

To get relief I had to do battle with the French bureaucracy. The French actually invented the word *bureaucratie* just after the Revolution (*Dictionnaire de l'Académie Française*, 5th ed., year 7, s.v. *bureaucratie*), and I quickly learned that the most appropriate definition of bureaucracy in France is actually something close to "Reign of Terror." In the weeks before school started, I carried my complaint up the school administrative ladder from office waiting room to office waiting room until I reached the *bureau* of the departmental inspector, the equivalent of a state superintendent of schools in the United States. Fortunately this gentleman, who had been duly warned by his staff about the crazy American, actually wanted to see me. He too had spent an exchange year abroad with his family—at the University of California—and his son, who spoke no English at the time, had been welcomed into the Berkeley public schools at the grade appropriate to his age. Glad to return the favor, the inspector ordered the headmistress of the Henri IV School to accept my daughter into the sixth grade and to provide her with a French tutor. That, it turned out, was just the start.

The French do not value the study of other languages, which they clearly regard as a threat to the purity of their own tongue, yet they begin second-language study in the elementary grades. François Truffaut presented a realistic portrayal of such study in the sadly comic English lesson sequence in his film *The Four*

Hundred Blows (1959). Clearly, French education hadn't changed much in the twenty years since the release of that film. At Henri IV, my daughter took English as her foreign language (the school steered the bright students to the other option, Russian, but for once we did not object), and she made herself unpopular by correcting the English *prof*, Mme Paillet, who insisted on such atrocities as *number phone* instead of *phone number*. When challenged, the teacher explained that phone number might be "OK" in American English (she evidently considered *OK* as un-American as *tarte aux pommes*), but that in her class only British English would do, and if *number phone* was good enough for the queen, it was good enough for her sixth graders.

During the year, my daughter picked up some French from the other students. The immersion method proved only mildly successful, and she missed out on such key areas as verb conjugation and the second person polite form, not to mention reading and writing. She learned no French from her teachers, who believed in sink or swim, or from her tutor, who was specially trained to teach French to foreigners using filmstrips. But I have no doubt that, because she was a middle-class kid with parents who were not awed by teachers and who knew how to protect her rights, she did better than the clean-shaven Portuguese teenager, the pupils from the North African ghettos on the outskirts of town, or the guest-worker children who were allowed to fail in school because their command of the official language was imperfect or nonexistent.

In the United States, as in France, we have linguistic problems that government language policy seems unable to resolve. Our cities and our schools are faced with the task of assimilating non-English speakers, a task that is not new, and one that we have yet to master. Fortunately, immigrants to America continue to learn English—or at least their children do—regardless of ethnic revivals or our inability to develop either an effective language pedagogy or a coherent national language policy. Nonetheless, the presence of non-English speakers on our streets and in our classrooms continues to generate friction and resentment.

Although we have seen over and over again that public and private efforts to maintain minority languages in the United

States are generally doomed to failure, many Americans continue to regard speakers of languages other than English as suspicious if not un-American. For two centuries, advocates of a monolingual, English-speaking America have proclaimed that nonanglophones cannot fully understand the principles upon which the United States was founded because these principles were articulated in English. For most advocates of official English, competence in a minority language—no matter how limited that competence may be—reflects a divided political loyalty. They further argue that lack of fluency in English bars residents of the United States from the economic mainstream, and that a polyglot society cannot be maintained efficiently. Moreover, speakers of English, conscious of its new-found power as a world language, have been quick to claim its superiority to other languages, which they characterize all too often as exhausted, inefficient, autocratic, or primitive.

On less ideologically enlightened or practical planes, settled Americans have been reluctant to accept newcomers, regarding them as socially, economically, and racially inferior, more insistent on special concessions like bilingual ballots, and on government handouts, and less willing to assimilate than earlier generations had been. These negative attitudes find their focus in attacks on minority languages, which are all too obviously badges of ethnicity—direct attacks on ethnicity are generally frowned on—and they result in calls for the establishment of an official language in America.

In this book, I will trace the history of official language policy—or the lack of such policy—in the United States, seeking by means of that history to explain the current highly charged attitudes toward official English and minority languages in America. My thesis is a simple one: the conditions producing today's official English movement have been present in the United States since before the country's founding two centuries ago, and the arguments both for and against official English have been repeated, with slight variations and little concrete effect, since that time. In short, little has changed in the past two hundred years, at least so far as official English is concerned.

Two notions, one philosophical, the other nativist, sometimes joined, sometimes independent of one another, support official English: perceived connections between language and nationality, and between language and race. American English is frequently held to reflect America's democratic social and political institutions. And the more or less open hostility on the part of established Americans of European descent toward newer immigrant groups or other nonanglophone populations is channeled into attacks on the supposed linguistic and racial inferiority of newcomers. (African Americans as well as Anglo-Saxons have shown hostility toward America's newest immigrants.) Both strands of argument assume English to be not simply a practical necessity for survival in an anglophone society, but, like New York's now defunct English literacy requirement for voting, the one essential test of Americanism.

Language was an issue in America in colonial days and during the federal period of the 1780s and 1790s. It surfaced again a century later, and during and after World War I as well. Language is an issue once again in the late twentieth century. Examining the history of attitudes toward English and minority languages in the United States will cast light on the official-language debate of the 1980s and 1990s and may help us see more clearly both sides of the issue. It should also help us to determine if either official-language legislation or minority-language support is appropriate at the present time, and what the effects of a national language policy might be, should Americans ever agree to have one.

The first chapter of *The English-Only Question* sketches the current legal status of English and minority languages and briefly discusses today's movement to make English the official language of federal and state government, a movement which is gaining some ground at the state level, but which is generating significant opposition as well. In chapter 2 I will examine the ideological relationship posited between language and nation, an ideology that is a major prop of the official-language movement. Focusing on the connection between American English and liberty that arose at the time of the founding of the United States, we will draw analogies with political and philosophical attitudes toward language in the Old World and other parts of the New World as well. Noah Webster proposed *American* (not English) as the nation's "federal" language, but Congress failed to act on his suggestion, which was clearly motivated by commercial as well as patriotic considerations. In any case, philosophers, politicians, and literary figures agreed that language reflected social organization, and many concluded that American English bore a special relationship to the nation's political institutions. Yet as an examination of the debate on English literacy at the New York State constitutional convention in 1915 shows, both supporters and opponents of official-language legislation argued that their respective positions were patriotic and American, while castigating those who disagreed with them as demagogic, both undemocratic and un-American.

Chapters 3 and 4 examine the other major force behind the official-English movement throughout its history: language and nativism in the United States. They focus on four states with large non-English-speaking populations: Pennsylvania, Louisiana, New Mexico, and Illinois. Benjamin Franklin feared the ever-increasing number of Germans in Pennsylvania, considering them both linguistically and racially inferior to Americans of British descent; yet Franklin also printed the first German newspaper in Philadelphia. And Thomas Jefferson, an early advocate of the study of English as a classical language, contemplated a mass settlement of English speakers in Louisiana to facilitate the formerly French territory's chances for statehood.

The United States has generally withheld statehood from territories until they contained English-speaking majorities. Louisiana is the one striking exception. It became a state in 1812 despite its French-speaking majority, and although the constitution of 1812 does not protect the French language in the state, the subsequent constitutional history of Louisiana reveals alternating periods of protection, toleration, and prohibition of the language (Kloss 1977, 112–15). Statehood was delayed for Michigan, originally settled by the French. State boundaries in the American Southwest were drawn to ensure English-speaking majorities for Colorado, Nevada, and Arizona (Mackey 1983, 177). And statehood was withheld from New Mexico for over sixty years because of nativist opposition in Congress to the territory's Mexican American majority population and to the prevalence of Spanish in New Mexican life. Spanish was both restricted and supported by legislation in the state. Hawaiian statehood was affected by a similar racial and linguistic prejudice, which could

preclude statehood for Puerto Rico as well. Illinois, which contained some early French settlements and later German ones,
opted for official English in its schools as early as 1845, made
American the state language in 1923, yet managed to tolerate
minority languages in public life more than many of its midwestern neighbors.

Changing immigration patterns, World War I, and isolationism all affected American attitudes toward speakers of other languages, and battles to save English or the minority languages
were fought in the press, the courts, and the legislatures of the
country. In the mid-nineteenth century, state and local statutes
protected English from the encroachments and presumed linguistic depredations of nonanglophone immigrants from northern Europe and Ireland, while interest in legislating a national
language policy revived in the 1920s during a period of reaction
against both the international role forced on the U.S. by World
War I, and the nation's newer and more visible southern- and
eastern-European immigrants.

The fifth chapter of *The English-Only Question* shows how
American schools have dealt with the question of official English
and the presence of large numbers of minority-language speakers
whose rights and education were in need of attention. Legislation
and lawsuits in the 1880s and 1890s sought to prevent non-
English languages—German was frequently singled out—from
proliferating, particularly in public, and from achieving any sort
of authority, particularly in the schools. After World War I there
was a severe backlash against the use of languages other than
English in the United States. Local ordinances were passed in
many areas requiring that English be used at all public gatherings,
and one midwestern governor forbade the use of foreign languages on the telephone. Many states sought to remove foreign-
language instruction from school curricula. In the 1920s several
states considered adding official-English provisions to their constitutions, and a bill was introduced in Congress giving *American* exclusive legal status on a national scale. That bill failed, and
the wave of linguistic protectionism proved temporary. By the
1930s the U.S. government was explaining the New Deal to
Americans in every language spoken in the union. Even today,
amid cries that America is turning polyglot, commentators like

Sen. Paul Simon of Illinois, author of *The Tongue-Tied American* (1980), frequently bemoan the adverse effect that the reluctance of Americans to study other languages is having on the country's economic and diplomatic dealings with the rest of the world.

The only United States Supreme Court decisions on official English and minority languages involve the schools. In chapter 5 we will examine two of these decisions, *Meyer v. Nebraska* (1923) and *Lau v. Nichols* (1974), the conditions that led to them, and their results. American schools, often credited as the primary agents of the Americanization of non-English-speaking immigrant children, were also forced to cope with the language problem. Initially, although many states required English language instruction in the nineteenth century, the public schools, particularly those outside of New England, competed with private and parochial schools to attract nonanglophone students by offering minority-language or bilingual instruction. In the 1880s there was a backlash as states forced schools—both public and private—to adopt English-only curricula, frequently excluding foreign language study altogether from the elementary or "common" branches. The English-only policy proliferated as levels of immigration increased, and America's schools, now firmly established as the nation's primary educators, freely ignored the problems of non-English-speaking students in the classroom.

Bilingual instruction had been abandoned in the United States during the late nineteenth century, and few attempts were made to teach English as a second language in the schools. Through a lack of resources, materials, and planning, the schools generally adopted a policy of language education by immersion. Nonanglophone children were forced to pick up what English they could informally, and lacking the academic English of the classroom, many of these children quickly fell behind. Educational authorities targeted foreign-born adults for specific English instruction in night schools, or on-the-job English classes, but teaching English to non-English speakers at any level was a relatively new enterprise in the early 1900s: materials and methods were few or nonexistent; not enough evening classes were established to meet enrollment demands; the classes that were formed were staffed by amateurs, and they were plagued by student fatigue and absenteeism. In sum, the schools were unable to cope with the language problem, and many students failed or dropped out. Nonetheless, linguistic assimilation did occur, hastened, perhaps, by the sharp drop-off in immigration between the two world wars: children and many adults learned English, and it quickly became apparent both to ethnic group leaders and to local governments that minority-language maintenance efforts were necessary in order to prevent serious generation gaps from developing in immigrant families.

Despite the high rate of English language learning among newer Americans, the post–World War II surge in immigration renewed the problem, and it has become clear once again that large numbers of nonanglophones are not being adequately served by American schools. Efforts at bilingual education were revived in the 1970s, in many cases ordered by the federal government. However, bilingual programs have proved controversial: bilingual methodology is not fully developed, many programs are inadequately funded or staffed with untrained teachers, and program success rates have been disappointing. Furthermore, such programs have become targets for those opposed to minority languages, who have turned the language assimilation issue into a political crusade.

The final chapter of *The English-Only Question* explores how other countries have dealt with the complexities of designating an official language and examines the latest congressional debate on the proposed English Language Amendment to the United States Constitution (the ELA). Pushed by opponents of bilingual education and bilingual ballots who raise the specter of Babel, such official-language laws attract the support both of those who would cut off immigration to the United States and homogenize its inhabitants, and of those whose aim is more altruistic or philosophical, who simply favor making explicit the long-held belief that English is in fact the official language of the land.

Both today's official-language statutes and those of the past depend for their success on interpretation by administrators and by the courts. Whether statutes were vaguely worded or explicit, whenever the language laws proved excessively prejudicial, they have been curbed. This was the case with the anti–minority language statutes common between 1919 and 1921. Similarly, when non-English speakers are failed or abandoned by the educational system, the courts and the federal government have intervened to attempt remedies. In the absence of such extremes, however, English continues to be recognized officially, often legally, even without the passage of explicit statutes. Perhaps the greatest barrier to the ELA has been the belief among constitutional experts that any official-language designation should be done not by constitutional amendment but by statutes with clearly defined intent and scope. They warn against using the federal Constitution to resolve a temporary social problem that could be better addressed through specific legislation and educational reform.

Language has always been an important symbolic issue in the United States. Debate over language generates passion and enmity. But as a symbol, language is also an issue that is easily eclipsed by more pressing economic, social, and political concerns. If the past cycles of protective legislation for English are any indication, whatever happens in the present debate over the ELA is likely to be minimally disruptive and only temporary. The issue of minority languages will not soon go away, and a constitutional amendment cannot force people to adopt English if they are unwilling or unable to do so. Nor will English cease to function as the nation's official language—the language of the laws, the courts, the government, and the schools—even if it does not have a constitutional amendment to establish it.

Acknowledgments

This thing of darkness I acknowledge mine.
—Shakespeare, *The Tempest*

In preparing this study I was materially assisted by a National Endowment for the Humanities Fellowship and through release time generously provided by the University of Illinois. In addition, I received help and encouragement from many colleagues. I wish to thank in particular John Algeo, Richard W. Bailey, Frederic G. Cassidy, Harvey Daniels, David Marshall, Geoffrey Nunberg, and Barbara Herrnstein Smith. Don Dripps, Eric Freyfogle, and Ron Rotunda, of the University of Illinois College of Law, helped me over the hurdles of legal theory and case law that initially seemed so daunting. I am indebted in particular to the work of Joshua Fishman and his colleagues, as well as that of Jim Crawford, Kenji Hakuta, Heinz Kloss, Arnold Leibowitz, and Calvin Veltman, who have pioneered in the various areas that underlie this study. Brenda Marder, editor of the *Brandeis Review*, first got me to focus my thinking on language and the Constitution. Ellen Graham, of Yale University Press, nudged me toward this book, and stayed with me patiently through repeatedly missed deadlines as my study in this complex, multidisciplinary area led me from one tangent to the next.

My own study of language history and attitudes toward language provided the springboard for this work and remains its chief focus. To cover the question of official and minority languages in the United States adequately, however, I have had to delve into areas where I cannot claim similar expertise: American history, education, immigration policy, law, philosophy, politics, psychology, and social theory, not to mention language policy in other countries. I do not pretend mastery of these areas, or even substantial insight into them, and the reader should ascribe to me and not my sources all glaring omissions as well as errors of fact or interpretation.

The

English-Only

Question

An Official Language

Section 1. The English language shall be
the official language of the United States.
Section 2. The Congress shall have the power
to enforce this article by appropriate legislation.
—*One version of the proposed English Language
Amendment to the U.S. Constitution*

Although many Americans assume that English is
the official language of the United States, it is not. That is, nowhere in the U.S. Constitution is English privileged over other
languages, and while a few subsequent federal laws require the
use of English for special, limited purposes—air traffic control,
product labels, warnings, official notices, service on federal juries, and naturalization of immigrants (Grant 1978, 3)—no law
establishes English as the language of the land.

On the other hand, Americans often assume that all the world
speaks English, or that it should: the image of the ugly American
abroad hinges in part on this frequently thwarted linguistic expectation. They further assume that everyone in the United
States speaks English, or should. Moreover, many English-speaking Americans tend to regard English not just as a language, but as
an essential human trait. In consequence, nonanglophones may
be regarded not simply as un-American, but as subhuman. To cite
one egregious example, Daniel Shanahan (1989) reports that in
1904 a railroad president told a congressional hearing on the mis-
treatment of immigrant workers, "These workers don't suffer—
they don't even speak English."

Just as the American stereotype assumes monolingual competence in English, American legislatures, courts, and schools have
always operated on the assumption that English is indeed the
official language of public expression—that English is the normal

1

vehicle of government, the courts, the schools, and the general business community in the United States. Although the legal record is generally silent or unclear on this matter, the assumption that English is or should be official has occasionally been voiced by American political leaders and by the federal courts. For example, in 1923 the United States Supreme Court, in a decision protecting foreign language instruction in the schools, ventured the opinion that it was desirable for English to be the American national language (*Meyer v. Nebraska*, 262 U.S. 390). As early as 1780 John Adams predicted that the United States would be the vehicle for making its national language, English, the next world language, "because the increasing population in America . . . will . . . force their language into general use, in spite of all the obstacles that may be thrown in the way" (1856, 7:250). John Quincy Adams (1875, 5:401) opposed the Louisiana Purchase because "it naturalizes foreign nations in a mass." In 1807 President Thomas Jefferson, who held similar fears that immigrants coming from absolute monarchies would be unable to adjust to American principles and would transmit their language to their children, proposed settling some thirty thousand Americans—whom he assumed to be speakers of English—in the newly acquired Louisiana Territory to prevent that area from remaining French in language and law (Jefferson 1903, 11:135–37; Franklin 1906, 99). In 1937 President Franklin Delano Roosevelt asserted in a comment on language policy in Puerto Rico that "English is the official language of our country" (Roosevelt 1941, 6:161). And in the case of *Frontera v. Sindell* (1975), the Sixth Circuit of the United States Court of Appeals flatly stated, "The common, national language of the United States is English" (cited in Leibowitz 1982, 117). Frontera was a carpenter who claimed that he failed the Cleveland Civil Service Carpenter's Examination because it was in English; he sought as relief a test in Spanish. The court's opinion continued, "Statutes have been enacted which provide exceptions to our nation's policy in favor of the English language to protect other interests and carry out the policies of the Fourteenth Amendment, but these exceptions do not detract from the policy or deny the interests the various levels of government have in dealing with the citizenry in a common language." In no instance, however, did either the executive or the federal court opinions endow English with official status, and the legal position of English at the federal level remains inexplicit, a situation which proponents of English as the official language of the United States find intolerable.

Although English may be the common, national language of the United States de facto—it is, after all, the language of the Constitution, laws, and government operations—it is not and has never been the exclusive language of the country. Besides the pre-Columbian languages of the Native Americans, now greatly reduced in numbers of speakers through deliberate policies of forced extermination and assimilation, and languages such as Spanish, French, Dutch, Hawaiian, and Russian, which coexisted with English in New World territories that eventually formed or were added to the United States, we find in the United States the many languages of those who immigrated or were brought under duress to its shores.

There are now, as there have been in the past, a considerable number of people in the United States for whom English is not a first language. For example, the 1970 census reported that at least 17 percent of Americans claimed a language other than English as their mother tongue, a figure "substantially larger" than that reported in 1940 or 1960, possibly due to the effect of the rise in ethnic consciousness during the 1960s (Fishman 1985, 109). The 1980 census reported that a lower figure, 10.9 percent of the population, claimed to use a language other than English at home, and that one out of every seven Americans spoke, or lived in a household with someone who spoke, such a language. However, the census also disclosed a significant degree of bilingualism among the members of this group: close to 82 percent of respondents indicated that they also spoke English well or very well.*

Despite the large percentage of bilinguals and nonanglophones who have always made up part of the American popula-

---

*U.S. Census 1980, table 99: Nativity and Language. Census data on total numbers of non-English speakers, in the years for which it exists, tends to be inaccurate, partly because the census has not always targeted language very precisely for investigation, and partly because respondents who are suspicious of the motives of the census takers often deny using languages other than English at home. In contrast, Fishman (1985) indicates that in 1970, respondents anxious to proclaim their ethnic heritage during a period of ethnic revival in American society may have exaggerated their fluency in languages other than English.

tion, English has frequently lived at peace with its linguistic neighbors. At other times, like the present, the language question has become a source of friction. Since colonial days, languages other than English have been used both privately and quasi-officially. However, at certain periods in American history attempts have been made to suppress at least the public use of minority languages. In the absence of overriding federal legislation, a number of states have made or are now contemplating laws to make English the official language of such public activity as education, voting, and legal and governmental services. Supporters of official-English legislation may further hope that the public restriction of minority languages will lead to their suppression in private as well.

The effect of these state official-language laws is not always easy to trace. Some of them simply give English the same honorary position as the state bird, flower, or fossil, while others seek *exclusive* status for English vis-à-vis the minority languages of the United States. For example, the Illinois statute, passed in 1923 and amended in 1969, simply declares that English is the official language of the state of Illinois, whereas California's more recent official-language law specifically protects English from the encroachments of other tongues.

In addition to general official-language laws, a good many states have designated English as the language of instruction in their schools, or the language of the state courts and government, and from time to time state ordinances have required English literacy for suffrage or jury service. Furthermore, by requiring American citizenship, which in most but not all cases presumes a knowledge of English, some states have limited entrance of non-anglophones into such professions as barber, private detective, or undertaker, and have even prevented them from obtaining hunting and fishing licenses (Foreign Language Information Service 1940).

The motives for laws privileging English are often simply practical or patriotic: proponents of official English assume that a nation functions best if its citizens share a common language, although it is clear that there are no monolingual nation-states today and that, contrary to the myth of Babel, plurilingualism may always have been the basic human condition (Calvet 1987,

32; Guy 1989, 153). In any case, supporters of official-language laws hope that imposing English by statute will accelerate its adoption among nonanglophones, though the furor over bilingual education and the generally disappointing experience with foreign language requirements in school curricula might suggest the futility of forcing anyone to learn a language.

Furthermore, supporters of official-English legislation frequently assume an identity between language and nation. This is a complex idea that has permeated scientific thought about language and has all too frequently taken on a reality outside of the purely linguistic arena as well. There it may have pernicious social and political effects, particularly in struggles between majority and minority languages. In elaborations of the age-old conviction that language reflects national identity, the philosopher Johannes Fichte (1808) and the philologist Wilhelm von Humboldt (1836) asserted the natural superiority of their native German in contrast to the failings of what they regarded as more primitive forms of speech. Their nationalistic essays drew legitimate charges of racism from their critics.

In a more scientific attempt to state the language-nation connection, the twentieth-century American linguists Edward Sapir and Benjamin Lee Whorf maintained that language controls the individual's perception of reality so that no two languages perceive the natural world in exactly the same way. Perhaps the most commonly cited example of the relation between language and perception is the number and variety of words for different kinds of snow in the Eskimo language. Eskimo has words for falling snow, snow on the ground, encrusted snow, and some twenty others, while English has only *snow, sleet,* and *slush.* While linguists today reject the strong, deterministic form of the Sapir-Whorf hypothesis, which would render translation, borrowing, and linguistic innovation virtually impossible, they do acknowledge a weaker version of the theory arguing that language influences perception without completely limiting or controlling it.

Languages carve up the color spectrum differently—the English shades of dark and light blue are two distinct colors in Russian. They also disagree on the linguistic spectrum. The very definition of what constitutes a language or a dialect is influenced by political factors as well as by linguistic ones. Though to an external observer Danish, Swedish, and Norwegian may constitute mutually understandable Scandinavian dialects, they are classified as separate languages by their speakers, who prefer that distinct tongues separate their distinct political units. In contrast, the Chinese consider the mutually incomprehensible spoken varieties of Cantonese, Mandarin, Hakka, Hunan, North and South Min, Wu, and so forth not as separate languages but as dialects of an all-embracing, culturally unifying Chinese.

The linguist Richard W. Bailey (1990, 84) has suggested that the language-nation problem has become even more complex in the late twentieth century, as nationality has frequently come to be defined in terms of structures that transcend individual political states (his examples are multinational corporations, which develop their own corporate culture, and global Islamic fundamentalism, which also transcends geographical boundaries). According to Bailey, "Like nation states themselves, these movements influence political affiliation, cultural loyalty, and language choice."

Language is central to national culture, as well as to the more genetically defined ethnos. When language functions as an essential token of cultural identification, changes in the linguistic status quo can produce disruption. In the early 1900s, for example, attempts to modernize the literary language of Greece resulted in violence: students and faculty at the University of Athens protested publicly in order to stop a performance of Aeschylus's *Oresteia* in modern, demotic Greek, and demonstrations at the university protesting a modernized translation of the New Testament led to several deaths.

So central is language to political organization that in many societies defining the language has become tantamount to defining nationality. The view that to be French is to speak French underlay official efforts to spread French from the capital outward, something that took over 150 years to accomplish. The official goal was to create the French people, and the French nation, by giving them the French language. Clearly, though, in another equally important sense, being French is a function of geography rather than language: there have been many residents of the Hexagon who were French—legally, socially, culturally, politically—without having French as their mother tongue. The complexity of the *questione della lingua,* an ancient and ongoing debate in Italy from the time of Dante to the present, similarly rests on the notion that defining the language is a necessary precursor to defining the group and ultimately the polity as well. In Europe, language played an essential part in the establishment of political units, both in the Renaissance and in the nineteenth century, and political turmoil in Europe during and after World War I, and at present as well, is frequently expressed in terms of calls for language rights and linguistic independence.

The situation may be slightly different for English in that nationality and political loyalty are often treated as distinct. Hence, in the United States, the conversational question What nationality are you? is frequently used to elicit information about the forebears of someone suspected of not being a Mayflower descendant. In England, too, native speakers of English are frequently classified as non-English in terms of their ethnicity: American, Scottish, Irish, Welsh, Asian, West Indian, Australian, and so forth.

In the United States, official-English advocates firmly subscribe to the language-nation connection, though frequently on a rather superficial and occasionally pernicious level. They would require English of American citizens in the belief that a nation's ideals are symbolized by and accessed through its language. Americanism, they argue, loses something in the translation, while English offers the only key to the nation's democracy, history and culture. Language thus becomes a literal shibboleth of nationality, a badge of true Americanism, and anything less than fluency in English—a foreign accent, let alone maintenance of a minority tongue—is perceived to threaten national security and subvert the national ideal. Some zealots in the cause have gone so far as to suggest changing the name of the language from English to American. (In fact, speakers of other languages sometimes consider English and American as distinct, hence the phrase occasionally appended to French translations of works by Americans, *traduit de l'américain,* while books of British provenance are labeled *traduit de l'anglais.*) But this linguistic chauvinism has a more damaging side: taking advantage of the presumed connection between English and democracy, anti-alien nativists insisted that nonanglophones could never understand the principles of American society, and produced statements like the following, by Clifford Walker, the governor of Georgia, to a national meeting of the Ku Klux Klan in St. Louis in the 1920s: "I would build a wall as high as Heaven against the admission of a single one of those South Europeans who never thought the thoughts or spoke the language of a democracy in their lives" (quoted in Bennett 1988, 223).

Even without the push toward official monolingualism in the name of Americanism, nonanglophones find themselves pushed by law and the conditions of American life not simply to adopt English but to abandon their mother tongue, and indeed immigration to the United States has generally been accompanied by a high degree of voluntary linguistic assimilation rather than permanent bilingualism, particularly in the second and subsequent generations. Concomitantly, there is a tendency for older generations of Americans, those already established and assimilated, to apply the bootstrap argument to newcomers: our ancestors had no special breaks, yet they assimilated; so can you.

Established ethnic groups perceive each new wave of immigrants as qualitatively different in its willingness to join the melting pot. In the nineteenth century, Germans and Scandinavians were often regarded by the Anglo-Saxon population as dangerous foreigners who were both racially distinct and bent on keeping their distance from American culture. In the early part of the twentieth century, newcomers from southern and eastern Europe were judged less adaptive to the American language and way of life than the northern and western Europeans who, after several generations in the New World, were finally shedding the linguistic trappings of their ethnicity. Today the same charges of unwillingness to assimilate are leveled at Hispanic and to a lesser extent at Asian Americans, despite linguistic evidence which shows that the children of these immigrants still learn English at an impressive rate.

This brings us to the less rational side of the official-English question. Since language retention is often the most visible badge of national origin, some English-only laws have not been attempts to ensure smooth-running government or statements of patriotism so much as thinly disguised attacks on race, religion, and ethnicity. In times of national emergency, American legislators have often questioned the loyalty of nonanglophones, pushing for stricter English literacy requirements to turn immigrants into 100 percent, unhyphenated Americans, while at the same time urging that immigration be sharply curtailed to protect the purity of the melting pot.* But these legislators have been opposed by colleagues reasoning that most if not all Americans trace their roots to someplace else, and celebrating the loyalty of newer Americans who spoke little or no English but managed to defend their country in all its wars.

Nevertheless, when the United States entered World War I, many localities banned the use of German in public while schools rushed to drop German from their curricula, and the 1920s saw an end to massive immigration. Many supporters of English-only laws today also favor immigration reform—by which they mean the exclusion from the United States of the "new" immigrants from the Soviet bloc, Asia, the Middle East, the Pacific, and Latin America.

While supporters of official-language laws emphasize their positive goal, the spreading of English, their opponents are wary of legislation perceived as threatening or punitive to minority-language speakers. Such fears are not without basis. Language legislation and immigration "reform" have served in the past as weapons against those who spoke little or no English, and supporters of today's official-language laws, in their fund-raising, routinely play on fears of the English-speaking population that they will soon find themselves at the mercy of foreigners.

The German, Spanish, Chinese, and Native American languages, among others, have been the targets of specific legal discrimination at various times over the past two hundred years. But while there have been both well-intentioned and glaringly discriminatory attempts to promote monolingualism in the United States, it would be wrong to assume from the foregoing that all efforts, public and private, have been directed toward the eradica-

---

*The phrase *hyphenated American* was common in the late nineteenth and early twentieth century as a derogatory reference to Americans of foreign birth, implying "a withholding of full allegiance to the adopted country" (*Webster's New International Dictionary*, 2d ed., s.v.). In this work I follow current, more neutral practice in omitting the hyphen in such compounds as *German American* and *Irish American*, as well as the more recent forms *African American* and *Asian American*.

tion of minority languages. Legislation to privilege English is sometimes balanced by policy supporting minority languages. French was encouraged in Louisiana, for example, even by Jefferson. He sought to make Lafayette the first governor of Louisiana, but Lafayette declined, and Jefferson then appointed William Claiborne, an English monolingual who insisted unsuccessfully that all laws be in English (Leibowitz 1969, 15). Jefferson was an untiring advocate of language study, and he promoted both Greek and Anglo-Saxon as academic subjects in the United States. He knew French as well: Jefferson concluded his letter proposing the settlement of anglophones in the Louisiana territory with a few words of French. A year later he affirmed that the French laws retained jurisdiction in Louisiana unless they had been specifically superseded by congressional action (1903, 11:58–59). Some of Louisiana's constitutions have protected French, and the 1975 constitution, without mentioning that language specifically, guarantees citizens the right to preserve their linguistic and cultural origins (Kloss 1977, 114).

Hawaiian is protected by the constitution of Hawaii (a symbolic gesture, since Hawaiian is for most a second language); and Spanish has been legally protected as well as attacked in New Mexico, a state which even today is proving strongly resistant to official-English legislation. In addition, local laws have favored specific minority languages (for example, German in the Midwest, German, Yiddish, and Italian in Pennsylvania), and while state courts have generally supported English-only legislation, two landmark decisions by the United States Supreme Court have protected minority-language speakers from discrimination within the context of an English-speaking country. In *Meyer v. Nebraska* (262 U.S. 390 [1923]), the court reversed state bans on foreign language instruction. More recently, in *Lau v. Nichols* (414 U.S. 563 [1974]), the court required schools to ensure that nonanglophone children were not excluded from the benefits of education. This resulted in the controversial proliferation of bilingual education programs, which we will examine more closely in chapter 5.

Although these decisions have significance for the language situation in the United States, it is important to note that, despite the popular misconception that such court decisions as

Meyer, Lau, or the *King* or Ann Arbor decision (473 F. Supp. 1371 [1979]) require minority-language or minority-dialect maintenance, none of these rulings guarantee language rights of any kind. Rather, these decisions deal with the rights of the individual. In the *Meyer* case, the court upheld the right of parents to direct their children's education and that of instructors to pursue their calling. In *Lau,* the court protected the plaintiffs from discrimination based on national origin. And in *King,* the court directed the Ann Arbor school board to ensure that black students learn to read standard English. In no cases have courts ordered minority-language-maintenance programs, or even transitional programs to teach English as a second or other language, though such programs have not been forbidden. Even the Bilingual Education Act of 1968 confers no minority-language rights (Macías 1979, 94). Federally sponsored bilingual programs, while not all equally accepted or effective, have all been transitional in intent: wary of permanently segregating minority language students, they are mandated to assist nonanglophones only until those students have mastered English and can join the regular curriculum.

In the nineteenth century the education community was more willing than it is today to permit non-English instruction: some states or cities provided public non-English or bilingual schooling (Ohio is the major example) in an effort to woo students from the private schools. Others at least conducted school assemblies and graduations in languages accessible to parents and grandparents (minority-language religious ceremonies were also common in the nineteenth century, and they too have declined).

In addition to historical and present-day bilingual education, there have always been strong efforts on the part of various ethnic groups to maintain minority languages through the foreign language press, radio, and television. Particularly challenging to the assumption that each new wave of migrants or immigrants retains its language and resists English is the fact that ethnic groups themselves continue to maintain private, supplementary schools to fight language loss among their children. These schools are deemed necessary because the children continue to pick up English and reject the minority language of their parents or grandparents, as generations before them have done. Such schools have sometimes been maintained in the face of efforts by the English-speaking majority to suppress them: in *Farrington v. Tokushige* (273 U.S. 284 [1927]), the U.S. Supreme Court ruled Hawaii's attempt to close Japanese supplementary schools an infringement of Fifth Amendment guarantees. (The Fourteenth Amendment, which pertained in the earlier *Meyer v. Nebraska* decision, did not apply to Hawaii because it was a territory, not a state, at the time; however, the Fifth Amendment applies to territories as well as states.)

While such supplementary minority-language schools are an important symbol of ethnic and cultural identity, they have not been particularly effective. Their mother-tongue instruction is more likely to resemble the foreign language instruction found in the public schools than the maintenance of a non-English first language (Fishman and Nahirny 1966, 104). In general, sociolinguists have concluded that despite maintenance efforts on the part of ethnic communities, minority languages tend to survive in the United States more as cultural artifacts—like ethnic restaurants—than as living languages transmitted across generations.

There is a practical side to the treatment of minority-language speakers as well as a legal one. While public support for minority languages has not always been strong, government officials and politicians, particularly those dealing with or representing ethnic districts, whether urban or rural, always manage to communicate with their constituencies in languages other than English when necessary. Similarly, like politicians on the lookout for votes, the business community, where money always talks, even now seldom hesitates to speak to customers in their native tongues. Non-English advertising thrives, particularly in urban markets, producing such materials as *Las Paginas Amarillas de Pacific Bell* (1988–89), a book which is somewhat shorter than the various English-language *Yellow Pages* for Los Angeles, but which contains many advertisements aimed directly at that city's Hispanics. According to Denis P. Doyle, Spanish-language television broadcasting has become "the fifth network" (*English Language Amendment* [henceforth, *ELA*] 1985, 229).

However, businesses do not always treat their employees with the same consideration they give their customers, and reports of workers fired for using Spanish or another language on the job continue to surface in the press. The courts have held that employers may require their employees to use English when dealing with the public, or when the language is otherwise essential to the job, while prohibitions on the use of languages other than English during work breaks tend not to be upheld. In 1987, though, a panel of the Ninth U.S. Circuit Court of Appeals ruled that, despite California's official-English law, a regulation requiring Los Angeles municipal court employees to use only English on the job was discriminatory, fostering an "atmosphere of inferiority, isolation and intimidation." The court further found California's language law "to be primarily a symbolic statement concerning the importance of preserving, protecting, and strengthening the English language" (*Gutierrez v. Los Angeles County Municipal Court*, cited in Gonzalez, Vasques, and Bichsel 1989, 196; the opinion was vacated on a technicality in 1988).

National Language Policy

The courts, the schools, and public opinion in general have vacillated on the minority-language question. In light of the checkered historical and legal record concerning English and other tongues, experts wonder whether the United States actually has any official-language policy, and if so, what that policy may be. Like American linguistic history, their conclusions are often contradictory. Shirley Brice Heath (1977) views the failure of the nation's founders to inscribe an official-English language policy into its laws as a conscious decision on their part to support cultural pluralism. In contrast, Steven Grant (1978) finds in American law a string of incoherent language policies all of which, whatever their stance on minority languages, assume that English is and ought to be official. As for linguistic assimilation and the retention of minority languages, Heinz Kloss (1977) presents clear evidence that nonanglophone Americans assimilated to English despite laws which consistently supported minority languages, while Jack Levy (1982) sees in the various language laws and lawsuits a calculated and explicit attempt to eradicate minority languages and force everyone in the nation to speak

English. Embracing these opposites, Richard Thompson (1982) concludes that while English *is* the official American language, the country's implicit language policy opposes linguistic discrimination, promotes bilingualism, and encourages—or at least should encourage—the study of foreign languages. Resolving these apparent contradictions, Joshua Fishman (1985, 59) accurately characterizes current American legal practice as favoring a kind of "parsimonious equity" with regard to language. Making the least effort necessary to assure that everyone is treated fairly, American laws are—in the long run—"neither mandatory with respect to English nor prohibitory with respect to other languages."

Ironically, since American language policy is indeed fragmented and inexplicit, the record supports all of these contradictory conclusions to some extent. Throughout its history, the United States has both encouraged and suppressed minority languages. American society and American law recognize the unofficial officialness of English. The federal government actively used minority languages to recruit settlers for its sparsely populated territories in the Midwest and West, then withheld statehood from territories that lacked English-speaking majorities. In addition, both economic pressure and consciously articulated public policy encourage minority language speakers to adopt English at the expense of their native tongue. And ironically, both business and government leaders—not to mention educators—bemoan the fact that Americans by and large are monolingual, a situation which, they contend, places American goods and services at a disadvantage in the international marketplace of the twentieth century. Even this support of second-language acquisition proves controversial. The linguist Peter Strevens (1988, cited in Bailey [1990, 84–85]) maintains that monolinguals dealing with language communities in a position of economic or political superiority to their own operate at a disadvantage. However, Geoffrey Nunberg (personal communication) warns that while there is much speculation, there is as yet no *proof* that monolingualism limits markets.

The pattern of American linguistic assimilation is perceived to adversely affect the position of the United States in international diplomacy as well as trade, and as a result the American tendency toward monolingualism is seen by many to affect national security directly. Since the Sputnik crisis of the 1950s and the subsequent passage of the National Defense Education Act, or NDEA, knowledge of foreign languages has been defined as a military asset. But the need to speak to the world's buyers and rulers in their languages has little overall effect on the retention of ethnic mother tongues at home. Although individuals often do become bilingual, learning English and retaining an ethnic language as well, bilingualism has not become institutionalized. For many, knowledge of a language other than English marks them as unassimilated and educationally deficient, not as scholars or national assets.

Fishman (1985, xiii) is not alone in seeing non-English languages as both persistent and inevitably peripheralized in the United States. Once the switch is made to English, few individuals are willing or able to maintain or return to their first language, or to learn a supplementary or foreign language. As Fishman shows, where the ethnic community remains physically or ideologically isolated from the society in general, as was the case in several areas in the nineteenth century, and as is the case today for the Old Order Amish and Hasidic Jews, the transition to English tends to be slower. And groups like American Hispanics, whose mother tongue is revitalized by continued immigration, tend to show a high degree of bilingualism which then disappears once the source of linguistic renewal dries up.

The American linguistic situation produces an almost inescapable paradox. Minority-language speakers are encouraged to abandon their native tongues and become monolingual in English to demonstrate their patriotism, their willingness to assimilate, and their desire to enter the economic mainstream. Once they do this, they are encouraged—with the same arguments of patriotism and economic advantage—to learn a foreign language in order to strengthen their country's position in the international arena. Supporters of minority-language maintenance regard this as wasteful, while more cynical observers insist that it is not a question of waste since two distinct and independent groups of people are involved. According to this view, those who need to adopt English are members of the poor and working classes whose linguistic handicaps cause them to fail in school and afterwards in adult life. Members of such a group will never become diplomats or international trade representatives. On the other hand, the argument goes, it is the monolingual middle class, the academically and socially successful, whose second-language skills need beefing up. However, both liberal and conservative analysts admit that a national policy which promotes second-language competence—whether it is in English or another language—as a cultural asset and not a social liability, rewarding it in the schools and in the workplace, would go a long way toward unifying these two distinct populations (Doyle, *ELA* 1985; Thompson 1982).

The English Language Amendment

Recently, recognition that the United States lacks any formal, coherent language policy has led to attempts to establish such policy. For the past thirty years the American social and legal systems have moved in the direction of increased civil rights protection for individuals and groups. This has been marked on the social plane by the civil rights movement, the women's movement, and the ethnic revival. On the legal plane this trend is reflected in a variety of laws and decisions protecting Americans from discrimination on the basis of race, religion, sex, and national origin: *Brown v. Board of Education* (1954), the Civil Rights and Voting Rights acts of the mid-1960s, the *Miranda* decision protecting the rights of the arrested, *Roe v. Wade* (1978) legalizing abortion, and *Lau v. Nichols* (1974), which has become the basis of bilingual education.

These events have all produced a significant backlash. Forced busing, the primary method of desegregating schools, continues to come under attack; the Equal Rights Amendment failed at the federal level, though it succeeded in many individual states; Miranda remains under siege; and the Supreme Court has remanded the regulation of abortions to the jurisdiction of the individual states.

In a reaction against the ethnic revival of the 1970s, the most pressing aspects of American language policy today pit official-English movements against supporters of minority-language rights. Bilingual schools, ballots, and street signs inflame those monolingual English speakers who resent or fear languages they cannot understand, while in the era of the bicentennial of the U.S. Constitution, more rational Americans wonder whether English can survive what seems to be a massive assault on its two-century hegemony. As a result, the 1980s have seen a renewed interest in official-language legislation. But reacting to the monolingual revival, a significant number of educators and community leaders have emphasized the importance of acquiring English while at the same time conserving minority languages as an important national resource.

In November 1986 the voters of California passed a referendum, known as Proposition 63, making English the official language of that state. Some three-quarters of the electorate voted to make it so, which perhaps was only to be expected, for most people in the United States either speak English or feel a need to learn it, and many view such a language law as a simple reflex issue, like voting for apple pie. For others, both those who support the English-first, or English-only, movement, and those who oppose the establishment of English, the official-language question has become a matter of deep concern.

The language question has always been an important legal issue in California. The 1849 California constitution called for the publication of the future state's laws in English and Spanish (California became a territory in 1848 and entered the Union in 1850). But in 1855 English became the official language of the California schools, and when the constitution was rewritten a generation later, Spanish was dropped and all executive, legislative, and judicial proceedings were ordered to "be conducted, preserved, and published in no other than the English language" (California 1879, 801). Debate at the 1878–79 California constitutional convention was spirited, with supporters of official bilingualism arguing that the Anglos were newcomers to the state who should observe the courtesy that was becoming of conquerors; that the Treaty of Guadalupe Hidalgo, through which California was acquired from Mexico in 1848, implicitly guaranteed language rights; that most states allowed publication of laws and other documents in minority languages; and that government and business were still conducted exclusively in Spanish in many parts of southern California, and restrictions on the use of

Spanish in these areas would represent not only an injustice but a very real hardship. But opponents of Spanish, who won the roll call vote 46 to 39, countered that the treaty of cession did not guarantee Spanish-language rights; that California's Mexicans had had some thirty years to learn English, which was more than sufficient; and that privileging Spanish would open the door for concessions to speakers of French, German, even Chinese. Although the Treaty of Guadalupe Hidalgo did confer American citizenship on Mexicans who chose to stay in the region, at least one delegate, complaining of the paperwork that goes with official bilingualism, considered them to be strangers still: "We have here in the Capitol now tons and tons of documents published in Spanish for the benefit of foreigners" (801). This sentiment clearly persists in California.

The question of an official language is now before Americans at the national level, as well, in the form of the English Language Amendment to the U.S. Constitution, first proposed in 1981 by the semanticist and then senator from California Samuel I. Hayakawa. The ELA would establish once and for all the primacy of English, defending it against the imagined onslaught of competing languages, and requiring the learning of English by immigrants.

On the surface, these seem laudable aims. After all, the ELA makes legal what happens anyway. There have always been non-English speakers in the United States, and those groups who have come to the country as permanent residents have always adopted English, a process which often takes three generations to complete. But the ELA is creating just the kind of furor we might expect from a proposed constitutional amendment. Turning on such controversial social issues as bilingual education and immigration policy, language loyalty and patriotism, it provokes heated and sometimes irrational debate among legislators, civic leaders, newspaper columnists, educators, and the public at large. To point to one blatant example, audience and panelists almost came to blows when the television talk-show host Phil Donahue broadcast a program on the official-language question from Miami in 1985.

Although Congress has taken no action on the ELA, with the exception of brief hearings before the Senate Judiciary Committee's Subcommittee on the Constitution in 1984 (*ELA* 1985) and the House Subcommittee on Civil and Constitutional Rights in 1988 (*ELCA* 1989), official-language laws were passed in Arkansas and defeated in Texas, Oklahoma, and Louisiana. In 1986 the issue was discussed in thirty-seven state legislatures. An official-English statute, explicitly targeted at Mexican Americans, initially failed in Texas, though state Republicans vowed to resurrect it. Official-language amendments to state constitutions have been defeated in Louisiana, traditionally protective of its French heritage, and Oklahoma, where opposition was led by a Native American state senator whose constituents strongly favor minority-language rights. In 1988 official-English measures succeeded in Florida (where the initiative gathered 84 percent of the vote), Colorado (where 60 percent of voters supported it), and Arizona (where the margin of support was a much narrower 51 percent of the vote), and Massachusetts will be the target of official English supporters in 1990. The ELA has been repeatedly introduced in Congress between 1981 and the present.

Clearly, interest in official-language legislation is high, and the status of such legislation is likely to change by the time this book is published. According to a recent issue of the newsletter of the English Plus Information Clearinghouse (EPIC), official-English laws are pending in Alabama, Connecticut, Kansas, Missouri, New York, Pennsylvania, West Virginia, and Wisconsin. English-only legislation was defeated in Maryland and died in New Hampshire and Utah. In addition, the concept of English-plus—that is, support for English *and* second-language study or minority-language maintenance—has won legislative approval in Michigan and New Mexico (*Epic Events* 1.6 [Jan./Feb. 1989], 5).

The language issue arouses fear and passion on both sides. Former senator Hayakawa recently warned members of U.S. English, a lobbying group that supports the ELA, that opponents of official English in Colorado were being aided by a "Soviet front group" of lawyers bent on undermining national unity (memorandum of 15 July 1988). However, included among the "enemies" of official English is the U.S. Department of Justice, which is clearly on the side of national unity. The department joined in an unsuccessful effort to remove the official-language amendment from the Florida ballot on the grounds that petitions had not been circulated in Spanish, as required by the federal Voting Rights Act. Moves are still afoot to invalidate the Colorado and Florida votes.

In the meantime, the scope and effects of the new statutes remain far from clear. The passage of state official-language laws does not create instant change, though it is often accompanied by anti–minority language incidents. California officials have treated Proposition 63 as symbolic, leaving minority-language services intact, though in one instance the mayor of Monterey Park, a city with an Asian majority, tried to prevent the public library from accepting a gift of ten thousand Chinese books on the grounds that "English is the law of the land" (Crawford 1989, 58). The Medical Center of the University of California at San Francisco permits its departments to require that English be spoken as a legitimate "business necessity," though ten employees filed a formal complaint alleging they were forced to observe the English-only rule in personal conversations and had been reprimanded for speaking Spanish and Tagalog (" 'English-only' rule" 1988; the university has since backed away from the rule).

Similarly, just after the 1988 election the Associated Press reported the suspension of a Miami supermarket cashier for speaking Spanish to fellow employees (*Champaign-Urbana News Gazette*, 13 November 1988, p. B7). The supermarket chain denied that the suspension was on linguistic grounds, pointing instead to "a store policy that prohibits personal conversation between employees during work hours," a policy that would seem to be unenforceable in the average grocery store. However, the employee contended a written notice clearly stated that his suspension was "for speaking a foreign language."

Passage of the Colorado official-English amendment to the state's constitution also prompted a brief wave of anti-Hispanic discrimination: the *Chicago Tribune* reported that a school bus driver forbade children from speaking Spanish on the bus; that Anglo schoolchildren told their Spanish American confreres they had just been made unconstitutional; and that a restaurant worker was fired for translating menu items into Spanish for a customer from South America. In response to such incidents, Colorado's governor Roy Romer and Denver's mayor Federico Pena ordered both state and city policies on bilingual assistance for legal and social services to remain in force. However, such orders were viewed by supporters of the state's English Language Amendment as contrary to the English-only spirit of the new law (*Chicago Tribune*, 15 January 1989, p. 6). In contrast, while Arizona's Proposition 106, amending article 28 of the state constitution, is the most restrictive of the current wave of official-language laws, requiring that "this state and all political subdivisions of this state shall act in English and no other language," the Arizona attorney general issued a nonbinding opinion that the law "does not prohibit the use of languages other than English that are reasonably necessary to facilitate the day-to-day operation of government" (Crawford 1989, 67–68; *U.S. English Update* 7 [March/April 1989], 2).*

U.S. English was rocked by controversy in 1988 when Dr. John Tanton, one of the group's founders, asserted that Hispanic fertility could lead to the disintegration of the nation. In response, a number of prominent supporters, including the group's president, Linda Chavez, and the television journalist Walter Cronkite, resigned from the organization. Tanton, whose concern that too many of the world's non-European tired, poor, huddled masses were making it to America's shores led him to found the Federation for American Immigration Reform (known, ironically, by the acronym FAIR), announced his own resignation from U.S. English. However, the group's October 1988 newsletter contained a prominent article by him debunking what he regards as the myth of the Swiss multilingual paradise. FAIR has also been accused of attempting to interfere with the publication of a recent study of bilingual education that is critical of the tactics of U.S. English (Crawford 1989, 7).

Opponents of the English Language Amendment fear it as an attack on bilingual programs, and it is true that many supporters of the ELA are opposed to bilingual education as well as continued immigration. But such an amendment may be purely symbolic and have little or no practical effect. This has been the case with

---

*In 1990 a federal court found the Arizona statute to be in violation of First Amendment speech guarantees.

official English in Arkansas, and it is clearly the case in Illinois, whose official-language law goes back to 1923. Illinois has always permitted foreign-language instruction, and it ordains English as its official language while offering bilingual ballots, bilingual education (Chicago has programs in some seventeen languages), and driver's license tests in Polish and Spanish as well as English.

On the other hand, the English Language Amendment and its ilk could add to the already negative climate for minority language maintenance, further impede the already difficult transition to English, and discourage much-needed foreign language instruction in this country. Unlike most state language statutes, the California official-English law has teeth, permitting ordinary citizens to sue if they feel the position of English has been harmed, diminished, or ignored in any way. U.S. English, which led the English-only drive in California, announced plans to sue several cities, including Los Angeles and San Francisco, under the provisions of the new law. An amendment to the U.S. Constitution will certainly guarantee the filing of lawsuits to test its implications.

Clearly, the ELA attracts a fringe of bigots and opponents of immigration; such has been the case with all nativist movements in American history. In addition, though, it appeals to middle-of-the-road Americans and even those who think of themselves as otherwise liberal, who express resentment toward aliens perceived to be illegal, intrusive, excessively fertile, and overly dependent on social services paid for by what they regard as an already overtaxed middle class. For example, the American Civil Liberties Union opposes English-only legislation. Its position, as articulated by ACLU Legislative Counsel Antonio J. Califa (1989), is that "entitlement to the rights of democracy . . . should not be predicated solely on a citizen's proficiency in the language of the majority." In response to this position, however, members and former members wrote to the ACLU newsletter to defend English-only laws and protest continued immigration. One such correspondent blamed "parochial or religious groups" for aiding "thousands and thousands of illegal immigrants," while another objected that "millions of aliens have forced their way into our country, and as they gain majorities in various areas they will change the law to force Spanish in the same way the French have done in Quebec."*

Further compounding the problem of designating an official language, the rational appeal of one nation speaking one tongue also attracts the support of well-meaning citizens—perhaps a majority of Americans, English and non-English speakers alike, and even some linguists—who find the idea of linguistic and ethnic prejudice otherwise abhorrent. It is more than likely that the massive support given California's Proposition 63, and the 1988 referenda in Arizona, Colorado, and Florida, came from these rationally motivated citizens, together with an increasingly discontented middle class—including a majority of the state's schoolteachers—and not just from the radical fringe with its campaign of fear.

By linking immigration with the question of a national language, the current English-first debate does not differ much from earlier attempts to deal with the fact that the United States is and has always been a multilingual country whose basic language is English. Furthermore, while many believe that the ELA is aimed primarily at Hispanics, who are stereotyped as reluctant to assimilate, recent studies show that Spanish speakers rapidly adopt English, and that Spanish can be maintained as a minority language only so long as Hispanic immigration continues (Marshall 1986; Veltman 1988). Spanish is then no different from any of the other minority languages in the United States. Nonetheless, researchers are now finding that the large numbers of Hispanics who have become monolingual English speakers are not reaping the promised benefits of assimilation. Their competence in English does not readily translate into increased salaries and greater job opportunities: apparently the discrimination against American Hispanics is deeper than language alone.

Seeing discrimination as the main threat of official-language legislation, some opponents of the ELA have countered with their

---

*Civil Liberties 366 (Spring 1989), 2. Although the British ended French dominance in Québec (and both groups beat out the original Native American population), it is the French who are blamed by the writer of this letter for seeking to reclaim their lost language rights. See chapter 6 for an analysis of the situation in Canada, so often alluded to by official-English proponents.

own constitutional amendment, the Cultural Rights Amendment (CRA), which seeks to bar discrimination on the basis of minority language and culture just as discrimination on the basis of national origin is already prohibited. Supporters of the CRA favor a government policy of English-plus, not English-first or English-only (Michigan recently adopted such a plan), though even if they could garner government support for minority-language maintenance, the problems of how to prevent erosion of minority languages may prove to be insurmountable. Both Doyle (*ELA* 1985) and Fishman (1985) conclude that private-sector maintenance programs have a limited appeal and effect despite their efficiency in responding to community demands. The public sector is poorly equipped to provide language maintenance in the face of ambivalence toward such programs at the community and individual levels.

One obstacle to the ELA's success is the uncertainty over the effect it might have. On one hand, it might simply prove symbolic. In the case of Arkansas and Illinois, English-only laws have not restricted minority-language rights or interfered with the assimilation process. On the other hand, it is difficult to predict the effects of an amendment to the federal Constitution on the basis of state precedents, since, as we will see in chapter 4, the states have been inconsistent in applying official-language laws, and individual statutes have been ruled unconstitutional by federal courts.

Although gauging the effects of an English Language Amendment is a difficult enterprise, it is possible also to see that the ELA might change language use in America profoundly. The House and Senate versions of the proposed English Language Amendment are quite different. The Senate version, which simply establishes English in the most general fashion, need not affect the status of other languages, though supporting legislation spawned by an ELA could either be restrictive or permissive. In and of itself, however, the Senate version of the ELA should not put bilingual education programs in jeopardy, nor should it require that ballots, street signs, and emergency services in multilingual areas be limited to English.

In contrast, the House version is more focused on protecting the domain of English in public life, and, by implication, in private life as well. It specifically prohibits the use of any language other than English except as a means of establishing English proficiency. This could restrict the use of multilingual tests, forms and ballots, as well as translators for legal and emergency services. The legal analyst Charles Dale (1985) concludes that an extreme interpretation of the ELA might not only outlaw foreign language requirements in college curricula, it could prevent the voluntary teaching of any foreign language except for the limited purpose of helping a non-English speaker to learn English. (In order to avoid such an interpretation, Arizona's recent official-language law specifically permits both transitional bilingual education and school foreign-language requirements.)

But whether statutes are broadly phrased or specific, there is always a danger that the adoption of official-language laws may backfire by producing an even more negative climate for minority-language speakers than presently exists. Ironically, an English Language Amendment may not only fail to facilitate the adoption of English, it may in fact deter the learning of English by isolating non-English speakers further from the American mainstream. However, it is not clear that a more balanced government approach to language learning of the kind anticipated by the Cultural Rights Amendment can succeed either. For example, writing in the *Chronicle of Higher Education*, Daniel Shanahan (1989), head of the Program in English Studies at the Monterey Institute of International Studies, describes a plan to make all Americans multilingual. Shanahan suggests calling English not the official but the "standard" language of the United States (he finds *standard* a more neutral term), at the same time requiring all students, regardless of their native language, to learn a second language. Minority-language speakers would learn English as their second language, while anglophones would choose some other language to study. Shanahan's regulations, which he would phase in over a twenty-year period, require all students to show competence in a second language for high school graduation and native-speaker fluency in that language for college graduation. While there is much to praise in such an optimistic approach to the problem of language learning, a problem which certainly merits government support, I strongly doubt that the fluency Shanahan requires can be established through coercive legislation and academic requirements alone.

On balance, the benefits of an English-only amendment to the federal Constitution are not entirely clear. Sen. Orrin G. Hatch of Utah, who chaired the 1984 hearings on the ELA, warned supporters of the measure against using the constitutional amendment process, instead of specific laws, to legislate social policy. That the framers of the Constitution, who dealt with the same problems of multilingualism that face us today, chose not to adopt an English-first stance is instructive: their attitude should lead us to question the necessity of an amendment whose purpose seems not purely linguistic but either naively idealistic or, more likely, both culturally and politically divisive and isolationist in its thrust. But in order best to understand the current status and possible effects of the official-language question, we must first trace its origins in ideas about language that have been brought to bear in American political theory and legislative history.

2 Language and Liberty

> The American Language will . . . be as distinct as the
> government, free from all the follies of unphilosophical
> fashion, and resting upon truth as its only regulator.
> —William Thornton, *Cadmus* (1793)

American ideas about official languages reflect both a desire to achieve the best possible fit between language and society and a resentment of aliens or other populations of non-English speakers perceived as outside the American mainstream. Such ideas derive from a complex of Western linguistic speculation that views language as the direct expression not only of culture and nationality, but also of political structure and moral rectitude. On one hand, official English espouses a simplistic idea of melting-pot ethnicity, where unity of language goes hand in hand with a cultural uniformity that distills the essence of Americanism. On the other hand, official-language movements—and the official-English movement is no exception—represent not simply instruments for the pious expression of nationalist sentiment, but elaborate though often ineffective strategies for social control and political reform. As such, they seek to mold a rational, unified, or modern society out of one perceived to be chaotic, pluralistic, or backward.

English is the speech of the Anglo-Saxon founders of the United States, to be sure, and many supporters of today's official-English, or English-first, movement want nothing less than to anglify everyone living within the borders of the United States, or to exclude them from the country entirely. At this level it is easy to see in much of today's official-English propaganda the essential elements of nineteenth-century American nativism: a not too thinly veiled attack on immigrants, racial minorities, and non-Protestants.

27

But in the eyes of many who support the official-language movement, both today and in the past, the idea of English-first or even English-only does not call up the hatred and exclusion of nativism. Rather, it is assimilationist in nature, fixing on language as the key to Americanism. Consequently, learning English is considered tantamount to Americanization. This is the logical outcome of an eighteenth-century sociolinguistic theory which celebrated American English as both the reflection and the enlightened instrument of American democracy. The popular expression of such a view, despite its grounding in seventeenth- and eighteenth-century language philosophy, is as simplistic in its way as its nativist counterpart. Extrapolating from the notion that language both reflects and influences worldview, it naively assumes that English is the language of liberty because British and American society are democratic in structure and because the United States was founded on principles of individual liberty. Furthermore, it supposes that immigrants to America who learn English thereby demonstrate their understanding and endorsement of the principles upon which the nation was founded, while those who decline to learn English, or who are unable to master it, pose a threat of subversion to the American system of government.

The Language-Nation Connection

In the eighteenth century American English had already become a target of derision by the British. They criticized it for borrowing terms from Indian languages, and for its innovations and its archaisms, which were perceived by many, though not all, English reviewers to be corruptions (Read 1933). In response to such treatment by the mother country, after the American Revolution, many influential American writers picked language as a political rallying point. No less a figure than John Adams ([1780] 1856, 7:249–51) believed "that the form of government has an influence upon language, and language in its turn influences not only the form of government, but the temper, sentiments, and manners of the people." According to Adams, in a democracy like the United States, excellence in the use of the English language, rather than accidents of birth and class, would serve to distinguish merit. Finding that republics had attained greater "purity, copiousness, and perfection of language than other forms of government," Adams predicted that "eloquence will become the instrument for recommending men to their fellow-citizens, and the principal means of advancement through the various ranks and offices" in American society. So strongly did Adams believe in the geographical expansion of the United States across the North American continent, and in its destiny to influence the affairs of the world, that he was convinced it was only a matter of time before American English would become the next world language (he was not so sanguine about the vitality or the future of English in the British Isles), and he recommended the study of the language to everyone (9:510).

The symbolic connection Adams makes between language and liberty has a long mythology behind it. The linguistic cosmography underlying the notion of official languages posits the existence of ideal states of language and contains parallel elements both of religious and secular ideology that tend to reinforce one another. On the religious plane, language myth begins with the Judaeo-Christian ideal of a monolingual Eden, where language came from God, and proceeds to the polylingualism following the incident at Babel—where the profusion of tongues reflects divine retribution for inappropriate human acts. This language myth presupposes a natural tendency of languages to decay along with public morality. It even singles out specific grammatical structures as evil or reprehensible. For example, in English, the passive voice is routinely charged with deception, equivocation, and the deliberate shirking of responsibility (see Baron 1989a, 1989b). And it assumes that, since a nation's language is evidence of its moral well-being, we must all honor an obligation to return, if not to the monolingual paradise whose loss provides clear evidence of human guilt, then at least to a linguistic state that signals through good grammar a return to sound moral principles.

Similarly, one secular view of language prevalent since the seventeenth century posits an ideal, classical, or golden age from which all languages have decayed, and to which they must strive to return if they are to survive. This view assumes that language reflects not so much moral character as social structure: democracies have democratic languages, so the argument goes, while despotic states are revealed in the hierarchic and oppressive nature of their languages (clearly, such arguments break down upon close analysis). It further supposes that language at its best must emulate logical processes. Indeed, traditional grammatical analysis borrows the terms *subject* and *predicate* from logic on the assumption that the major linguistic unit, the sentence, must be a logical structure. Clearly, although language shares certain features with formal logic—languages do exhibit rule-governed structures, for example—not all aspects of language conform to the demands of logical rigor. Idiom, to cite the most common example, frequently defies logic in its general resistance to grammatical analysis. Nonetheless, linguistic chauvinism sometimes leads to the unwarranted claim that a specific language embodies the power of logic. Such claims have occasionally been advanced for French which, because of its ordering of subject, verb, and object, is supposed to mirror the structure of human thought. And thought, according to the myth of French rationality, is, in its ideal state, purely logical. Conflicting claims have been made by Westerners for Chinese, some regarding it as an ideal, transcendental language where word equals thing, thus reflecting the structure of the mind, others condemning it as intentionally obscure and impossible to learn.

Taking its cue from the religious myth, the secular one views human language, like humans themselves, as springing from a common ancestor, though it replaces the divine creation of language that operates when Adam, in Genesis, names the animals, with an evolutionary process dependent on functionality and survival of the fittest. The secular myth also supposes that imperfect languages may be improved through the rigorous application of logic and analogy, and that a purely and transparently rational language may one day be constructed—either from the perfection of a natural language or from the invention of an artificial one—that will serve to unify the peoples of the earth.

Common to both these views is the feeling that at any given point in time, language is not as good as it should be; that language is constantly under siege from external and internal forces, both competing languages and the ineptitude or the malice of its native speakers; and that a perfected language will somehow reflect an improvement in the condition of the individual or the state. If we add to the religious and rational myths of language the notion revived and augmented by nineteenth-century literary romanticism and European political nationalism, that language directly reflects the collective or national soul of its speakers, then we may have some idea of the underlying whirlpool of language myth that underlies the official-language debate in the United States and other nations.

The facts and mythology surrounding the language-nation connection affect our attitudes toward language as they affect its use. It is no wonder then that the question of an official language raises issues of morality, nationalism, social policy, education, and ideology. As we shall see, the official-language question in the United States can reflect a direct concern for ensuring an efficient and democratic society, but it can be used as well to mask less worthy efforts to mold American society by excluding certain ethnic, racial, or religious elements from full and equal participation in it.

In considering the question of an official language, we must look not only at myth but at linguistic reality. Ronald Wardhaugh (1987, 22) conservatively estimates that there are some four thousand languages spoken in the world today, and only some 160 national states. Enforcing monolingualism at the national level—were such a thing at all possible—would result in language loss on a massive scale. (Wardhaugh also presumes that language loss is not necessarily an evil to be avoided, nor is monolingualism in all cases a goal to be pursued.) While multilingualism may therefore be the way of the world—and most likely it has been since humans first began to use languages—monolingualism has often been posited as the ideal state from which we all arose and toward which we all must aim again. The notion of an eternal and immutable language has always been attractive to language theorists and critics uncomfortable with the messy facts of linguistic variation and change. Some speculators have even gone so far as to attempt to recreate the lost ideal language, though a more practical result of the Babel myth is the widespread belief that our native language is endangered and must be safeguarded from further assault.

While the example of Babel is commonly held up as a warning

against multilingualism, particularly in the United States, and particularly by those with little or no expertise in language study, nationalism frequently provides a stronger motive for enforcing language policy and reinforcing linguistic protectionism. Political theorists also view the community of language presupposed by monolingualism as an asset: it allows them to clarify their ideas of nationality and offers a neat, symbolic representation of national behavior. In addition, on a practical level, the concept of one nation, one language facilitates the day-to-day internal operations of the state and simplifies the tasks of education and commerce.

Because they are so attractive and so apparently useful, we tend to forget that both concepts, that of an ideal, static language and that of a unified, national language, are in essence myths that clash with everyday linguistic reality. Nonetheless, it is these powerful myths that underlie the language policy, or the lack of one, in the United States.

The First Official Language

The Old Testament story of the confusion of tongues at Babel informs most Western linguistics from the Renaissance to the eighteenth century. It explains the current multilingual status of the human race while offering a tantalizing golden age extending from Eden through the building of the Tower of Babel, when only one pure language was spoken, dialect-free and immune to decay. The Babel myth assumes that present-day languages are corrupt amalgams of a once pure ancestor, and it spurs the search for the original human language, identified by various Western speculators as, among others, Phoenician, Chaldee, Greek, Hebrew, Swedish, Celtic, Teutonic, even Chinese. The myth further offers a challenge to distill from the multitude of mixed languages one common, universal language which will be, if not identical to the pre-Babel tongue, at least its equivalent.

It was the challenge to construct an Edenic language, together with support from the Royal Society, that spurred Bishop John Wilkins (1668) to produce his *philosophical* (that is, 'natural, universal') language. Wilkins hoped that his work would remedy "the Curse of the Confusion" as well as "facilitating mutual Commerce, amongst the several Nations of the World," together with improving human knowledge and both spreading religion and correcting erroneous beliefs (a2, verso–b1, recto). Wilkins observed that one common reason for language change—whether language loss or linguistic borrowing—derives from contact situations, and he concluded without surprise that immigration has a negative effect on linguistic purity:

> The Laws of forein Conquests usually extend to Letters and Speech as well as Territories; the Victor commonly endeavouring to propagate his own Language as farre as his Dominions; which is the reason why the *Greek* and *Latin* are so universally known. And when a Nation is overspread with several Colonies of foreiners, though this do not alwaies prevail to *abolish* the former Language, yet if they make any long abode, this must needs make such a considerable *change* and *mixture* of speech as will very much alter it from its original Purity. (6)

For Wilkins, contact produces change, and change results in impurity. Citing versions of the Lord's Prayer at various stages of English, Wilkins demonstrates that all spoken languages vary over time. And he insists that language is the object of rational, conscious human control: Wilkins finds Malayan to be the newest of the world's languages, a lingua franca invented by fishermen from the Indies who "for the more facil *converse* with one another . . . agreed upon a distinct *Language*, which probably was made up by selecting the most soft and easy words belonging to each several Nation" (10).

The equation of nationality with linguistic homogeneity that is so prevalent today is also an ancient idea. According to the Old Testament, one crucial—and potentially fatal—linguistic difference, the pronunciation of the initial sound in the word *shibboleth*, separated the Ephraimites from the people of Gilead (Judges 12). Similarly, though the ancient Greeks were well aware of the local variations in their own language, they defined themselves linguistically as distinct from the *barbaroi*, or barbarians, whose speech was clearly not Greek.

Many eighteenth-century language commentators considered

classical Greek an ideal language because they thought it free from dialect variation and unchanged for a millennium (see, for example, Webster 1789, 35). The fact that Greek was also the language of Athens, the West's first and most idealized popular democracy, strengthened the connection between language and government as well. Of course, such early views of Greek were simplistic and incorrect. The Greek language had many dialects (the major ones were known to seventeenth-century linguists) and varied with time as all languages do. As for the connection between language and democracy, Athenian democracy excluded women, the lower classes, and slaves, as well as foreigners, a fact that bothered theorists two hundred years ago less than it might today.

With the development of the concept of national language— for example, Greek—comes the identification of a linguistic *other* which usually carries with it a deprecatory connotation. While the original meaning of *barbaroi* is something like 'stammerers,' which suggests a people who are linguistically impaired, initially designating non-Greek speakers by this term is likely to have been hyperbolic. To the Greeks, the *barbaroi* were simply speakers of non-Hellenic, and therefore unimportant, languages— hence two linguistic meanings of *barbarism* in English, 'improper borrowing; speech error or solecism.' But to the Romans, the barbarians loomed as uncivilized and predatory enemies whose language and culture threatened to overrun the Latin world, and the language of the barbarian became something to be feared rather than mocked or patiently tolerated.

Language in the New World

Latin itself eventually became an official language of what would develop into modern Europe, and though today's Romance languages developed from a Latin source (*Romance* means 'of Roman origin'), they and the non-Romance European languages as well labored for centuries under the shadow of an official administrative and literary Latin before finally breaking free. Because of this struggle for independence from Latin, the European powers were already committed in varying degrees to a policy of linguistic protectionism at home when European settlers came to North America. It is no surprise that they brought their linguistic baggage with them.

The Europeans managed their initial encounters with speakers of new Western languages according to established patterns: they ignored the Indians' language; they set about converting the natives to a less *barbaric* means of communication; or, in a few cases, motivated by the desire to trade or to gain converts to Christianity, the Euro-Americans learned Amerindian languages. As Stephen Greenblatt (1976, 562) shows, language was perceived as an instrument of empire by the Spanish as early as 1492, and Europeans naively supposed that the American natives, possessing little of value in the way of language or culture, were a tabula rasa waiting to be inscribed with Spanish, Portuguese, English, or French. Louis-Jean Calvet (1974) documents similar attitudes and a similar pattern of linguistic colonialism in Africa.

So convinced were they of their own linguistic superiority, it is even possible that the first voyagers to the New World found the natives to be entirely without language. Greenblatt cites the journal of Christopher Columbus, who intended to capture six Indians to bring back to Spain "that they may learn to speak" (562). Like the Greek view of barbarians, such a comment is most likely hyperbolic, though: a contemporary analogy is our propensity to regard as illiterate someone with whose language we find fault, or whose views simply differ from our own. Other Europeans saw in the native languages that bore no connection to anything they had heard before a reflection of Satan or of Eden, while others, perhaps thinking they had stumbled on a true *philosophic* or universal language, pretended—at least in print—that they had no trouble conversing with the noble savages, whose speech was perfectly rational, transparent, and in no need of translation. David Simpson (1986, 205–28) describes the idealization of the language of American Indians, a phenomenon which increased on the American East Coast as the Indians were driven further west. For example, Roger Williams saw connections between the Indian languages of New England and Hebrew and Greek. Thomas Jefferson and Philip Frenau thought the Indians were descendants of the Carthaginians, while others saw in them a lost tribe of Israel. Delaware was incorrectly imagined to be a language in which there was no distinction between the self and other, no separation of the verb and noun.

We must assume that most Europeans who came in contact with New World natives reacted more realistically. Through practical necessity, they either picked up an imperfect version of the local speech or, if possible, imposed their own upon their contacts, and we can document a number of contact situations where pidgin languages arose, attesting both to the difficulties of communication and the will of participants on both sides to overcome these difficulties. However, the official policy of all the colonial powers was one of benign, or more often malign, neglect. They simply ignored or devalued the native languages, a pattern that continues in force to this day in all of the Americas, even in areas where the Amerindian language remains strong—for example, Navajo in the Southwestern United States and Quechua in Peru. (While the latter is now recognized as a national language, it remains one of low status and limited sway [Paulston 1986, 119].) Even the common designation of Central and South America as Latin America (a designation found in Spanish and Portuguese as well as English) underscores the invisibility and sense of unimportance of the indigenous, non-European languages of the New World.

The English in particular saw the New World—in the words of Samuel Daniel's poem, *Musophilus* (1599), "th'yet unformed Occident"—as a place to plant their language and thereby enrich the ignorant natives. At least one early writer, however, was aware that such a project of imperialistic enlightenment could backfire. William Shakespeare, in *The Tempest* (first performed, 1611), has the New World native Caliban—a humanoid monster whose name is an anagram of *cannibal*—tell his master, the magician Prospero, "You taught me language, and my profit on't / Is, I know how to curse. The red-plague rid you / For learning me your language!" (I.ii.363–65).

Although, as Greenblatt rightly points out, the Europeans do leave Prospero's magic isle at the end of *The Tempest* (569), the historical conquest of the New World by the Old continued to the point where pre-Columbian languages were not simply ignored by the colonists, but exterminated or relegated to the lowest status. Europeans came to the Americas with a sense of cultural superiority engendered by their extensive literary tradition and their ultimate linguistic triumph, the Bible, and with the expectation that their language would spread and prosper. However, they also feared the linguistic contamination and decay that their new environment threatened.

Ignoring the fact that the history of European vernaculars is one of derivation and amalgamation often resulting from the contacts between migrating or conquering populations, many Latin American colonies had official-language policies early on, and declared Spanish or Portuguese as official languages when they became independent states. As a further safeguard, they set up academies, on European models, to protect and purify American Spanish and Portuguese, and to prevent its divergence from the language of the parent country or its corruption through contact with the languages or the natives of the New World (see, for example, Guitarte and Quintero 1968).

No New World English academies survived, perhaps because no British model served as precedent, though such institutions were occasionally suggested or even tried (see Baron 1982a, 99–118). But it was clear from the outset to the inhabitants of new as well as old England that linguistic differences were arising between English and American; some observers went so far as to warn of the eventual severing of linguistic ties to the mother country. But no linguistic break accompanied American independence from Britain, and British and American English continue to be mutually intelligible, at least in their standard varieties. Furthermore, it was always clear to the founders of the United States that Samuel Daniel's musing would come true, that the English language would dominate all others in the thirteen original states, spread across the North American continent, and eventually become the next world language. The international spread of English (not always, to be sure, the American variety) has ensured the maintenance of a common core of intelligibility for English speakers around the globe, despite the emergence of new localized forms of the language. However the warning that British and American will develop into separate languages was repeated as recently as 1978 by no less a figure than the editor of the massive supplement to the *Oxford English Dictionary*, Robert Burchfield (*Chicago Sun-Times*, 29 June, p. 77).

Democratic Language

Europeans in the New World were well aware of the power of language as a vehicle for subjugating or submerging conquered populations, or for separating or uniting nations. In particular, the challenge of consciously remodeling or revising language to achieve enlightened social or political goals has appealed to many Americans. To some extent we can trace a connection between language, politics, and social reform to new attitudes that accompanied Europeans to North America. The New World originally presented an attractive if ambiguous prospect to the European mind, a chance to extend the sway of Western culture as well as a vision of Eden where civilization might be designed anew. Here government, industry, and the arts would flourish at a level of rationality that had not been possible since the Fall. Here even the cities would reflect not the chaotic historicity of their Old World counterparts but the deliberate order of the universe, ranging their inhabitants along streets and avenues set out to follow the compass points, and neatly numerated, alphabetized, and grouped into arrangements of trees, counties, states, and presidents.

Language in the New World offered a similar prospect for extension and perfectibility, and while some reformers of the English language occupied themselves with efforts to keep the colonial tongue from straying too far from its origins, others did not hesitate to suggest that the time was right and the iron hot, that English in the New World could be forged anew in the image of democracy or rationality, or, in the more extreme cases, in the image of both.

Seventeenth-century speculation about the relationship between words and things, between language, the world, and the mind, touched on the connection between language and the polity, and this in turn influenced the way Americans regarded their special linguistic position. John Locke, in his *Essay Concerning Humane Understanding* ([1690] 1694), employs the political imagery of liberty, democracy, and dictatorship to portray the arbitrary relationship between the word and that thing or idea to which it refers. While Locke defines language as a unifying social phenomenon, a position that supports the connection between language and nation, he goes beyond this commonplace to treat language as the concrete representation of political forces. In phraseology reminiscent of a revolutionary manifesto, Locke defends the basic human liberty to coin new words, arguing as well for our right to make language mean what we will. In turn, he objects to that despotism which forces us to accept other people's meanings: "Every Man has so inviolable a Liberty, to make Words stand for what Ideas he pleases, that no one hath the Power to make others have the same Ideas in their Minds, that he has, when they use the same Words, that he does" (225). Such liberty produces confusion, of course, and lies behind the fundamental dilemma of linguistic interpretation: because of it, Locke argues, we cannot know exactly what a word or a set of words means to someone else.

The German biblical scholar and linguistic philosopher Johann David Michaelis extended Locke's metaphor of language and liberty in his *Dissertation on the Influence of Opinions on Language and of Language on Opinions* ([1759] 1769), an essay which won the prize of the Berlin Philological Society and which encouraged Noah Webster to write an essay with the same name. Like Locke, Michaelis describes the operation of language—particularly etymology and word formation—in political terms. Considering language to be a democratic system, he protests against the use of borrowed (that is, Greek and Latin) words in scientific or technical vocabulary because they reinforce the class distinction between the learned and the common people, excluding the masses from participation in the process of scientific discovery. Echoing Locke's imagery, Michaelis's objection to the jargon of botanists reads like a declaration of political rather than linguistic independence: "Words cannot be deprived of their received meaning, but by the consent of the people, and the gradual introduction of a contrary custom; whereas an author treats the technical language he makes use of, with all the arbitrariness of despotism" (88).

Here Michaelis diverges from Locke: for him the truly democratic language precludes the possibility of misunderstanding, while the autocratic one all but guarantees that language will not be clear to the masses. Citing Horace as his authority, Michaelis argues that language is democratic because use or custom is decided by the majority. This "democratic form of languages" is in turn a means of preventing confusion and ensuring successful communication that no individual, whether government leader or language expert, can change (89). Michaelis reminds us that even the Emperor Augustus acknowledged his inability to legislate the adoption of new Latin words. And ironically, Michaelis, who was himself a scholar of language, regards the opinion of the linguist as suspect too: "Scholars are not so infallible that every thing is to be referred to them. Were they allowed a decisory power, the errors of language, I am sure, instead of diminishing, would be continually increasing" (78; this attitude is voiced by many language commentators from Noah Webster and Richard Grant White to John Simon).

While he privileges the role of the educated in directing the linguistic tastes of the common people—a condition that he finds inherent in all democratic systems—Michaelis reserves for classic authors, "the fair sex," and, above all, the people, "who are indeed the supreme legislators," the inalienable right to create language: "This is a right invested in every one who is master of the language he speaks: he may form new words, and form new phrases, provided they coincide with the genius of the language, and be not over multiplied" (79).

Language reform is to be accomplished in the same way other reforms are instituted in a democracy, through the rule of law, or, failing that, through public ridicule, which provides an important unofficial corrective. Furthermore, reform is not to be accomplished "by any act of private authority; that would be a flagrant infringement on the rights of language, which are democratical" (79). Michaelis is pessimistic about the success of artificial or philosophical languages, such as the one proposed by John Wilkins (1668), because they are the product of an individual and are therefore not only more liable to error, but are also opposed in their nature to the democratic spirit of linguistic evolution.

Unfortunately, Michaelis observes, there are times when the people as a whole, like the individual, are also prone to error. Discussing folk etymology, the transformation of difficult or foreign words into more familiar ones (for example, the formation of *woodchuck* from the Cree Indian *wuchak*), Michaelis warns that, just as language may influence the formation of correct opinion, it may also serve to perpetuate popular error: "Credit no proposition purely because the etymology implies it, or seems to imply it. Etymology is the voice of the people; which the philosopher always suspects, yet always attends to it" (73).

Language and Americanism

Primed by such applications of political thought to linguistic theory, from the outset political leaders, language commentators, and foreign observers saw a link between democracy and the state of English in the United States. Two strains fuse in the discussion of the role of American English in the United States. One focused on the philosophical issues of how the American language expressed and facilitated the democratic spirit of the nation, as well as how a common, standardized American speech could unify a diverse land; the other evolved a more reactive, nativist view of English as the key to Americanism and the Americanization process. Both of these strains are evident in the debate over language regulations concerning voting in English, which we will consider later in this chapter, and in laws mandating English as the language of education, to be examined in chapter 5.

Americans were conscious that their English was different from that used in England, if only because their situation in the New World forced them to name plants, animals, and geographic conditions that had not existed in the Old World. Like Michaelis, for example, the American physician Benjamin Rush (1787, 805) objects to the "stupid reverence" of using Latin terms for the classification of native plants and prefers substituting home-grown American names or, if foreign ones are de rigueur, borrowing them from Cherokee instead of the classics.

The British frequently chided Americans about the differentness of colonial English, deriding them both for their innovations and for their occasional preservation of language forms that had gone out of fashion in the mother country. Sometimes, though, a British observer praised the linguistic adaptability of the Americans, and French travelers found that the citizens of the New World identified closely with their own brand of English, particularly after the American Revolution.

The marquis de Chastellux, traveling in the new United States, noted that Americans resented visitors calling their language *English* as it reminded them of their oppressors: instead, he observed a distinct preference for calling the language of the United States *American* (1787, 2:265). And in 1789 the French revolutionary minister Roland de la Platière forcefully expressed his admiration of American culture, philosophy, and politics, predicting "the language of such a nation will one day be the universal language" (Baldensperger 1917, 92).

Anti-British sentiment after the Revolutionary War even led to possibly apocryphal suggestions that the newly emerging United States speak a language different from English. Some reformers advocated Hebrew, felt by many eighteenth-century language experts to be the language of the garden of Eden (many of the early colonists had identified themselves as Israelites in a new promised land, while a popular belief that persisted through the nineteenth century also derived the American Indians from the ancient Hebrews). Other anti-English patriots suggested Greek, a language thought to embody the structures of democracy, or French, considered by many, and particularly by the French, to be the language of pure rationality. The impracticality of converting Americans to any new language was always clear, however, and one revolutionary wag advised Americans to retain English for themselves and instead force the British to learn Greek (Baron 1982a; Guitarte and Quintero 1968, 567, document a similarly deliberate, though less radical rejection of Old World Spanish by newly independent Latin American nations in the nineteenth century).

It was Noah Webster who seized on the issue of linguistic consciousness in much of his early writing and firmly established the connection between language and Americanism that persists to this day. The paradox raised by Michaelis—that the people rule in matters of language, but that the people can also be wrong—presented few problems to a patriotic language reformer like Webster, who in the late eighteenth and early nineteenth centuries offered his spelling books, grammars, and dictionaries as guaranteed models of correctness to be adopted in America by popular acclamation, thereafter to function with the force of law, much in the manner of the federal Constitution. Webster advocated a "federal language," a standardized form of English, to be based on his own language reference works, which would "prevent the formation of dialects in this extensive country" (1831).

While British linguistic and legal standards derived to some extent from the oral traditions of the speech of the royal court and the common law, the American language, like the American Constitution, seems to rely more on the written word, which is regarded by some critics as a sign of colonial insecurity but may also be viewed as an attempt to base the new nation on documentable official standards. Accordingly, Webster's idea of Federal English was a language uniformly spelled according to his occasionally aberrant notions of orthography. It was to be made free from the regional variations in pronunciation and usage that plagued English in the mother country through the establishment of national standards which, in many cases, happened to correspond to the peculiarities of Webster's own New England dialect. For example, Webster preferred to pronounce *deaf* as if it rhymed with *reef*, and he favored saying *beard* as *bird*.

Like Michaelis, Webster accepted the idea that language reflects social and political organization. In *Dissertations on the English Language* (1789, 106), his own declaration of linguistic independence, Webster argues, "I should ascribe the manner of speaking among a people, to the nature of their government and a distribution of their property." According to Webster, the rich, who are used to owning slaves or commanding servants, "form a habit of expressing themselves with the tone of authority and decision" (107). On the other hand, he regards New England speech as diffident and respectful of the opinions of others, reflecting the region's egalitarian social structure, "where there are few slaves, and less family distinctions than in any other part of America":

> Instead of commanding, [New Englanders] advise; instead of saying, with an air of decision, *you must*; they ask with an air of doubtfulness, *is it not best?* or give their opinions with an indecisive tone; *you had better, I believe*. Not possessing that pride and consciousness of superiority which attend birth and fortune, their intercourse with each other is all conducted on the idea of equality, which gives a singu-

lar tone to their language and complexion to their manners.
(107)

Webster strongly believed that the American Revolution had placed the United States in "a situation the most favorable for great reformations" of the language. In the post-revolutionary fervor, "attention is roused; the mind expanded; and the intellectual faculties invigorated. Here men are prepared to receive improvements, which would be rejected by nations, whose habits have not been shaken by similar events" (405–06).

Webster's arguments for the establishment of an independent American language, while designed in part to promote the projected series of textbooks which he tried unsuccessfully to persuade Congress to adopt as the "Federal school books," echoed both the political and philosophical sentiments of the times. In establishing the vernacular in the new nation, Webster sought to base the grammar of American English not on the tyranny of outmoded or inapplicable Latin rules that he found dominating grammars of British English, but on the demands of logic (18). A rationally based grammar, together with the spread of schools using a standard set of textbooks, would in Webster's view create a uniformity of speech serving the national interest: "A sameness of pronunciation is of considerable consequence in a political view; for provincial accents are disagreeable to strangers and sometimes have an unhappy effect upon the social affections. . . . Our political harmony is therefore concerned in a uniformity of language" (19–20). Furthermore, for Webster, using the same variety of English guaranteed American social equality and political liberty (25).

According to Webster, this uniform American language, whose usage is "founded on the common law of the nation" (169), is governed in much the same way that the affairs of the United States are governed. The American language should therefore be independent of, and even consciously different from, British practice: "As an independent nation, our honor requires us to have a system of our own" (20). Although he did not favor abandoning English for some other language, as some rabidly anti-British Americans reportedly wanted to do, Webster in his *Dissertations* goes so far as to reject British language standards even when they are demonstrably correct, finding it against the national interest to introduce "any plan of uniformity with the British language, even were the plan proposed perfectly unexceptionable" (171).

Instead, Webster foresees a time when American English will go uncontested in the world, when one hundred million Americans will spread across the entire continent, all speaking the same tongue "like children of the same family," while English in Britain will still be confined to a small island population, and Europe as a whole will continue to be "embarrassed by differences of language" (21). Webster regards this European Babel as a source of linguistic contamination. According to him, the nations of the "Eastern Continent"—including Great Britain—are so close to one another that their languages are growing together. In contrast, Webster finds America's isolation from the Old World a protection against this contamination, though it is certain to mean a divergence of American from British English (22).

For Webster the prospect of creating an American language, along with other distinctly American institutions, is the direct outcome of the notion of New World perfectibility and the revolutionary chain of political events: "We have . . . the fairest opportunity of establishing a national language and of giving it uniformity and perspicuity, in North America, that ever presented itself to mankind. Now is the time to begin the plan. The minds of the Americans are roused by the events of a revolution . . . the danger of losing the benefits of independence, has disposed every man to embrace any scheme that shall tend, in its future operation, to reconcile the people of America to each other" (36).

Although English-speaking Pennsylvanians feared the ever-increasing German population (see chapter 3), Webster was confident that no other language could compete with English in North America: "It is contrary to all rational calculation, that the United States will ever be conquered by any one nation, speaking a different language from that of the country" (35). In fact, he finds the purest English spoken among the "American yeomanry," that is, those of English descent (288). In order to preserve this purity from the vagaries of change, Webster proposes a reformed, phonetic spelling of "the American tongue" (394). Such a reform would have important social consequences: "All persons, of every rank, would speak with some degree of precision and uniformity. Such a uniformity in these states is very desireable; it would remove prejudice, and conciliate mutual affection and respect" (397). Webster's new orthography would also create a distinction between British and American spelling that would reinforce American nationalism: "A *national language* is a band of *national union*. Every engine should be employed to render the people of this country *national*" (397).

Webster repeatedly stresses that American "customs, habits, and *language*, as well as government should be national" (179). He argues that without a federal language America will lose both self-respect and the respect of other nations. He further warns that inaction in the establishment of the American national language "is treason against the character and dignity of a brave independent people" (406). And using terms even stronger than Locke or Michaelis, Webster concludes the *Dissertations on the English Language* with nothing less than a revolutionary call to linguistic action: "*NOW* is the time, and *this* the country, in which we may expect success, in attempting changes favorable to language, science and government. . . . Let us then seize the present moment, and establish a *national language*, as well as a national government" (406).

The Democracy of the Word

American linguistic independence was encouraged as well by Jacques Pierre Brissot de Warville, a French revolutionary who traveled in the United States in 1788, later became the leader of the Girondists, and was guillotined in 1793. Brissot also stresses the need for developing a distinct American language: "The Americans must detest the English; they must, if possible, seek to erase their [English] origins, to remove every trace of them. But because their language will always give them away, they must make innovations in their speech, as they have in their laws (1791, 1:69).

Brissot imagines America as a universal asylum, and Americans as being "in rapport with all the inhabitants of the earth." As such, Americans must make themselves understood by all, "and above all, those with whom they have the most communication, for example the French." In order to do this, Brissot urges that Americans make their language independent from England by making it more like French, a practise that Webster himself had violently opposed. This process of "universal naturalization," adding Gallicisms to American English, will have a double advantage: it will bring Americans closer to other peoples, while distancing them from the British. And in doing so, Americans "will create a language of their own, an American language" (1:69–70). It becomes clear to Brissot, however, that this linguistic hybrid is far from a fait accompli. Hearing of the language difficulties suffered by a French farmer he meets on his travels, Brissot advises his French readers against settling in the United States unless they speak its language.

In the nineteenth century, Webster's radical attempt to make American English fit the nation's politics gave way to a subtler form of linguistic Americanism. In his early writings Webster had argued that, in addition to underscoring American independence, an American spelling would boost the national economy, for it would encourage the printing of books in the New World rather than their importation from England (1789, 397). Webster's national spelling benefited his own economy as well, as his locally produced blue-backed speller replaced textbooks imported from England. However in the 1830s, when the balance of the book trade was reversed and Webster began to sell his dictionaries in England, he quietly retracted his spelling innovations, together with his advocacy of an American English independent from its British parent, and focused instead on the universality of his American product.

Other writers continued to celebrate American English as the most visible strength of Americanism—or condemn it as the nation's most visible weakness. Writing in the *North American Review*, Walter Channing finds the United States deficient in literature "because it possesses the same language with a nation, totally unlike it in almost every relation" (1815, 308). Channing calls not for a new national language so much as a peculiarly American one. He romanticizes the language of Native Americans: unlike European Americans, they are "most perfectly contented with their language," which Channing describes as poetic and unshackled, rich as the soil, ornamented as the flower, soaring as the eagle, in short, as genuinely original, a quality necessary for producing great literature.*

Webster's dream of a federal language was revived by William S. Cardell, a grammarian and author of children's stories, who founded the short-lived American Academy of Language and Belles Lettres (1820–23). Cardell's goal was to achieve national uniformity in language among all classes of people, a uniformity destined to arise not from the "artificial, perplexing, contradictory, and impracticable, systems taught in [British] colleges and schools" but from the genius of "a nation of plain men." Cardell argues that the success of every American institution, and of American society in general, depends on "the goodness of our national language" (1825, vii; 30–31), which in turn can only come about not through free enterprise, but through government regulation (1822, 21; 30–31).

The notion of an independent American language remained strong to foreign observers as well. Perhaps the most famous French commentator on the American scene, Alexis de Tocqueville, was convinced that democratic social and political conditions had influenced the development of the spoken language of the United States. According to Tocqueville, in aristocracies, language, like society, is conservative and traditional, intellectual and philosophical. As a result, European languages, including British English, have been heavily larded with Greek and Latin learned coinages which seldom trickle down to the speech of the masses. In contrast, Tocqueville finds democracies both unsettled and stimulating in their effect on language: "The constant agitation that prevails in a democratic community tends unceasingly, on the contrary, to change the character of the language. . . . Besides, democratic nations love change for its own sake, and this is seen in their language as much as in their politics. Even when they have no need to change words, they sometimes have the desire" ([1835] 1945, 2:65).

Tocqueville observes that since the majority in a democratic society prefers commerce and politics to philosophy or literature, "the words coined or adopted . . . will mainly serve to express the

*Pages 313–14; this view of Indian languages is quite the opposite of the one taken later by the federal government's Bureau of Indian Affairs, which for a century operated on the assumption that such languages must be eradicated; see chapter 5.

wants of business, the passions of party, or the details of public administration" (65–66). Occasionally speakers of democratic languages will opt for an aristocratic classical phraseology, though the result may be comically inept: "The eminently democratic desire to get above their own sphere will often lead them to seek to dignify a vulgar profession by a Greek or Latin name. The lower the calling is and the more remote from learning, the more pompous and erudite is its appellation" (66). But Tocqueville finds that more often democracies borrow words from the modern rather than the classical languages, though their most effective agent of change is adding new meanings to already existing words.

Tocqueville cites speakers of democratic languages as preferring "generic terms or abstract expressions" which "enlarge and obscure the thoughts they are intended to convey; they render the mode of speech more succinct and the idea contained in it less clear" (69). While this may sometimes be a fault, obliterating the niceties of style and leading to a potentially fatal indeterminacy in word meaning, Tocqueville sees it as a strength as well, a simple reflex of the democratic state of mind: in democracies, people "are apt to entertain unsettled ideas, and they require loose expressions to convey them" (70). While the multiplication of meanings increases the potential for ambiguity—Tocqueville argues that "without clear phraseology there is no good language" (67)—he strongly favors the democratic idiom that has developed in post-aristocratic Europe and the New World, where class and caste distinctions have disappeared, and where majority rule applies to language as well as law.

Tocqueville views language change within a democratic milieu as a kind of secret-ballot social Darwinism which ensures, if not survival of the fittest, at least survival of the most popular. The result is a linguistic uniformity paralleling social amalgamation: in short, a melting pot. When all the words of a language mix together freely, only those words "which are unsuitable to the greater number perish; the remainder form a common store. . . . Almost all the different dialects that divided the idioms of European nations are manifestly declining; there is no patois in the New World, and it is disappearing every day from the old countries" (68).

Despite Webster's reversal on the issue of the distinctness of American English, the notion that language and social organization were related persisted in the nineteenth-century stereotype of American English as plain and efficient, though generally undistinguished. The marquis de Chastellux had earlier confirmed a common European stereotype that the American language reflected the practical nature of the Americans: "If the people characterize any particular tree, it is from the use to which it is applied, as the *wall-nut*, from its serving to the construction of wooden houses" (1787, 1:41–42; in a note, the English translator of the work points out the marquis's error in etymologizing *walnut* literally). In *Notions of the Americans* (1828, 1:153), James Fenimore Cooper, then resident in England, also idealized his compatriots as living more simply, and communicating more naturally and directly, with less deviousness and artificiality, than their English counterparts. However, upon his return to the United States Cooper decided the language was not as he had imagined it to be. Instead he found American English to lack simplicity, and in *The American Democrat* (1838, 117–18) he accused Americans of ambiguity, perversion of meaning, excessive formality of speech, and inflated diction. Despite this disillusionment, Cooper did retain the idea, common on both sides of the Atlantic, that the development of a bourgeois society is a great linguistic leveler. He writes elegantly, and perhaps with a tinge of regret: "While it is true that the great body of the American people use their language more correctly than the mass of any other considerable nation, it is equally true that a smaller proportion than common attain to elegance in this accomplishment, especially in speech" (118).

Whitman's American Primer

Pointing to Athens and Rome as proof of the connections between liberty, prosperity, glory, and language, the politician John Adams had unsuccessfully urged Congress to establish an academy to oversee the American language. Like Adams, the novelist Cooper hoped that democracy would raise the common denominator of American speech. For the journalist and poet Walt Whitman, better English meant a truly democratic extension of the language beyond the standard to include elements that are usually regarded as outside the range of acceptability: slang, regionalisms (particularly place names), neologisms, technical vocabulary, borrowings from other languages, and vulgar speech. In his *American Primer*, written in the 1850s but not published until 1904, Whitman revives the notion that the United States—now somewhat older than when Webster proposed his federal English, but still perceived as a new nation—needs a new language: "The new world, the new times, the new peoples, the new vista, need a tongue according—yes, what is more, will have such a tongue—will not be satisfied until it is evolved" (ix). Whitman rejects the words of the past one thousand years, all of which must be superseded in his "renovated" English: "These States are rapidly supplying themselves with new words, called for by new occasions, new facts, new politics, new combinations. —Far plentier additions will be needed, and, of course, will be supplied" (5).

For Whitman, as for Webster before him, this new tongue, called into being by the newness of the American situation, bears the stamp of American democracy: "Words follow character—nativity, independence, individuality" (2). Whitman's linguistic embrace includes the nonstandard along with the standard. Going Webster's already classic lexicon one better, Whitman's *Real Dictionary* "will give all words that exist in use, the bad words as well as any," and he describes in revolutionary terms a grammar that is equally revolutionary: "The Real Grammar will be that which declares itself a nucleus of the spirit of the laws, with liberty to all to carry out the spirit of the laws, even by violating them, if necessary. —The English Language is grandly lawless like the race who use it—or, rather, breaks out of the little laws to enter truly the higher ones" (6).

Assuming that language reflects the national soul as well as the national government, Whitman finds the English character reflected in the American language, which is "full enough of faults, but averse to all folderol, equable, instinctively just, latent with pride and melancholy, ready with brawned arms, with free speech, with the knife-blade for tyrants and the reached hand for slaves" (6–7).

But Whitman's populist view of the American language is only part of the picture, for he is also a reformer keen on taming the nation's linguistic independence. Although Whitman celebrates the American language with his own brawned tongue, his linguistic embrace is exclusive as well as inclusive. Writing during the height of American nativism just before the Civil War (see chapter 4), Whitman strongly objects to the influence of Catholicism in American place names, urging that Baltimore, St. Louis, St. Paul, and New Orleans be renamed despite the fact that not all of those names were self-evidently Catholic, and that "aboriginal," or Native American, names replace the saints' names so common in California. Recapitulating the nativist Protestant fears of an international Catholic theocracy, Whitman asks, "What do such names know of democracy?" (35). He urges the development of native place names if America is to become an independent nation and a world leader: "A nation which has not its own names, but begs them of other nations, has no identity, marches not in front but behind" (34).

Whitman was never one to deny his self-contradictions, and—to stretch an image—in his comments about language Whitman appears to be writing out of both sides of his pen. His America-for-the-Americans stance, which rejects the "ultramarine" words and names of a papist Europe, is counterbalanced to some extent in an article, written about the same time as the *Primer*, in which the largely monolingual Whitman recommended over one hundred words, most of them French but some from the Italian, for which he sees a strong need in English. And if this lapse in the celebration of home-grown words—the bad as well as the good—were not enough, Whitman's devotion to the democratic speechways of the common people is tempered by his assumption that the new borrowed words will percolate from the literary elite to the language of the folk, for the items on his wish-list "have been more or less used in affected writing, but not more than one or two, if any, have yet been admitted to the homes of the common people" (1856, 185).

Like Whitman in his more generous moments, though more evocative and less specific, Vachel Lindsay (1928) romanticizes the "real American language" in an expansive and rambling essay for H. L. Mencken's review *The American Mercury*. Lindsay does not discuss democracy or liberty, but seeks instead the elusive speech of the common people, "the United States language," as he also calls it, which in its "colonial purity" contains the essence of Americanism. Returning to his roots, Lindsay locates this "U.S.A. language" not in urban areas, but among the folk, along the back roads, and in the fields where the real wheat grows. It is heard not in speakeasies but in temperance meetings. It is not the language of "professors of so-called English," nor is it what Lindsay calls "the British language," his term for the more formal talk heard only on Sundays, though it is equally correct, spoken by folks who "believed in grammar just as they believed in paying their debts" (258). It is not dialect or slang, moreover, and although United States language is not the public language of oratory and world affairs, it is eloquent and revolutionary, coming forward "during completely national upheavals" and recalling the language of Thomas Jefferson and Andrew Jackson.

The Linguistic Failure of Democracy

As with Whitman, it is difficult to pin Vachel Lindsay down, and his essay swerves from a nostalgic consideration of American English to the telling of some completely unrelated anecdotes. It is clear, nonetheless, that Lindsay is describing what he regards as a national asset, and a heroic one as well, which serves its country well in times of trial like the War of 1812 and World War I (Lindsay 1928, 258). But not all associations between language and liberty are positive ones. A good number of British and American commentators have dismissed John Adams's dream of American eloquence as unfulfilled, and many have blamed social egalitarianism in the United States for the nation's supposed literary and linguistic mediocrity. While critics of the state of the English language may be reluctant to reject a democratic system of government, for that would be altogether too revolutionary, they are quick to assert that too much personal liberty can produce linguistic decline, if not anarchy.

Unlike his predecessors, the American expatriate novelist Henry James found that the liberty inherent in American democracy had produced not a democratically organized language, but a linguistic anarchy traceable directly to American social excess. James specifically attacked the language of American women, attributing what he heard as their faulty pronunciation to the overly democratic fabric of American society.

According to James, American women, unlike their European counterparts, speak not as ladies but as they like. He claims, in a uniquely Jamesean version of the political diction we have come to associate with descriptions of American English, that "we might accept this labial and lingual and vocal independence as a high sign of the glorious courage of our women if it contained but a spark of the guiding reason that separates audacity from madness."*

In James's view, the general decline of American English has come about because the country's political and social democracy confuses independence with anarchy. He charges that in its rebelliousness, the nation resists any rule of law, and grammatical law suffers along with the rest. Specifically, James supposes that an American, if asked about linguistic standards, would reply, "Well, we don't here, you know—in the matter of speech or any thing else—acknowledge authority!" (41:19).

A century earlier, Adams and his like saw in democracy the opportunity for citizens to distinguish themselves rhetorically, and many commentators praised the American system as a great linguistic leveler, but the anti-egalitarian James maintains that in America's perverted sense of social equality, Americans have considered it their duty, not to rise to new heights, nor even to dwell content among the mediocre, but to sink instead to the lowest possible linguistic level. Although in his experience European men and women, comfortable with a hierarchically ordered society, do all they can to emulate the language of the elite, James finds throughout America "an innumerable sisterhood, from State to State and city to city, all bristling with the same proclamation of indifference, all engaged in reminding us how much the better sisters may, occasion favoring, speak even as the worse" (40:1105).

James's description of language bristles with political metaphors. For him, American women speak poorly on purpose in

---

*1906–07, 40:982; for a discussion of the antifeminist context of James's linguistic commentary, see Baron 1986.

order to proclaim not simply their indifference to the laws of speech, but also their social as well as linguistic emancipation (41:113). James combines his antifeminism with his notion that the New World has not lived up to its promise. To him, the pronunciation of American women is an affront to their country's national honor. So, apparently, is women's emancipation. An autocrat responsible to no electorate, James characterizes language as democracy, then stages a coup to restructure the grammar as a dictatorship. While his syntax is complex, James's message to American women is plain: since they cannot rule their language democratically, he will rule for them, paternalistically.

While commentators who were sanguine about the future of American English spoke of the language in terms of its congruence with American democracy, for James, as for many more recent critics of American English, the bloom is off the rose. The noble experiment of the New Eden is a cultural failure: American democracy may be an effective political system but it has not produced a language worthy of Greece, or Rome, or even England, with its constitutional monarchy. Instead, American democracy has produced linguistic anarchy, and the only solution to the country's language problems is to replace free market forces with a strong, authoritative system of government language regulation.

Today's language commentators are equally strident in their denunciation of the language-liberty connection. Edwin Newman (1974, 11), who fears that America will be the death of English, traces what he regards as the current decline of English in the United States to the social upheavals of the 1960s and "a wholesale breakdown in the enforcement of rules, and in the rules of language more than most." The Society for Pure English, a loosely structured language academy founded in England by the poet Robert Bridges in the early 1900s, characterized its aim as "democratic." But Arnold and Charlene Tibbetts (1978, 168–69), in their proposal for an American Society for Good English, agree with Newman that in a democratically constituted English language, too many rules are being broken. The Tibbettses argue that to correct problems of language, American society must become "more authoritarian in matters of usage."

Voting in English

Ironically, then, the special relationship posited between English and American democracy is also blamed for the supposed decline of English in the New World. Proponents of official English continue to insist that language is the key to Americanization. When he introduced the English Language Amendment in 1981, then Senator Samuel I. Hayakawa maintained that English is necessary to establish "a common basis for communicating and sharing ideas." He later testified during congressional hearings on the ELA that it is mainly through classes taught in English in the schools that immigrants learn "the social imperatives of being an American, the attitudes and customs that shape the American personality, the behavior that makes a good American citizen" (*ELA* 1985, 55).

Official-English supporters continue to suggest as well that only the national language can reveal the mysteries and guarantee the continued benefits of the American way, that only through an understanding of the English language can anyone comprehend the spirit and the subtleties of the Declaration of Independence, the American Constitution, American laws, and the philosophy on which the United States was founded. A pamphlet issued by U.S. English and entered into the written testimony of the 1984 English Language Amendment hearings characterizes English as nothing less than "the living carrier of our democratic ideals" (*ELA* 1985, 135). Gerda Bikales, then the executive director of U.S. English, warned at the same hearings that language may be the *last* of the ties that bind Americans together (*ELA* 1985, 110). Subsequently, in an (undated) letter on the U.S. English letterhead mailed in 1989, the television personality Alistair Cooke reminded his readers of the importance of English in providing the unity described by the motto on American coins "E pluribus unum" ('Out of many, one').*

Proponents of official English also agree with critics like James, Newman, and the Tibbettses that the existence of English is threatened by the very democratic structures of American so-

---

*Cooke did not comment on the significance of the fact that the American motto is in Latin.

ciety and government—popular rule and the protection of individual liberties—that once were thought to give the language its strength. There is a further paradox: supporters of official English regard as purely and uniquely American their proposal to remedy the situation by requiring English in public life, while their opponents consider such a forced Americanization to be blatantly un-American.

This question of language and Americanism has of course been played out on the political as well as the literary/philosophical plane. Uppermost on the English-first agenda has been required English literacy for the naturalization of immigrants or, failing this, an English literacy requirement for voting.

As we shall see in the next chapter, there was some sentiment in mid-eighteenth-century Pennsylvania to teach English to immigrant Germans. As early as the 1880s it was suggested at the federal level that immigrants be forced to learn English. An immigration bill excluding persons over sixteen years of age "who could not read and write the English language or some other language" was vetoed by President Cleveland in 1897. The Senate report on the issue specifically targeted the "recent" immigrants from eastern and southern Europe who furnish the greatest number of "paupers, diseased and criminal" and who "are most alien in language and origin to the people who founded the 13 colonies and have built up the United States." The report guaranteed that the proposed literacy test would "exclude a larger number of undesirable immigrants, so far as statistics can be relied upon, than any restriction which could be devised" (Immigration Commission 1911, 21:47).

In 1906 the House of Representatives again debated the question of an English literacy requirement for immigration and naturalization. The proposal, as reported by Rep. Robert W. Bonynge of Colorado for the House Committee on Immigration and Naturalization, would require an immigrant to speak, read, and understand English, and write either English or another language. It was attacked by Richard Bartholdt of Missouri, who favored the acquisition of English but argued that nonanglophones "conduct themselves as loyal citizens of the country" and rejected a law that would penalize them for "a difference of a twist of the tongue" (*Congressional Record* [1906] 40:3649). Other representatives wondered aloud about the degree of grammaticality that would be required for naturalization. One quipped, "Many a man can parse and not be fit for citizenship" (3652), while William B. Cockran of New York, who opposed the measure, emphasized that an immigrant's usefulness should be measured in terms of contribution to the work force, not ability to learn English: "We do not want linguists, but we do want laborers" (7733). Cockran eventually supported the amended version of the bill which dropped the literacy test, requiring for naturalization simply the ability to speak English. Cockran commented on the final version, "I think it infinitely better for the country that every recruit to citizenship should be able to work in one language than that he be able to speak in a dozen" (7875).

Although a knowledge of spoken English did become required for naturalization, many observers noted that since no agency had set objective standards for testing this knowledge, the law was enforced erratically, with some judges exhibiting extreme leniency and others being so strict as to (illegally) require candidates for citizenship to read a passage (Gavit 1922, 120). The English literacy debate continued for some time. Early in 1915 President Woodrow Wilson vetoed a bill requiring immigrants to be literate in some language on the grounds that such a measure was contrary to America's traditional stance as the protector of human rights (the bill was later passed over his veto). Later that year, when the delegates to the New York State constitutional convention debated an English literacy requirement for voting, the relationship between language, liberty, and patriotism was raised by both sides. In 1890 Mississippi had establish a literacy test as a means of preventing blacks from voting. The New York literacy test, which had been put forth unsuccessfully in 1894 as well, would have given residents of the state two and one half years to acquire English. Its author, the physician and hospital administrator Charles H. Young, of Westchester County, considered it both a "liberal" and a "modern" proposal, replacing earlier "aristocratic" property qualifications for suffrage with more democratic educational requirements (New York State 1916, 3:3001). But state (later U.S.) Sen. Robert F. Wagner called the measure "un-American," as did legal author Alfred Gindy Reeves, who labeled it "anti-New York" and anti-democratic as well: "People of New York do not want an aristocracy of so-called culture" (3165).

Both supporters and opponents of the New York English literacy test insisted that their positions represented the true, liberal, patriotic spirit of American democracy. Young argued that an English literacy requirement would help the foreign born to "become acquainted with the spirit of our institutions. . . . [and] acquire patriotism from knowledge of our history and government." He warned that giving women the vote, a move that was in the offing in New York, would add some two hundred thousand illiterates to the rolls. And he raised the specter of an electorate not simply untutored but disloyal as well: although America had not yet entered the war, Young reminded the convention of the menace of German Americans "who have not yet learned the English language and who are reading papers in sympathy with [Germany]" (3002).

The engineer Olin Landreth supported Young's measure as a way of regularizing a situation that already existed de facto: "[English] is the national language, it is the official language, and it should be recognized." Landreth agreed that English "is the only language by which [voters] can get immediately in touch with patriotism," and he punched home his theme in a style reminiscent of Walt Whitman: "It is the real language" (3044). Another supporter, delegate Gordon Knox Bell, appealed to the Anglo-Saxon heritage of the United States, recalled the Magna Charta, and urged Americans to tell immigrants, "You have got to learn our language because that is the vehicle of the thought that has been handed down from the men in whose breasts first burned the fire of freedom" (3016). Bell also characterized English as the mystical key to Americanism: "Let that be the language which, although it may fetter our immigrants, it will also open to them, and lead them upward into, the path of comprehending the blessed vision of liberty which we, more than any other nation, now possess" (3017).

Delegate-at-large Louis Marshall, an attorney and Jewish community leader who would later serve on the New York State Immigration Commission, strongly opposed the English literacy requirement. He told the convention that knowing English was not a precondition for patriotism. Marshall reminded his listeners of "the thousands who were unable to read and write the English language who hastened to defend the flag of their adopted country" (3018). He argued that while literacy itself was valuable, the language of literacy should not be dictated. Marshall further maintained that the English literacy test specifically sought to disfranchise New York's one million Yiddish speakers, whose tradition of literacy was more ancient than that of the Anglo-Saxons, and at least as significant in terms of world culture. He pointed out that the illiterate barons at Runnymede in 1215 "signed" Magna Charta by making marks, not by writing their names, while the ancestors of New York's Jews, "who had no English or Anglo-Saxon blood flowing through their veins, were able to read and write. And although they did not participate in the Magna Charta, and although they were made the objects of hateful discrimination in that document, those of their speech had previously educated the world in the Decalogue. They had developed a literature rich in every department of thought and one branch of them had given to the world the Sermon on the Mount" (3019). In response, delegate Edward E. Franchot raised the now familiar objection that certain immigrant groups simply do not want to assimilate. Franchot insisted that the Jews had voluntarily chosen not to identify themselves with American institutions, or to learn English, "the language which is almost essential to the due appreciation of those institutions" (3046).

However, other opposition delegates found the English literacy requirement inconsistent with the modern spirit of toleration and liberalism, labeling it repeatedly as "dangerous" and "un-American" (3022), and two delegates even suggested that literacy might not be an absolute good after all. Senator Wagner claimed, "The most dangerous criminals in the community are those that use their knowledge of letters to consummate their insidious designs" (3025), while delegate Green asserted, "The prisons are filled with men highly educated, a very small proportion, as shown, are of the uneducated variety" (3160).

Delegate Frank Mann considered the English literacy requirement an attack not just on New York's Jews but on all other immigrant groups, the Germans in particular. Mann objected to Young's characterization of German Americans as subversive. Referring to the war in Europe, Young told the convention, "We are confronted by a possibility [of] war with a power many of whose people are in this land at this time, and these people, who have not learned the English language and are reading papers in sympathy with the foreign country, are a menace" ("Literacy Test" 1915). But Mann went so far as to claim that German immigrants were even more American than their British counterparts, citing figures to prove that a greater percentage of Germans were literate and became citizens than English immigrants, and that the British rulers, the Hanovers, had all descended from the German nobility (New York State 1916, 3039–40).

The English literacy test was finally defeated in a party-line vote at the constitutional convention of 1915. But the issue did not die. Aided by the nativist ferment following World War I, New York State passed a constitutional amendment in 1921 requiring new voters to demonstrate the ability not only to speak and read English, but to write it as well. In an editorial, the *New York Times* favored the English literacy requirement as a measure of Americanization (7 November 1921, p. 14). One letter to the editor of the *Times* supporting the amendment warned, "Our melting pot will melt little if Babel continues" (29 October 1921, p. 12). However, Max J. Kohler (1921), an expert on immigrant literacy, warned that the measure would disenfranchise hundreds of thousands of immigrant women. (According to the Dillingham Commission report of 1911, about two-thirds of male immigrants had some knowledge of English, while only 47.7 percent of women did [Forbes and Lemos 1981, 80].)

Convinced that speaking English meant being true blue American, and appalled by the threat of a return to the undesirable state of Babel, New York's voters readily adopted the English literacy test. However, similar postwar literacy measures, buttressed and opposed by the same sorts of pro-American, anti-Babel arguments found in the New York debate, failed to pass in Illinois, Indiana, and other states (see chapter 4).

It is clear from the thread of literary and political language commentary we have followed in this chapter that Americans both treasure the national language and perceive the learning of English by nonanglophone residents as a symbolic rite of passage, a declaration of faith in the United States. Whatever one's feelings about minority languages, official English is still a strong symbol and one that is not completely illusory, for our attitudes toward language inevitably affect the way that language is used. With few exceptions, minority-language speakers, like their majority-language counterparts, have always supported English acquisition, a fact repeatedly chronicled by opponents of official-language legislation yet denied by supporters of such measures. Arguing against New York State's English literacy test for voting, Max J. Kohler (1921) cited government statistics demonstrating the commitment of immigrants to Americanization through English: the illiteracy rate of the children of foreigners was 0.9 percent, significantly lower than the 4.4 percent rate of native born children. Like the majority, minority-language speakers see English as a practical tool for economic advancement, a means by which anyone in America can make it to the top. Nonetheless, English for them is not simply a "language of wider communication," as some of today's sociolinguists have designated it. It remains as well a powerful badge of Americanism.

Unfortunately, Americanism evidenced by the adoption of English is not always enough. The idealism and patriotic sentiment expressed by supporters of official-language legislation are undercut by the nativism that inevitably accompanies such measures, a nativism which rejects certain groups of Americans no matter what language they speak.

The language critic John Simon (1980, xiv) attributes at least some of the faults of American English to the nation's misguided protecting of minority rights. Ignoring the fact that women are not a minority in the United States, Simon decries "the notion that in a democratic society language must accommodate itself to the whims, idiosyncrasies, dialects, and sheer ignorance of the underprivileged minorities, especially if these happen to be black, Hispanic, . . . female or homosexual." Had he been writing a century earlier, Simon, who himself came to English after learning several other languages, would probably have singled out Germans instead of Hispanics in his complaint.

Indeed, the very same charges leveled at Hispanics by today's supporters of official-language legislation were aimed by more established Americans at German immigrants from the mid-eighteenth century until that group's visibility declined shortly after World War I. The Germans, who until recently constituted America's largest ethnic language minority, were variously accused of clinging stubbornly to their European customs, including Catholicism (although many of them were Lutheran), refusing to assimilate, supporting German-only or bilingual schools, having too many children, and, most important from our point of view, seeking to undermine English as the official language of the American colonies, and later, the United States. In the next chapter, we will look at this less attractive, nativist side of putting English first.

3 Defending the Native Tongue

> The tendency . . . to preserve a sameness of language throughout our own wide spreading country, that alone would be an object worthy of the public attention.
> —*Chief Justice John Marshall, 1822*

The English-first movement in America was reinforced by the political identification of the American language with Americanism, but it began locally at least a generation before the establishment of the United States, as a defensive reaction to German immigration in Pennsylvania, and it continues unabated in areas with large non-English-speaking populations. Many English-speaking Americans in the eighteenth century, as now, reacted to nonanglophones with suspicion, if not outright fear and intolerance of those considered racially inferior to the Anglo-Saxon stock. However, politeness occasionally led their nativist concern to be expressed as anxiety over the preservation of American ideals and a desire to assimilate foreigners, newcomers, and conquered peoples. Ethnic, religious, and political battle lines were drawn, and language early on became an important nativist issue as well as a cultural and philosophical concern.

Writing in the *American Magazine* (1758, 631), one observer—most likely the review's editor, the Philadelphia cleric and educator William Smith—warned that the presence of a large number of nonanglophone immigrants should prompt efforts to defend English in America from the encroachments of minority tongues: "For as we are so great a mixture of people, from almost all corners of the world, necessarily speaking a variety of languages and dialects, the true pronunciation and writing of our own language might soon be lost among us, without . . . a previous care to preserve it in the rising generation." As we shall see from remarks

he published elsewhere, which are cited below, Smith was thinking of the German population of Pennsylvania, who were accused
by their English neighbors of everything from sedition and stealing
jobs from Anglo settlers to popery and causing bad weather (Feer
1952, 403). Other voices, particularly in areas with a significant
nonanglophone population, agreed that the English language
needed official protection. Noah Webster complained that French
phrases were entering English at an alarming rate, and he was
disturbed as well that "the language in the middle States is tinc-
tured with a variety of Irish, Scotch and German dialects" (1783, 7).

The German Question

According to Albert B. Faust (1909, 2:147–48), the
children of Pennsylvania's Germans picked up English quickly in
the eighteenth century, a phenomenon of assimilation noted by
observers of many immigrant groups in the twentieth century as
well. The consequent language loss among the young people
prompted organized efforts to preserve German in the Pennsylvania colony, largely through the institutions of the schools and
churches, though the main factors supporting German were social isolation, most prevalent in rural areas, and continued immigration: earlier German settlers had to keep up their language to
deal with the newer Germans coming into Pennsylvania.

The German community also lamented the contamination of
its language with English words. One eighteenth-century visitor
from Europe complained that "the language which our German
people make use of is a miserable, broken, fustian, salmagundi of
English and German. . . . People come over from Germany forget
their mother tongue in part while seeking in vain to learn the new
speech" (quoted in Von Hagen 1976, 103). The German press in
Pennsylvania spurred efforts to defend the language against the
encroachment of English.

Just as German speakers reacted to the threat posed by English, Pennsylvania's Anglo-Saxons frequently voiced their fears
of being swamped by German immigrants. While in the 1730s
Benjamin Franklin published some of the first German books and
the first German newspaper in America, and in 1749 his English
Academy in Philadelphia became the first non-German school

where German was taught (Bartel 1976, 98), by midcentury Franklin regarded the German settlement in Pennsylvania— which at the time had reached roughly one-third of the colony's population—with some apprehension. Writing in 1751 to his fellow printer James Parker, Franklin expressed his fear that Pennsylvania "will in a few Years become a German Colony: Instead of their Learning our Language, we must learn their's [sic], or live as in a foreign country" (Franklin 1959, 4:120). Franklin complained that the Germans, whom he also called the Dutch, worked for lower wages, thereby taking jobs away from English workers, and he suspected them of disloyalty to the Crown: "How good Subjects they may make, and how faithful to the British Interest, is a Question worth considering" (4:121). Franklin berated the American Germans for speaking a nonstandard variety of their own language and for refusing to learn English, making communication with them impossible.* And Franklin, who considered the Spanish, Italians, Russians, Swedes, and all Germans except Saxons to be a "swarthy" racial group distinct from the English, objected to continued German immigration into the Pennsylvania colony: "Why should the Palatine Boors be suffered to swarm into our Settlements, and by herding together establish their Language and Manners to the exclusion of ours? Why should Pennsylvania, founded by the English, become a Colony of Aliens, who will shortly be so numerous as to Germanize us instead of our Anglifying them, and will never adopt our Language or Customs, any more than they can acquire our Complexion" (4:234). Franklin's widely publicized comment on the "Palatine Boors" haunted him for years, eventually costing him a Philadelphia county election in 1764, when he came in next-to-last in a field of fourteen (10:394).

On balance, however, Franklin was a moderate on the German question. In 1753 the English naturalist and former Quaker Peter Collinson sent his friend Franklin a list of radical recommendations for assimilating Pennsylvania's Germans. Collinson favored establishing English schools in German areas; making En-

---

*4:484; today as well it is common to hear claims that nonanglophone immigrants are illiterate in two languages, their native tongue and English, by which it is generally meant that they learn nonstandard varieties of each language.

glish a requirement for holding public office; requiring English
for deeds and contracts; offering a bounty for intermarriage between Germans and English and the settling of Germans in the
less populated colonies of Georgia, North Carolina, and Nova
Scotia; and prohibiting both the local German press and the im-
porting of German books (5:21). Franklin, who was of course a
printer in possession of a font of German type, supported all of
Collinson's recommendations except those encouraging intermarriage and limiting the printing and sale of German-language
materials.

WILLIAM SMITH'S BILINGUAL EDUCATION

Franklin's friend William Smith, who became the
first provost of the Philadelphia College, Academy and Charita-
ble School (the forerunner of the University of Pennsylvania) in
1750, as well as the editor of the *American Magazine* in 1757,
held views identical to Collinson's and similar to those held today by many supporters of English-first. As an educator, Smith
was active in the movement to establish English schools among
the Germans. Smith feared that the French settlers in Ohio
would seduce Pennsylvania's "uncultivated Race of *Germans*,"
and in a 1755 pamphlet he called for parliamentary action to
restrain and forcibly assimilate the colony's German population.
Complaining that the Germans had become "insolent, sullen,
and turbulent"—Smith's evidence for this was their alignment
with the Quakers in a recent election—Smith warned as well of
their "Popish" leanings and concluded, "I know nothing that will
hinder them, either from soon being able to give us Law and
Language, or else, by joining with the *French*, to eject all the
English Inhabitants" from their own colony (Smith 1755, 29).

Smith assumed that ignorance of English was prima facie evidence of low intelligence, a view that remains common: opponents of New Mexican statehood a century later repeatedly set
the alleged low level of intelligence of the territory's Hispanics
against the intellectual achievements of the rest of the nation,
and twentieth-century psychologists attributed the supposed inferior intelligence of the new immigrants from central and southern Europe directly to their lack of English. Smith was optimistic
that Pennsylvania's Germans, whom he characterized despite

their high literacy rate as "a Body of ignorant, proud, stubborn Clowns (who are unacquainted with our Language, our Manners, our Laws, and our Interests)," could be assimilated if German immigration to the colony were cut off. Nonetheless, he urged Parliament to enact a law that would "suspend the Right of Voting for Members of Assembly from the Germans, till they have a sufficient Knowledge of our Language and Constitution," an educational mission that he estimated would take about twenty years to complete (40).

As a further incentive for learning English, Smith, like Collinson, hoped "to make all Bonds, Contracts, Wills, and other legal Writings void, unless in the *English* Tongue." Although Smith himself had helped establish a German newspaper in the colony (Franklin 11:294–95n), he urged Parliament to discourage the printing of potentially seditious material by banning all foreign language newspapers and periodicals in Pennsylvania, or if that was considered too harsh, at least requiring them to publish "just and fair" English translations alongside the originals (42; such requirements became law much later, and only temporarily, during World War I). An anonymous line-by-line attack on Smith's anti-Quaker pamphlet managed to agree with only one of his points: the writer judged Smith's English-only proposals to be a "certainly proper and necessary" way of dealing with the Germans (*An Answer to an Invidious Pamphlet* 1755, 78), though the Commonwealth of Pennsylvania's early constitutions (1776, 1790) repudiated such thinking with their uncompromising stand on freedom of the press.

Like his contemporaries, William Smith assumed that a common language was a prerequisite for national unity, and despite his legal recommendations, his primary efforts were in the area of schooling. Smith proposed sending teachers and ministers among the Germans "to bind them to us by a common Language, and the Consciousness of a common Interest" (41). Smith commented privately to Franklin that the Germans needed an English education because they were unused to liberty, and he maintained that bilingual schools were necessary to bring English to the Germans (Franklin 5:215–18). In a subsequent pamphlet, Smith suggested extending the benefits of the English language to Native Americans in order to secure their loyalty in the struggle against the French. He boasted that an Indian chief friendly to the British cause had sent his two sons to the Philadelphia Academy, "where now they begin to read and to speak *English*" (Smith 1756, 49).

In 1753, working with the newly founded British Society for the Propagation of Christian Knowledge (SPCK) among the Germans in Pennsylvania, Smith planned a school that would bring together English- and German-speaking children in the same classrooms, to be taught by bilingual instructors, or at least by teachers willing to learn whichever language they lacked. Instruction would take place in both languages, and bilingual catechisms would be distributed among the poor. It is clear, though, that Smith's motivations were political as well as religious. He was alarmed at the prospect of a large body of Germans living separately in the English colony, maintaining their own language and customs. Smith sounded a theme that would be frequently repeated over the next two centuries: by being taught English the Pennsylvania Germans would learn "to feel the meaning and exult in the enjoyment of liberty, a home and social endearments." Through intermarriage and the acquisition of a common language, Smith hoped to create better British subjects resistant to the blandishments of the French. More important, perhaps, from the point of view of language, Smith's schools would bring English to those most able to adopt it: "The old can neither acquire our Language, nor quit their national manners. The young may do both" (Smith 1879, 1:30). The ultimate result of Smith's bilingual education, then, would not be the creation of a bilingual citizenry. Rather, Smith's goal was to assimilate Germans to the point where "all the narrow distinctions of extraction, &c., will be forgot—forever forgot—in higher interests" (1:31).

The German language would certainly be one of the distinctions of extraction to be lost in Smith's "bilingual" schools. Smith says as much when he evokes the glories of the republican Rome of Cincinnatus in describing the melting-pot society that he envisions for Pennsylvania: "Difference of manners, language & extraction, was now no more [in Rome]. . . . The rising generation acquired a conformity in all things. No distinction remained but between a virtuous and vicious citizen" (1:33). Repeatedly,

Smith stressed the importance of a universal knowledge of English. Nonanglophone Germans would remain "strangers to the sacred sound of liberty in the land where they were born [Germany], & uninstructed in the right use & value of it in the country where they now enjoy it." Without English, he insisted, "it is scarce possible to remove any prejudices they once entertain," while he perceived the maintenance of German as a subversive activity, allowing "such prejudices . . . daily [to] increase among them, unknown to us" (1:36).

In a description of the SPCK charity schools printed by Benjamin Franklin in 1755, we find one of the earliest statements of the common argument that a knowledge of English is essential for economic success in America. The purpose of the schools "is to qualify the Germans for all the Advantages of native English Subjects. But this could not have been done without giving them an Opportunity of learning English, by speaking of which they may expect to rise to Places of Profit and Honor in the Country" (Weber 1905, 44). Smith had an additional motive in advocating German-English schools: the use of the new Philadelphia Academy to train Pennsylvania Germans to teach in them. He warned that teachers recruited from abroad are not to be trusted. On the other hand, Smith's home-grown teachers would be bilingual in English and "High Dutch," and they would "be educated under the Eye of the public in the colonies where they are wanted; & thus we will not only be certain of their principles, but also have them complete masters both of the English & German languages" (Smith 1879, 1:35).

While Smith was supported by a number of influential Germans, including Henry Muhlenberg, the "virtual founder of the Lutheran church in America" (*Dictionary of American Biography* [hereafter *DAB*], s.v.), his assimilationist leanings drew opposition from Christopher Sauer, the German printer whose newspaper and other publications helped form popular opinion among the German Americans of Pennsylvania. In 1754 Sauer alerted the readers of the *Pennsylvanische Berichte* that the charity school scheme sought to deprive them of their religion, their language, and their ethnicity: "German ministers are urged to learn to preach in English so that the Germans may by degrees become one nation with the English, and be provided with English clergymen." Sauer decried suggestions that the Germans would prove disloyal in a political crisis. He observed, "The Irish, the Swedes and the Welsh keep their languages, yet for all are not looked upon as a disloyal people." Why, Sauer asked, are they not sent English teachers as well? (Weber 1905, 38–39).

Sauer's assessment of the evangelical as well as the assimilationist motives of the founders of the charity schools is undoubtedly correct. The statements of many of Pennsylvania's Anglos bear this out. In 1756, for example, Smith wrote to the bishop of Oxford, "Till we can succeed in making our Germans speak English & become good Protestants, I doubt we shall never have a firm hold of them" (Smith 1879, 1:146). And Rev. Thomas Barton proposed in 1764 that a law requiring Germans "to give their children an English Education, which could not be deemed an abridgment of their liberty (as British Subjects)," would inevitably lead to their conversion to the Church of England (Weber 1905, 62).

Sauer's continued attacks in the press, together with faltering financial support from England, contributed to the failure of the SPCK schools, the first of which opened in 1755. They proved to be largely monolingual English schools after all (the school in Lancaster, an area of heavy German settlement, taught English, Latin, and Greek), and in 1757 the complaint was lodged against them by a leader of the Reformed Church that "the Directors try to erect nothing but English schools, and care nothing for the German language" (Weber 1905, 59), bearing out Sauer's contention that the English hoped to strip the Germans of their language and literature. In all, there were about thirteen such schools, never gathering more than one thousand pupils, and all had closed by 1764.

PROFESSING ENGLISH ONLY

The idea of German-English schools did not die with the 1760s. Benjamin Rush (1951, 1:365–66) advocated the retention of German in Pennsylvania: "The German youth will more readily acquire knowledge in the language in which they have been taught to express their first ideas than in any other." Rush also felt that Germans could not defend their property or attain eminence in the country without a knowledge of English acquired *through* German. This bilingual approach he deemed "*the only possible means*, consistent with their liberty, of spreading a knowledge of English among [the Germans]." Interestingly, Rush (1951, 1:493) foresaw as well a day when English and Spanish would dominate the hemisphere: "When we consider the influence which the prevalence of only *two* languages, viz., the English and the Spanish, in the extensive regions of North and South-America will have upon manners, commerce, knowledge, and civilization, scenes of human happiness and glory open before us which elude from their magnitude the utmost grasp of the human understanding." Rush served on the board when the German-sponsored, bilingually oriented Franklin College (named after its primary benefactor, Benjamin Franklin, and later merged to form Franklin and Marshall College) opened its doors in Lancaster in 1787.

Rev. Joseph Hutchins was appointed Franklin College's first professor of English language and belles lettres. The college trustees asked Hutchins "to show that the College is founded for cultivating the English language as well as for other literary purposes," though they were so outraged by the insensitive, hectoring, English-only sermon Hutchins delivered at the institution's opening ceremonies that the publication of his remarks was deferred for nearly twenty years.

In his blunt comments belittling German and lamenting the handicaps German students brought with them to the classroom, Hutchins demonstrated an extreme insensitivity to the clientele he was supposed to educate. Hutchins set out by characterizing Franklin College as "unluckily instituted under some peculiar disadvantages" because its students all came from German backgrounds ([1787] 1806, 9). He then warned his audience that, despite their wishes, English must replace German in the inevitable Americanization of their children:

> Whatever impediments you throw in the course of spreading [the English] language in its true pronunciation and elegance among your children, will be so many obstructions to their future interest in private and public life . . . to their future eminence in the public councils of America . . . and to that national union with their fellow citizens of the

United States, which [all] are anxiously wishing to promote. As the limited capacity of man can very seldom attain excellence in more than one language, the study of
English will consequently demand the principal attention
of your children. (14–15)

Despite his abrasiveness, Hutchins's words were prophetic:
Franklin soon became a monolingual English school.

Speaking two years before Webster put into print his own ideas
about Federal English, Hutchins strongly advocated the idea of a
national American language. He acknowledged that, were he in
Germany, he would support the universal study of German. However, since despite their German antecedents, the Franklin students were American, they would have no choice but to function
in English, which had already come to be viewed as the nation's
official language: "Although the English language is nervous,
copious, and beautiful, yet I do not recommend your preference of
it on that account; but solely because it is the national language
of the United States; because it is the language of those laws and
of the courts of judicature, by which your posterity must be governed, and their privileges secured" (16).

Hutchins acknowledged that German might be studied as a
secondary language, though his negative characterization of such
study seems surprising in one whose professional interest purport-
edly lay in philology. Rather, he expressed what was already the
typical American attitude that proficiency in languages is an
educational frill: all "English Americans . . . must allow a skill
in languages to be frequently a *useful*, and at all times an *orna-
mental part* of a liberal education" (16). Hutchins himself
proudly admitted knowing no German, a fact that did not endear
him to the Franklin community. He further angered his audience
by acknowledging that he had not understood the sermon delivered in German at the opening ceremonies by Henry Muhlenberg, by then one of Pennsylvania's most prominent citizens, and
by insisting that Germans in America could hardly object to
making English the language of their religion.

But object they did. German immigration to the United States
continued strong through the late eighteenth and the nineteenth
centuries. With the failure of the SPCK schools, and the faltering

early history of Franklin College, German continued to function as Pennsylvania's second language. In fact, though, a shift to English was occurring at a slow but regular pace. In many areas, according to Kloss (1940, 230–31), trilingualism was becoming a way of life. Though English commonly served as the language of religion and the sciences in Philadelphia in the early 1800s, and somewhat later in the middle and southwestern part of the state, High German persisted in the press and the arts, and Pennsylvania German, or Pennsylvanish, remained the language of everyday communication for many German Americans in the state up to World War I. Official state publications were routinely issued in German as well as English, including the minutes of the state constitutional conventions of 1776 and 1789–90. Sessions laws were published in German as well as English from 1786 to 1856 (Kloss 1977, 143). And German schools continued to exist: neither section 44 of the 1776 constitution, nor article 7 of the 1790 constitution, both dealing with the common schools, prescribes an official language of instruction, though one section of article 7, guaranteeing the rights of religious societies, implies protection for the German parochial schools of the commonwealth.

The Pennsylvania Constitutional Convention of 1837–38

The language issue surfaced again in Pennsylvania during discussions to amend article 7 at the constitutional convention of 1837–38, at a time when the nativist movement was beginning to gain some ground in the Northeast. At the convention, the writer and lawyer Charles Jared Ingersoll proposed the establishment of free public schools to provide for education "in the English and German languages" (Pennsylvania 1837, 5:186). Ingersoll argued that the constitution's silence on the question of German in the schools had too often resulted in the imposition of English in the classroom and banishment of German. This he regarded as "an act of despotism" worthy of tsarist Russia: "Who is the conqueror, except it be Nicholas of Russia, in the instance of the poor Poles, who would oblige his victims to un-learn their mother tongue, and to learn another?" (259).

Ingersoll faulted English education for ignoring the German

population, thereby making them the least-educated ethnic group in the state: "They were obliged to be educated by their masters, and . . . they were obliged to be educated in a language they did not relish" (254). Citing a letter from the philologist and legal philosopher Pierre Du Ponceau complaining of the degeneration of German in the commonwealth, Ingersoll called for integrating the Germans into the public schools, enabling them "there to read and write their own vernacular, instead of dictating to them our own tongue" (189). Ingersoll reminded the convention that there were no monolingual nations: even in England, France, and Germany several languages existed side by side, and he insisted that English and German would not interfere with each other if German were to be thus encouraged in Pennsylvania.

Opposition to Ingersoll's amendment mounted quickly, and the debate lasted several days. Misreading Ingersoll's coordinate wording which called for schools in "English and German"—a pairing that suggests an approach similar to our notion today of bilingual education—delegate James Dunlop warned that the disjunctive "English or German" in Ingersoll's amendment might be taken as giving school districts the choice of excluding German, and while he admitted that multilingualism existed throughout the world, he reminded the convention that no other nation willingly *supported* two languages: "We would look upon them as being deranged, to think of such a thing." Even unofficial multilingualism in Dunlop's view creates distrust and causes both "public excitement" and dirty partisan politics (227).

Delegate Benjamin Martin objected that German could not be favored without considering the Scotch, Irish, Spanish, or French, who might also wish their children to learn in their own vernacular.* Both Almon Read and Joseph R. Chandler preferred leaving the choice of language up to the local school district. Chandler further observed that Spanish was becoming increasingly important for political and commercial dealings with neighboring nations, and that there were sections of Pennsylvania where only

*Page 194; this too has become a common theme in the attack on minority-language rights: if you make concessions for one language, you must make them for all, and that would lead to chaos.

Welsh was spoken (219, 243). Chandler characterized bilingual education as "mongrel education." Noting the difficulty of finding qualified bilingual teachers, he added, "and when they are found, they seldom either teach the German or the English in such manner as any person would desire to have their children taught." Though he accepted the existence of German schools in areas where German prevailed, Chandler favored education in the national language: "Do not let us fix upon any portion of the commonwealth, the evil of living within a language. . . . The Saxon, the Russian, the French and the Irish, when they come among us, should come into our language, as well as into our country" (195). And though he claimed to admire the German language as much as anyone, Chandler would prohibit German schools in order to protect the English language from corruption. He did "not wish to see our own language destroyed by the introduction of any foreign idiom, any more than he wished to see our institutions altered in order to correspond with those of Germany" (243).

There was some debate among the convention delegates over the extent to which German immigrants had either maintained their native language or shifted to English. It was a question that had concerned Pennsylvanians for close to a century. In 1750 the Swedish botanist Peter Kalm observed the deviation of Swedish in America from the Old World variety and predicted that Swedish in the New World was doomed to extinction (Kalm [1937] 1966, 2:683–87). Kalm found Dutch disappearing as well, particularly among the young, who "scarcely ever spoke anything but English and . . . became offended if they were taken for Dutch, because they preferred to pass for English" (626). Similarly, the bishop of the Swedish churches in America, Israel Acrelius, noted as early as 1758 that there was a school on every Pennsylvania hillside, and that "none, whether boys or girls, are now growing up who cannot read English, write, and cipher" (Weber 1905, 22).

This is clearly an exaggeration—both as to the number of schools and as to the number of English-speaking Germans—as are Benjamin Franklin's complaints that the Germans know no English at all. But in 1820 Edward Everett's *North American Review* ("German Emigration," 12) cites the visiting German writer Von Furstenwarther complaining that German is disappearing from the churches of Pennsylvania and from its towns, and that what remains of the language has become a corrupt dialect of English. (The reviewer, most likely Everett himself, who had recently returned from studying in Germany, then criticizes the quality of Von Furstenwarther's German.) Von Furstenwarther further decries the negative attitude toward German prevalent among the young: "The children of German parents are commonly ashamed of the country and language of their fathers, so that in the third generation, at the present day, the traces of their origin disappear." This the reviewer finds laudable, and after an ironic comment on the difficulties of bilingual debate in the Dutch parliament, he turns the question of official language against another American language minority in order to make a joke about the U.S. Congress: "Were our leaders in Congress, who think it incumbent on themselves to make a long speech on every subject that comes up, obliged to translate their harangue, first into Chickahominy, and then into Kickapoo, we apprehend it would prove a damper." In advocating universal English in the states, the writer goes on to raise the fear of Babel in a comment that is particularly telling if he is indeed Everett, who held the chair of classical Greek at Harvard and was the master of several classical and modern languages: "We recommend to all German and other emigrants . . . instead of wishing to cherish and keep up their peculiarities of language and manners, to get over and forget them as soon as possible; remembering, that from the days of the tower of Babel to the present, confusion of tongues has ever been one of the most active causes of intellectual and political misunderstanding and confusion" (18).

In 1837 we find constitutional convention delegate James Clarke insisting that the German intelligentsia universally favored assimilation. According to Clarke, the German clergy want all Germans to speak English. And delegate Thomas S. Cunningham, who longed for a monolingual United States, agreed that most Germans "learn their children the English language" because of the advantages it offers them (Pennsylvania 1838, 5:224).

James Dunlop, the English-first delegate who praised the German language and who came closest to claiming that some of his best friends were German, insisted that virtually all the young

Germans in the state spoke English; that the Germans did not want any special favors for their language; and that he saw no need for maintaining the German language in Pennsylvania. It was not so much their language that Dunlop resented as the power of the German voting bloc to elect only Germans to the governorship, while excluding those, like himself, of Scots-Irish descent (228–29). Andrew J. Cline agreed that "most of the enlightened Germans had given up all desire of perpetuating the German language," acknowledging that German was used not for learning or literature, in Pennsylvania, but only for religious studies (244–45; Ingersoll too rejected the claim that the Germans no longer used their language in their worship [259]).

In contrast, delegate Charles A. Barnitz observed, probably correctly, that only the urban Germans had adopted English, and that German remained very much alive in the countryside, where "we may as well have these schools in the Greek language as the English" (271). Joseph Konigmacher, of Lancaster, refuted assertions that most Germans were shifting to English, though he opposed Ingersoll's bilingual education amendment (284). Joshua F. Cox insisted that while most of his constituents who were of German descent spoke English, they wanted their children to be educated in German: "They retained a very natural attachment to the mother tongue, and did not like to see it neglected or disused" (266).

The delegates to the 1837–38 convention were also split then—as we are in the United States today—on the relative value of immersion and bilingual education as ways of spreading English across the land. Charles Barnitz insisted that children "must be instructed in that language which they have been accustomed to hear" (278). Robert Fleming agreed that immersion would not work: "If the Germans are sent to an English school and, at home, have nothing but German, they will improve but very little in English studies" (242).

Delegate James Merrill recognized that while many of Pennsylvania's Germans had learned English, many others had not. However, Merrill saw the position of English as secure: "Nobody can suppose that the German can ever supersede the English in this state, or in this country." He therefore favored German-language schools, warning that German-speaking children immersed in English-language schools would surely fail (199; for a confirmation of such predictions, see chapter 5). His eloquent argument in favor of transitional bilingual education—naturally he does not use this modern name for the practice—has been applied over and over in the past two centuries: "If it is our object to make our people become homogeneous, will you do it by coercing this class of our citizens to come into this system of English education at the outstart, or will you give their minds a start in their own language? Give them a chance to obtain some intelligence in their own language, and then they will be more able to see the necessity of coming into the language of the state" (199).

Many delegates claimed to agree with Ingersoll that German schools should be permitted, but argued either that the state constitution already permitted them, or that the matter should be dealt with not in the constitution but in the legislature. Supporting Ingersoll's amendment, Charles Barnitz maintained that unless German-language schooling were explicitly authorized in the constitution, local school officials would interpret it as being prohibited (240–41). Daniel Saeger pointed out that in some parts of Pennsylvania, the school law had already been narrowly interpreted as forbidding German public schools because they were not explicitly permitted, and other delegates confirmed that this was the case in their districts. Daniel Saeger agreed that a constitutional basis for such schools would appease German residents who were reluctant to pay taxes for the state-sponsored English-language schools which they did not use (215). Delegate James M. Porter suggested that German public schools would also serve to attract pupils away from the parochial schools (this argument supported bilingual public schools in Ohio later in the century), though he supposed no constitutional mandate to be necessary because Pennsylvania schools were already bilingual where the population required it. Porter lamented the decline of German in the New World, though delegate Sturdevant did not feel that German-language schools could correct this. Porter concluded that it did not matter what language children were educated in, so long as they were educated.

Surprisingly little time is spent during the debate on the Ingersoll amendment in celebrating English as the language of liberty. Rather, the emphasis is on the utility of English as what we now call a language of wider communication, and as the means of unifying the American population. Many delegates did remark that a knowledge English was requisite for performing the duties of citizenship (these duties are neither specified nor elaborated). Delegate Thomas H. Sill praised German as a copious and learned language, but objected that if a child were to learn only one language in school, then English would be the most useful "because it is the prevailing language of the country, and all business, both of the general government and of this state, is conducted in that language, as well as the business of the courts of justice" (201–02). Sill saw English as necessary in order for citizens to function beyond the German neighborhood or to represent the German population at the state and national level. He reminded the convention that German instruction was already permitted in Pennsylvania's German communities, but he warned that passing Ingersoll's amendment to article 7 would set a dangerous precedent of support for two languages in the state: it would acknowledge "that there are, and ought to be two languages and, in some degree, two communities of people kept up for all time to come, in the commonwealth of Pennsylvania" (202).

Sill opposed both the active suppression of German and the designation of English as the official language of instruction in the schools, but he cited a speech made by the educator and biblical scholar Calvin Ellis Stowe (the husband of the future novelist Harriet Beecher Stowe) at Columbus, Ohio, praising the Prussian school system for requiring the national language, German, and not the local dialects. According to Stowe, a student of many languages, "This uniformity of language is of great importance to a nation's prosperity and safety; it is necessary, as a common bond of union and sympathy, between the different parts of the state; and without it, a nation is a bundle of clans, rather than a united and living body." Stowe is cited as further warning that "the facility of business and the progress of intelligence require uniformity of language, and parents have no right to deprive their children of the advantages, which a knowledge of the prevailing speech of the country affords" (203). Sill himself viewed monolingualism as essential: "I think that the whole people of this state should be amalgamated as soon as that end can possibly be accomplished; and that they should be made one people in sentiment—in principle—in language" (202).

Perhaps most damaging to Ingersoll's position was the opposition of U.S. Rep. William Hiester, an assimilated German who objected to the bilingualism prevalent in the Louisiana legislature, found the need for German schools declining each year, and argued strongly for unhyphenating all hyphenated Pennsylvanians:

> All the public records of every kind are kept in the English language, and it seems right to me that the Germans should be made to accommodate themselves to it. . . . I believe that all intelligent Germans entertain the opinion, that it would be much better to dispense with the German language in the schools. I hope to see the day when the people of this commonwealth will not be distinguished by the title of German and English, and when we shall be known only by the common title of Pennsylvanians. (281)

The convention eventually rejected Ingersoll's bilingual amendment by a vote of 51 to 68. It similarly rejected proposals to require German of local officials in German areas of the state, though the convention supported, with virtually no opposition, the publication of its journal in German as well as English. Had the debate on revising article 7 of the Pennsylvania constitution taken place a year later, there might have been more support for authorizing German as a language of instruction in the schools. In December 1837, one month after the Pennsylvania constitutional debate, the Ohio General Assembly published Calvin Stowe's report on European education. This widely circulated study (the Pennsylvania House of Representatives reprinted it in 1838, at the request of the state commissioner of education), which, as delegate Sill reported to the convention, praised the Prussian system of education in the national language as the most advanced in the world, also acknowledged the necessity of bilingual education. In his report, Stowe observed with evident approval that in the Polish region of Prussia, both German and Polish were taught in the elementary schools. In fact, Stowe concluded his report with a summary of the special needs of the children of non-English speaking immigrants to the United States in which he supports bilingual education as a means of ensuring a smooth transition to the national language of his own country:

> It is essential that [the children of immigrants] receive a good English education. But they are not prepared to avail themselves of the advantages of our common English schools, their imperfect acquaintance with the language being an insuperable bar to their entering on the course of study. It is necessary, therefore, that there be some preparatory schools, in which instruction shall be communicated both in English and in their native tongue. The English is, and must be, the language of this country, and the highest interests of our State demand it of the Legislature to require that the English language be thoroughly taught in every school which they patronize. Still, the exigencies of the case make it necessary that there should be some schools expressly fitted to the condition of our foreign emigrants, to introduce them to a knowledge of our language and institutions. A school of this kind has been established in Cincinnati.... The instructions are all given both in German and English, and this use of two languages does not at all interrupt the progress of the children in their respective studies. (Stowe 1838, 46)

Both a German-language revival in the 1850s and a resurgence of German immigration later in the century kept the issue of German in the Pennsylvania schools before the public. In 1852 the state superintendent of schools affirmed that "if any considerable number of Germans desire to have their children instructed in their own language, their wishes should be gratified," though he added that no one could force school directors to implement German classes (Kloss 1940, 1:268–69). In 1857 the state school superintendent repeated the opinion that directors could not be compelled to cause German to be taught, noting that only 7,000 of the state's 541,000 pupils were German-speaking, and that bilingual education did not work well: "The teaching of German and English in the same school and the transition of German pupils to the English is attended with great embarrassment. An adequate remedy is very desirable; but probably time and the increasing prevalence of the English language in the common conversation will prove to be the only available one" (269–70).

Bilingual schools persisted in the heavily German city of Lancaster until 1895, and in 1905 Pennsylvania required the publication of official notices in German, Italian, and Yiddish newspapers (Kloss 307; see chapter 4 for a discussion of court challenges to the validity of such publication orders in other states). In 1918 German was banned from all Pennsylvania schools. That law was repealed in 1921, however, though Pennsylvania did join with the majority of the United States in mandating English instruction from English texts (except for foreign languages taught as such) for all private as well as public schools.

Bilingual Louisiana

The legal history of Louisiana shows a similar shift from early protection of languages other than English (French was not initially a *minority* language in Louisiana) to a more decidedly English-first policy by the later nineteenth century. Settled originally by the Spanish around 1542, Louisiana was claimed by the French in 1682, ceded to Spain in 1762, and returned to France in 1800 before it was sold to the United States in 1803 (Kloss 1977, 107).

The Territory of Louisiana, or Orleans, as it was also called, was clearly multilingual long before it became a state in 1812. There is no official recognition of French in the state's first constitution of 1812, which ordains that "the laws, the public records and the judicial and legislative written proceedings of the State shall be promulgated, preserved and conducted in the language in which the constitution of the United States is written" (Louisiana 1845, *Journal*, 313). However, both the first constitution and the accompanying motion to annex West Florida were ordered printed "in the two languages," a phrase whose lack of specificity indicates that the equivalent status of French and English for all other purposes was accepted as a matter of course (Louisiana [1814] 1844, 5, 10). Indeed, until 1830 the majority of Louisiana's population was of French descent.

The proceedings of the 1812 Louisiana constitutional convention were printed in French and English, as well, and the French journal was reprinted for the convenience of delegates to the second constitutional convention, in 1845, where the issue of official recognition of French proved controversial. The 1845 convention passed without discussion article 103, a continuation of the 1812 requirement that laws and public records be written in English, and there was apparently no hesitation in passing article 132, which read, "The constitution and laws of this State, shall be promulgated [that is, 'published' or 'printed'] in the English and French languages."* However, there was considerable opposition to the proposed amendment requiring two major legislative officers to be bilingual: "The secretary of the senate and clerk of the house shall be conversant with the French and English languages; and members may address either house in the French or English language."

Explaining his amendment, Bernard Marigny told the delegates that while French was clearly on the decline in the state legislature, the proposal would prove a courtesy for the older members of government who had not learned English. Opponents to Marigny's amendment labeled the measure unnecessary. George S. Guion remarked that "the day is not distant when every citizen will speak [English]" (Louisiana 1845, *Proceedings*, 870). Thomas H. Lewis observed that the French-speaking legislators always addressed their colleagues in English (836), and he objected that requiring bilingual competence for the secretary and clerk would not "force the French language to be employed, if in the nature of things, it was destined to fall into disuse" (865). Thomas M. Wadsworth claimed that if French were to be privileged, Spanish should be protected as well (866). Wadsworth facetiously supported the right of legislators to speak in any language at all—"a member might address the chair in Choctaw" (835)—but he clearly favored English-only, arguing, as had been done earlier in the German debate in Pennsylvania, that the youth of the state were already abandoning French in favor of English: "We have a national language, and that language must predominate. It

*Journal, 313–15; the legal distinction between the two articles is not entirely clear, though the latter seems merely to permit French translation of what were initially English laws.

will be the language of the rising generation of French descent" (867).

Marigny pointed out that French was not protected in the 1812 constitution because at the time the French had a three-fourths majority of the state population. He complained bitterly that "within the last thirty-three years . . . the Anglo-Saxon race have invaded everything," and boasted, "We could have become Americans without you." Marigny described his colleagues' hostility to French as a none too subtle attack on the "civil system of law" (866; Louisiana at the time operated under a combination of the French *code civile* and the English common law). His passionate defense of the measure ensured its passage, though there was no support for another proposal to create French criminal courts (bilingual civil courts already existed) or for a move requiring bilingualism of all appointed or elected officials and their staffs.

The language articles of the 1845 constitution were continued without change in the 1861 secessionist state constitution, including the provision for writing laws in the language of the U.S. Constitution, despite the fact that the convention had repudiated the Constitution in favor of that of the Confederate States of America (Louisiana 1861). After the Civil War, the Louisiana constitution was rewritten once again, and during the debates some delegates clearly opposed French language rights. Alfred C. Hills, who was new to the state, felt Americans should speak English or go back where they came from:

> I believe the English language is the official language of this country. I believe in a homogeneous people, in one language and one system of law, and I believe that the publication of the laws of this State, or the proceedings of any convention, or any English court, in the French language, is a nuisance and ought to be abolished in this State or any other. . . . If there are any in the State who cannot speak, read or write the language, they should learn to do so before they reside in the country any longer. (Louisiana 1864, *Proceedings,* 47)

Delegate John Henderson, Jr., declared his patriotism by claiming, "I never will vote for any other language but the American" (47), while A. Cazabat challenged the notion that English was the constitutional language of the state, urging that French be permitted as a courtesy to Louisiana's many wealthy and concerned nonanglophone citizens (48). In practice, this courtesy was observed: French was recognized as an important Louisiana language, if not an explicitly official one. Opening prayers at the 1864 convention sessions were conducted in English and French, convention proceedings were printed in French, as usual, and the constitution itself was ordered to be printed in English, French, and German newspapers. Support for Spanish and Irish, called for by several delegates, was not forthcoming at all.

Language first emerged as a school issue at the 1864 convention. The committee on education recommended that English be the sole language of instruction in the state's schools. Delegate Alfred Hills explained that the education committee had not sought to prohibit French, but rather to require English, "because we have schools in the State now in which no language except French is taught, and the result is the children grow up unable to speak English, and we wish to provide against this evil" (*Debates*, 478). Cazabat's attempt to include French as an official language of instruction was defeated (Louisiana 1864, *Journal*, 138), though the measure finally adopted as article 142 was then amended so as not to exclude French entirely: "The general exercises in the common schools shall be conducted in the English language" (*Debates*, 479).

Support for French was not as strong in 1864 as it had been at previous conventions, though this may simply reflect an increase in assimilation rather than an attempt, as Kloss (1977, 114) suggests, to punish the Louisiana French for favoring secession. The laws and proceedings of the state of Louisiana were still required to be written in the language of the U.S. Constitution, though they were no longer to be "promulgated" in French as well, and the secretary and clerk were no longer required to be bilingual. Instead, according to article 128, which was adopted without discussion, English was named as the only language that could be required of public officials: "The Legislature shall pass no law excluding citizens of this State from office for not being conversant with any language except that in which the constitution of the United States is written" (*Journal*, 182).

By 1870 earlier bilingual provisions in many Louisiana legal matters were replaced by English-only requirements, though statutes mandating bilingual publication of legal notices, and in some cases publication in German as well, continued to proliferate until 1914, when English-only laws took over nationwide (see Kloss 1940, 1:190–213, for details of the various statutes). After 1864 constitutions and school legislation permit French-language schools "where the French language predominates, if no additional expense is incurred thereby," although, as was the case with Pennsylvania, in 1921 the Louisiana constitution once again required only English in the schools (Kloss 1940, 1:165–67). However the Louisiana constitution of 1974 implies protection of French once again in guaranteeing the right to preserve "historic linguistic and cultural origins" (Grant 1978, 10).

A Federal Case

The states accommodated their ethnic populations to a greater or lesser extent, all the while defending English as the "native" tongue of the land, but little or no action was taken at the federal level in the eighteenth and nineteenth centuries to support minority languages. From the outset, lawmakers and public officials frequently sought to address the large number of German speakers in their native language, not so much to assure language maintenance (that was the goal of some, but clearly not all, German Americans) as to appeal to an ethnic voting bloc and to ensure communication between government and the citizenry.

In the 1770s the Continental Congress printed German translations of some of its proceedings, including the Articles of Confederation, and German Americans actively supported the Revolution. (French translations of the articles and other documents were printed as well in an attempt to attract Quebec to the Union.) Kloss (1977, 27) maintains that German was the language of command of the German battalions, which consisted of young, American-born Germans. However, nativists opposed making any concessions to ethnic groups and from the outset advocated an English-only approach as a means of defending not simply the native tongue but the native American as well. (The term *native American* became widespread in the early to mid-nineteenth

century, in association with the Native American, or Know
Nothing, party. It generally referred not to the American Indian,
its primary sense now, but to native-born, typically Anglo-Saxon
Protestant, Americans.)

THE GERMAN VOTE

On 13 January 1795 a proposal in Congress to print
all federal laws in German as well as English lost by only one
vote—or so it has been made to seem by pro-German historians
and English-only activists: in actuality, the final vote on whether
or not to translate federal laws into German, which took place
after another congressional debate one month later, is not record-
ed. The translation proposal itself originated as a petition to Congress on 20 March 1794 from a group of Germans living in Au-
gusta, Virginia. A House committee responding to that petition
recommended publishing federal statutes (in English) and dis-
tributing them to the states, together with the publication of
three thousand sets of laws in German, "for the accommodation
of such German citizens of the United States, as do not understand the English language" (*American State Papers* ser. 10, v.
1:114). According to the succinct report in the *Aurora Gazette* on
the House debate over the proposal on 13 January 1795, "A great
variety of plans were proposed, but none that seemed to meet the
general sense of the House" (22 January 1795, p. 3). A vote to
adjourn and sit again on the recommendation failed, 42 to 41.
This was clearly interpreted by the House as a vote of no confidence both in the committee's recommendation to publish laws
in German and in its recommendation on the distribution of the
sets of laws once they were published. A new committee was
then formed and asked to report again, and the House adjourned.
It is from this close vote, not on an actual bill but on adjournment, that the so-called German vote legend has probably been
based.

On 16 February 1795 the House once again considered the
question of promulgating the laws, and among the issues, once
again, was translating federal statutes into German. This time,
some of the actual debate has been preserved. Rep. Thomas
Hartley argued that "it was perhaps desirable that the Germans

should learn English; but if it is our object to give present information, we should do it in the language understood. The Germans who are advanced in years cannot learn our language in a day. It would be generous in the Government to inform those persons. Many honest men, in the late disturbances [the Whiskey Rebellion], were led away by misrepresentation; ignorance of the laws laid them open to deception."

William V. Murray, who opposed translating into German, countered "that it had never been the custom in England to translate the laws into Welsh or Gaelic, and yet the great bulk of the Welsh, and some hundred thousands of people in Scotland, did not understand a word of English" (*Annals of Congress* 4:1228–29). The House finally approved publication of current and future federal statutes in English only. The bill was agreed to by the Senate and signed by President Washington the following month.

The January vote on adjournment became known as "the German Vote" or "the Muhlenberg Vote," after the first Speaker of the House of Representatives, Pennsylvania's Frederick Augustus Muhlenberg, a Federalist and son of Henry Muhlenberg, well known as a pro-English German. Although the roll call vote does not survive, tradition has it that Muhlenberg stepped down to cast the deciding negative. Tradition notwithstanding, too much weight should not be given to the fact that the Speaker was not in the chair on this occasion. It was, of course, common for the Speaker to step down, and Muhlenburg did so on many other occasions during the Third Congress. Even a positive vote on the adjournment issue would not necessarily have led to approval of German translations of the laws, a concession which the Congress has repeatedly refused to make ever since.

On a number of occasions during the nineteenth century the Congress again rejected motions to print laws or other documents in German as well as English. Nonetheless, this January 1795 vote has been transmuted by English-first supporters (with the help of some inaccurate nineteenth-century German accounts of the event) into a myth that German came close to replacing English as the national language of the United States (Kloss 1977, 28; Kloss 1940 1:86–92). A correspondent in a recent Ann Landers column alluded to this myth as a fact that demonstrated the tenuous position of English in the new nation, although the date was changed to the more patriotically crucial year of 1776.

FEDERAL ENGLISH-ONLY VOTES

German was not the only language dealt with by the Congress. In 1810 legislators rejected a petition from Michigan to translate the laws into French, arguing that such an action would confuse the law and discourage assimilation to English:

> Great inconvenience and confusion might result from having two separate texts for the same law, susceptible, as they necessarily would be from the imperfection of all languages, of different and perhaps opposite interpretations. The policy of legalizing any other than the prevailing language of the country is also objectionable, on the ground that it would tend to encourage and perpetuate the other dialects which partially prevail in different parts of the Union, and which, it is believed, ought rather to be discouraged.

On a more political note, the Congress concluded that a national language might prove even more important than an informed citizenry: "In a Republic, where the operations of Government are the result of the combined opinions of its citizens, it is important that the people at large should possess, not only enlightened, but similar views of the public interest; and it is not, therefore, of more consequence that information should be generally disseminated, than that the avenues to it should be common" (*Annals of Congress* 21:1886).

In December 1837 nine hundred members of the Native American Association, a group dedicated to opposing immigration and Catholicism, met and drafted a memorial to Congress warning of the danger posed by foreigners and urging that they be denied citizenship. According to the group's report, which accused Europe of dumping its paupers and criminals on the United States, the framers of the Constitution could not have imagined that by allowing immigration they would "place a large portion of the power of this Government in the hands of adventurers from every clime, before they could have time to acquire a knowledge of our language, much less before they could have learned the first principles of a republican government" (Native American 1838, 3). Congress did not act on this or other similar anti-alien measures (Bennett 1988, 51).

In 1843 Rep. Alexander Ramsey of Pennsylvania (later governor of Minnesota and U.S. senator from that state), who was of German and Scottish extraction, introduced a proposal to print fifteen thousand copies of President Polk's annual message in English, and another three thousand copies in German. Rep. John Slidell of Louisiana insisted that French was "the constitutional language" of his state (as we noted earlier, French was not mentioned in the Louisiana constitution until 1845). Accordingly, Slidell amended Ramsey's bill to add two thousand copies in French, and a South Carolina representative called for copies in Low German as well. Charles Jared Ingersoll, who had earlier supported bilingual education in Pennsylvania, favored this measure as well, remarking that bilingualism was common both in Europe and in his home state. However, other representatives opposed both the Ramsey-Slidell bill and an expanded version introduced by Ramsey after his initial version failed. Rep. Henry Murphy of New York argued, facetiously, that he was "at a loss himself to discover in what way advantage was to be derived to this country by printing these documents in these different languages, unless it was by combining the copiousness and richness of all into one, and making from the whole an American language" (*Congressional Globe* 1843, 43–44), while others feared the excessive costs of printing federal documents in what might be an ever-increasing number of languages, and Rep. Samuel Beardsley of New York expressed dismay that the House might "break in upon its established practice, and fall back and adopt the language of a foreign country" (44). Rep. Daniel Barnard of New York was perhaps most direct in his nativism, and least patient with nonanglophones, holding "it to be the duty of every American citizen who may have had the misfortune to be born in any country but this, and educated in any other land, when he comes here and takes upon himself American citizenship, to devote himself to learning the English language" (45).

Ramsey's motion was tabled without a vote, and subsequent attempts to authorize German translations of federal documents met with derision. In 1844 a proposal by Rep. John Wentworth of Illinois to print two thousand copies of the president's message in German was facetiously amended to include "every other tongue talked in the United States of America." It went down to defeat amid outcries of "What! In the Cherokee?" and in "the Old Congo language" (*Congressional Globe* 1844, 7). Similar moves were defeated in 1845, 1846, and 1847. In 1862 a proposal to print twenty-five thousand copies of the Patent Office Report on Agriculture for 1861 in German brought forth the opposition comment from Rep. Justin Morrill of Vermont that Germans knew English better than the members of any other immigrant group. Morrill characterized the proposal as "utterly subversive of the true doctrine of the country." Ignorant of the long if largely unsuccessful history of previous considerations of printing in German, Morrill feared, "for the first time in the whole history of our Government, a departure . . . from the sound and correct principle which has heretofore been acted on, of printing our documents in the English language" (*Congressional Globe* 1862, 1821). The measure passed, but on reconsideration several days later Rep. Eliakim Walton of Vermont worried "whether we are to have a national language or not," while Rep. Horace Maynard of Tennessee echoed his concern over "whether, in point of fact, we have any legal language or not." The decision to print the reports in German was reversed by voice vote (1843).

Not every nineteenth-century language observer shared the nativists' fears of German and the other minority languages. In an essay published in 1855, Charles Astor Bristed, the grandson of John Jacob Astor, explaining the American linguistic situation to a British audience, dismissed fears that the supremacy of English in the New World was in any way threatened by nonanglophones: "As to foreign intruders, we may partly infer their destiny from the fate of the languages which existed in the colonies simultaneously with, or even anterior to the English" (1855, 76). Bristed celebrated the disappearance of Swedish in New Jersey, Spanish in Florida, and Dutch in New York, and he observed that French hung on in New Orleans only through the isolation of the Creoles: "Whenever they have wished to gain influence and power . . . their adoption of the English tongue has been the first requisite. And the same holds good with regard to the more recent [French] emigrants" (76).

Bristed allowed that German emigration had lately become "excessive" and he admitted that the German language constituted the only true rival of English: "Whole districts of [New York City] are peopled by [Germans]; in street after street you see only German signs outside of the shops, and hear only Teutonic accents inside of the houses" (77). But according to Bristed, the new German would be as quick to die out as the old had: "We have seen that where the German language was originally established—in Pennsylvania—it was so far from making any encroachments on the English, that the English sensibly encroached on it. . . . The descendants of the original settlers have preserved it [German] at the expense of much loss both of power and progress" (77). Echoing Hutchins's earlier admonition to the German community of Pennsylvania, Bristed told his British readers, "If the German citizens of America wish to take that part in the affairs of the country to which their numbers, their abilities, and their education entitle them, the first condition will be their adoption of the general speech of the country. . . . We conclude, then, that the supremacy of the English language in the United States is menaced by no serious danger" (77). Nonetheless, as we shall see in the following chapters, from the 1870s to 1923 many Americans did not doubt that the English language continued to be menaced by an ever clearer and more present danger.

4 Language and the Law

Although a number of legislators had considered Spanish, at least in passing, as a language worth promoting in the United States, Charles Astor Bristed (1855, 57), in his essay on the English language, echoed the common nineteenth-century American rejection of New World Spanish, completely underestimating the political and literary influence that language would achieve only a century later, and dismissing it instead as beneath notice: "Little . . . is known, and as little cared about, the nature and extent of the modifications which the Spanish language may have received in the Hispano-American republics, for these countries occupy but an insignificant place in the political world, and what is more to the point here, are absolutely nowhere in the literary world." This negative attitude toward Spanish greatly affected the political status of New Mexico in its relations with the United States.

The Spanish Question

Although Pennsylvania and Louisiana dealt with the minority-language issue internally, the question of Spanish, for many years the majority language in New Mexico, was initially an external one. At the end of the Mexican War the United States formally annexed New Mexico with the Treaty of Guadalupe Hidalgo (1848), promising in article 9 of the treaty to make the territory a state "at the proper time." (Congress then substituted article 3 of the Louisiana Purchase treaty for article 9, promising statehood for New Mexico "as soon as possible"; neither article specifically mentions language rights, though both guarantee territorial residents the protection of the U.S. Constitution.) Responding to the treaty promise of statehood and an implied invitation by President Zachary Taylor in his 1849 annual message to Congress, in 1850 the New Mexico Territory held a statehood convention, drew up a constitution, and went so far as to elect state officials and delegates to Congress. But while gold-rich California was admitted to the Union in 1850 with a constitution protecting Spanish, impoverished New Mexico was refused statehood and given a territorial government instead. Repeated petitions for admission to the Union were denied, and New Mexico did not become a state until 1912.

Language was not immediately an issue within the New Mexico Territory, there being relatively few English-speaking settlers in that part of the Southwest. The 1850 constitution, sent to Congress with English and Spanish letters of transmittal from the governor, does not mention language rights, though the convention, sensitive to the mounting anti-Catholic nativism of the states, attempted to protect New Mexico's Hispanic citizens by instructing its congressional delegate, Hugh N. Smith, to "secure the Catholic population in the full and free enjoyment of all their religious rights and privileges" (U.S. House 1850, 11).

According to Bancroft (1889, 709), the early territorial legislatures of New Mexico conducted their business in Spanish as a matter of course, though because of the need to produce English documents for Washington, "the journals and laws had to be translated into English for publication." Indeed, the territorial legislature petitioned Congress in 1869 for additional funds to hire a second official translator at an increased salary so as "to have all bills, memorials, and resolutions written in both languages" (U.S. Senate 1869, 3). It is clear that many New Mexico laws were drafted in Spanish and then translated into English, for in 1874 a territorial statute gave precedence to the language of the original version of any future laws, whether Spanish or English, rather than that of their translation (Kloss 1977, 130).

However, from Washington's point of view, race and religion, as epitomized by the Spanish language, proved obstacles to New Mexican statehood. In 1876 both the House and Senate committees on the territories recommended passage of a statehood bill as long overdue. However, three members of the House committee opposed statehood on the grounds that New Mexico was thoroughly backward: it possessed no internal improvements, "and though various railways point in its direction, none have yet entered the Territory" (U.S. House 1876, 2). The minority report notes that the territory possessed only five public schools in 1870, and that in the year of the nation's centennial the territory was an embarrassment to an otherwise enlightened Union: it was settled "by a people nine-tenths of whom speak a foreign tongue, most of whom are illiterate, and the balance with little American literature" (7). The report, which claims that even the Catholic bishop was shocked at the degraded state of the church in the territory, emphasizes the undesirability of the Hispanic population by comparing them to the frequently reviled "uncivilized" Indians: "But few are pure-blooded or Castilian, . . . the rest being a mixture of Spanish or Mexican and Indian [living in a] condition of ignorance, superstition, and sloth that is unequaled by their Aztec neighbors, the Pueblo Indians" (12).

In 1888 Rep. William M. Springer of Illinois presented a similar minority report for the Committee on the Territories, opposing statehood for New Mexico (at the same time, Springer sponsored legislation admitting Washington, Montana, and the Dakotas to the Union). Alleging that New Mexico was not sufficiently advanced "in civilization and education," Springer cited with alarm the 1881 opinion of Territorial Governor Sheldon that requiring English in the schools "would prevent a majority of the children from being educated in the public schools" (U.S. House 1888, 45). In words reflecting the spirit of nineteenth-century know-nothingism and opposition to the new and visibly Catholic immigration to the states, Springer complained of the Hispanic influence on the New Mexico Territory, in particular the Spanish language, the Mexican style of dress, the adobe houses, illiteracy, the practice of enslaving Indians (a system of peonage was reported in the territory), and the prevalence of vice (that is, prostitution, adultery, and common law marriage) and Catholic idolatry, all of which, Springer charged, were inherited from Southern Europe (39).

By the 1880s minority-language populations had become a political issue in the United States (see, for example, the discus-

sion below of Illinois's Edwards Law), and Congress was targeting
the preponderance of Spanish-speaking New Mexicans as a major
reason to deny statehood to the territory. In 1892 a House report
by the Committee on the Territories recommending statehood
directly addressed the racial issue: "Objections [regarding 'the
character of the population of the Territory'] have been urged
against the admission of New Mexico which are not usually
brought forward against the admission of other Territories" (U.S.
House 1892, 16). The House report specifically confronted the
issue of language and allegiance: "It has been asserted that the
people of New Mexico are not Americans; that they speak a foreign language and that they have no affinity with American institutions" (43). While admitting that some older New Mexicans
were monolingual Spanish speakers, the report reassured the
Congress that young Hispanics in the territory were switching to
English: "There are very few persons in New Mexico under thirty
years of age who are unable to speak English, and . . . year by year
the use of the English language is taking the place of Spanish"
(43). The report expressed confidence that, while the "familiar"
use of Spanish might never be entirely eradicated, "the people of
New Mexico realize that they are a part of the United States, and
that the English language is the national language, and it is a fixed
and definite principle among them all that the English language
shall be taught to every child in New Mexico" (43).

In the area of New Mexican education, assimilation is claimed
for all but extremely remote rural areas. The House report count-
ed 143 English-only schools, 92 bilingual ones, and 106 which
were taught exclusively in Spanish, though the state superintendent of public instruction insisted that English was taught in all
the schools (17). Former Governor S. B. Axtell of New Mexico
testified before the committee to refute contentions that the
state's Hispanics were reluctant to learn English: "I know a number of men who have been educated by the Christian Brothers
who speak the English language as well as we do, and they learned
to use it properly." He further estimated that "75 per cent of the
adult population of New Mexico can understand the English language and speak it well enough to do business, to buy and sell, and
talk to laborers, and reply to questions" (19–20).

The House report also addressed the issue of patriotism in

what by the 1920s would become a common theme in the defense of minority-language populations. It strongly objected to the classification of New Mexico's "Spanish-speaking citizens" as a "foreign race" (43), pointing out that the proportion of native- to foreign-born inhabitants was higher in New Mexico than in Dakota, Montana, or Washington, and arguing that New Mexican natives were surely as loyal as foreign-born Europeans: "Can it be said that a native of New Mexico who renounced his allegiance to the Republic of Mexico over forty years ago has less interest in the Government of the United States, less devotion to republican principles, or less fitness for full American citizenship than a subject of European kingdoms who has within a few years left his native home?" (44). The report, which did not refrain from its own brand of stereotyping, found New Mexico's "slow and nonprogressive" conservative Hispanic population an ideal corrective for "our overzealous Americans" (17). It predicted that the combination of the two peoples through intermarriage was certain to produce "orators, poets, artists, and statesmen of the highest rank" (44).

In its conclusion, the House report reminded the Congress that the statehood pledge in the Treaty of Guadalupe Hidalgo "contained no condition that all the inhabitants should learn the English language" (43). And it cited the patriotic contributions of New Mexican soldiers and officers during the Civil War: "In the storm of battle they proved their title to American citizenship" (45). But despite a similar positive recommendation by the Senate Committee on Territories, the vote for statehood failed.

In 1902 the 57th Congress rejected yet another in the long series of petitions for New Mexican statehood (along with statehood for the territories of Arizona and Oklahoma). The historian Albert Jeremiah Beveridge, a "progressive" Republican senator from Indiana, chaired hearings on the statehood bill in New Mexico and in Washington, D.C., and ultimately recommended against its passage. While party politics had always been a factor in the New Mexican statehood question, during the hearings and in his subcommittee report, Beveridge—who believed in "America first! Not only America first, but America only" (*DAB*, s.v.)— focused exclusively on the prevalence of Spanish in New Mexico's public and private affairs. The New Mexico historian Ralph

Twitchell (1912, 2: 575–76n) describes the Beveridge hearings as "the most dastardly performance by a committee of congress ever witnessed." Beveridge's subcommittee arrived in New Mexico unannounced, summoned witnesses, placed them under oath, and interrogated them one at a time behind closed doors. According to Twitchell, the subcommittee had clearly decided in advance to deny statehood to New Mexico: "Never before in the history of the American people were the qualifications and fitness of the people of a territory subjected to and passed upon by a committee of either branch of the American congress."

Beveridge and his subcommittee, which included freshman Sen. William P. Dillingham of Vermont, who would later chair the Immigration Commission and become a leading exponent of quota restrictions in immigration (see chapter 5), toured Las Vegas (then a part of the New Mexico Territory), Albuquerque, Santa Fe, Las Cruces, and Carlsbad for nine days, expressing distress at the many business signs in Spanish, worrying over the presence of Spanish-language newspapers, and interrogating children in schoolyards, only to find them unable to reply in English. Witness after witness before the Beveridge subcommittee was forced to admit that in New Mexico, ballots and political speeches were either bilingual or entirely in Spanish; that census takers conducted their surveys in Spanish; that justices of the peace kept records in Spanish; that the courts required translators so that judges and lawyers could understand the many Hispanic witnesses; that juries deliberated in Spanish as much as in English; and that children, who might or might not learn English in schools, as required by law, "relapsed" into Spanish on the playground, at home, and after graduation. Subcommittee witnesses also confessed that Hispanics committed more crimes than Anglos, although several witnesses reminded the subcommittee that the territory's crime rate was extremely low and blamed the majority of the few felonies that were committed on outlaws from Texas entering the territory through Mexico.

Both Anglo and Hispanic witnesses used the term *Mexican* to refer to Hispanic natives of New Mexico as well as immigrants from "old" Mexico. Everyone else, in New Mexican parlance, was an *American*. Benjamin S. Baker, an associate justice of the New

Mexico Supreme Court, told the subcommittee, "When I use the term 'American' I mean all other nationalities except Mexicans" (U.S. Senate 1902, 46). At one hearing, Senator Beveridge criticized the English of one such "Mexican" school principal, saying, "I observe that you talk a little bit brokenly; how long have you spoken English?" (10). The reply was, "Since 1874," or twenty-eight years. The "American" superintendent of the East Las Vegas schools (an Anglo area of settlement) confirmed the subcommittee's suspicion that "it is very hard to teach [Mexicans] English well" (24), while just as the Pennsylvania Germans were criticized for not using standard High German, an Anglo justice of the peace, who testified that he knew no Spanish, informed the subcommittee that the Spanish used by New Mexican Hispanics was far from adequate: "They speak the Spanish language, or try to; but I understand that it is not the pure Castilian; it is a sort of jargon of their own" (18).

Pro-statehood witnesses (only one subcommittee witness actually opposed entering the Union) denied that Spanish was permitted in the public schools and emphasized the rapid assimilation to English of the young. The journalist Thomas Hughes implied that the minority language situation in New Mexico resembled that in Senator Beveridge's home state of Indiana: "Spanish is taught as a side issue, as German would be in any State in the Union. . . . This younger generation understands English as well as I do" (64–65). One sympathetic senator reminded his audience, "These people who speak the Spanish language are not foreigners; they are natives, are they not?" (347).

But Senator Beveridge did not consider Mexicans to be natives. He was so troubled by the Spanish problem that he appended to the record of his hearings several exhibits demonstrating his contention that the territory was more Mexican than American: a series of legal notices in Spanish and English; and a list of grand and petit jurors for 1902, together with a list of criminal indictments for 1900–1902, both containing a very high proportion of Hispanic names. Beveridge ignored witnesses who explained that Anglos always managed to get themselves excused from jury duty on trumped-up medical grounds, and he implied that the crime statistics attached to the report, which show assault, adultery, and fornication to be the most common misdemeanors punished in the territory, clearly reflected the moral degradation of the Mexican population.

Many witnesses before the Beveridge subcommittee testified that while older Spanish-speaking residents of New Mexico spoke little English, the younger generation was quickly becoming anglophone. But not quickly enough for Senator Beveridge, who categorized the "Mexicans" of the American Southwest as "unlike us in race, language, and social customs," and who concluded that statehood must be contingent on assimilation. He recommended that admission to the Union be delayed until a time "when the mass of the people, or even a majority of them, shall, in the usages and employment of their daily life, have become identical in language and customs with the great body of the American people; when the immigration of English-speaking people who have been citizens of other States does its modifying work with the "Mexican" element" (U.S. Senate 1902, Report, 9).

Seven years later Beveridge finally supported a New Mexico statehood bill (a promise of statehood for the territories had been a plank in the Republican platform that President Taft was determined to keep). However, there is some suggestion that Beveridge and his Senate colleagues backed the legislation only because they were certain it would fail in the House. In any case, Beveridge rewrote the enabling act which eventually passed Congress in 1910 to include a variety of provisions reflecting his English-only preference. The House version of the New Mexico and Arizona statehood bill permitted school instruction in languages other than English, and while it required English of state government offices and officials, it did not require English of state legislators. Beveridge imposed a stricter official-English requirement on New Mexico as a condition of its entrance into the Union. The Senator complained,

> One of the most serious difficulties of . . . the Territory of New Mexico, has been and is the disposition of the Mexican population to continue the Spanish language from generation to generation. . . . Had the provisions of the Senate bill been in force in the Territory for a generation the conditions above described would not now exist. Since we are about to admit this Territory as a state of the Union, the

disposition of its citizens to retain their racial solidity, and in doing so to continue the teaching of their tongue, must be broken up. (U.S. Senate 1910, 25–26)

The enabling act as amended by Beveridge permitted New Mexico to form a constitution and state government and provided for the establishment of a system of free public schools that "shall always be conducted in English." It also required "that ability to read, write, speak and understand the English language sufficiently well to conduct the duties of the office without the need of an interpreter shall be a necessary qualification for all State officers and members of the state legislature" (New Mexico 1910, 257).

Despite these restrictions, the enabling act passed the House unanimously. But New Mexico was still bilingual, and one of the first orders of business at the 1910 constitutional convention at Santa Fe was the election of an interpreter. All proceedings and committee files were ordered to be printed in English and Spanish (23). One hundred thousand copies of the constitution were ordered printed, fifty thousand in each language (96), and the constitution of the incipient state of New Mexico was ratified by means of bilingual ballots (76).

At the 1910 convention, the education committee report provided for the mainstreaming of Spanish-speaking children: "That children of Spanish descent in the State of New Mexico shall never be denied the right and privilege to attend the public schools or other public educational institutions of the state, and they shall never be classed in separate schools, but shall forever enjoy perfect equality with other children" (116). This was followed by a provision for separate schools for "children of African descent," a section which was opposed by a minority committee of three Hispanics and which was ultimately omitted from the final draft of the constitution.

In addition to requiring English of officeholders and the schools, the first official New Mexican constitution contained several other language-specific provisions. One supported transitional bilingual education, ordering that "the legislature shall provide for the training of teachers in the normal schools or otherwise so that they may become proficient in both the English and

Spanish languages, to qualify them to teach Spanish speaking pupils and students in the public schools and educational institutions of the state; and shall provide proper means and methods to facilitate the teaching of the English language and other branches of learning to such pupils and students" (234).

The constitution also ordered that "for the first twenty years after this constitution goes into effect, all laws passed by the Legislature shall be published in both the English and Spanish languages" (241–42), a provision that was subsequently extended. In protecting minority languages within the state, it classed English and Spanish as equal, providing that "the right of any citizen of the State to vote, hold office, or sit upon juries, shall never be restricted, abridged or impaired on account of religion, race, language or color, or inability to speak, read or write the English or Spanish languages except as may be otherwise provided in this constitution" (New Mexico 1911, 47–48). Furthermore, "in all criminal prosecutions the accused shall have the right . . . to have the charge and testimony interpreted to him in a language that he understands" (14–15).

Although the constitution and enabling act were passed in 1910 and ratified early in 1911, statehood was delayed yet again. During the delay, the House Committee on the Territories recommended dropping the English-language requirement for New Mexico state officials and legislators. In its report, the committee found the disqualification imposed on the Spanish-speaking New Mexicans potentially unconstitutional as well as a violation of the letter and the spirit of the Treaty of Guadalupe Hidalgo. The House committee observed that the U.S. Constitution does not deny citizens the right to hold office if they cannot speak English, and it pointed out that article 9 of the treaty guarantees the constitutional rights of the territory's Hispanic population (U.S. House 1911, 6).

Although the language of the enabling act was not revised, the English-only requirements for education and office holding in New Mexico were softened. The constitutional provision mandating English for state officials and legislators was repealed in 1912, over the governor's veto, after the granting of statehood (New Mexico 1912, 272), and subsequent school legislation provided that "Spanish may be used in explaining the meaning of

English words to Spanish-speaking pupils who do not understand English" (New Mexico 1915, 133) and required bilingual reading instruction in the first three grades if a majority of parents demanded it (New Mexico 1917).

Although the constitutional mandate that schools always be conducted in English (article 21, sec. 4) remains in effect, in 1941 the New Mexico legislature enacted a paradoxical law ordering Spanish instruction in grades five through eight, while at the same time giving county school authorities the option of excluding such instruction. Furthermore, it assured "that no pupil attending any public school in this state shall be required to take the course in Spanish . . . where the parent . . . specifically objects in writing" (New Mexico 1941). Naturally, this sort of equivocal minority-language protection did little to enhance the status of Spanish in the schools. Indeed, for much of the twentieth century, despite legal efforts to protect Spanish speakers, their language was stigmatized in New Mexican schools, and students were punished for using Spanish on school grounds (see chapter 5).

In writing the Senate version of the Arizona and New Mexico Enabling Act of 1910, Senator Beveridge treated the two territories differently. While he opposed Spanish in New Mexico, he simply deleted from the Enabling Act an Arizona territorial law requiring voters to demonstrate their ability "to read the Constitution of the United States in the English language in such manner as to show [they are] neither prompted nor reciting from memory," a statute that had twice been vetoed by the Arizona governor (U.S. Senate 1910, 5).

Beveridge's opposition to the Arizona English literacy statute was no doubt prompted by two political considerations: first, the law had been passed in a party-line vote by a Democrat-controlled legislature and vetoed by the Republican governor, Joseph Kibbey, who was a presidential appointee (Beveridge, as we noted, was a Republican); and second, the Hispanic voters it would disenfranchise constituted only 10 percent of the electorate in Arizona, a minority Beveridge could afford to protect without endangering the spread of official English. Naturally, Beveridge did not cite political motives for his action. Instead, he quoted the arguments put forth by Governor Kibbey rejecting the Arizona En-

glish literacy requirement on the grounds that it was both unpatriotic and unfair.

In his first veto of the Arizona law, Kibbey spoke with pride of
those Americans in the states who spoke only German, French,
Hebrew, or what he referred to as Scandinavian, who could understand the Constitution "quite as well as" those able to read it in
English. He reminded the legislators that the first Anglo settlers
in the Arizona Territory learned Spanish, which was both the
majority language and the official one. And he noted that the
Treaty of Guadalupe Hidalgo made residents of the territory
American citizens even if they did not speak English, and that
linguistic assimilation was both a slow and an involuntary process:

> A people does not, nor, indeed, do individuals, usually
> change their speech voluntarily. The acquisition of a new
> language voluntarily is a refinement of education confined
> to few individuals as a mere accomplishment. That a whole
> people should change their language denotes that there was
> a necessity more or less urgent to do so, or the acquisition is
> the result of years and often generations of association and
> intercourse with a people speaking a different language
> who have become predominant. (6)

In enacting the English literacy measure, the Arizona legislature found a precedent in the Maine constitution of 1893. As
early as 1879 Maine's school superintendent had proposed "to
educate all its children in the language of the State and Nation
and to make them an English-speaking people" (Kloss 1940, 1:
511). However, as Arizona's Governor Kibbey noted in his second
veto message (the bill had been slightly rewritten and passed by
the legislature again), the parallel between Arizona and Maine did
not hold. While both regions had similar non-English-speaking
populations, the Maine rule on voter qualification, aimed at the
state's French inhabitants, required English of new voters and did
not apply to those already enfranchised or to those over sixty
years of age, who were assumed to be too old to learn English,
while the Arizona law had no such provisos and would actually
disenfranchise many who had been voting all their adult lives.
Kibbey objected further that the Arizona law would disenfran-

chise not only Hispanics, but Scandinavians, Germans, and Italians as well (10). His successor, Gov. Richard E. Sloan, further charged that the English literacy requirement was a racial and not an educational test, aimed directly at the best class of Arizona's Hispanic voters, and he found it therefore "unjustly discriminatory" (13–15).

Although Pennsylvania, Louisiana, and New Mexico have dealt with their German, French, and Spanish speakers differently at different times, sometimes supportively, sometimes repressively, a number of striking similarities emerge. In these states, minority-language speakers typically strove to preserve their language rights while fighting a losing battle against language shift among the young and in the face of opposition from English speakers.

In all three states, supporters of minority-language rights emphasize both an obligation to translate for citizens who are too old to learn English, and a need to recognize the patriotic contributions of nonanglophones to the nation's war efforts. In contrast, proponents of English-first—both anglophones and minority-language speakers favoring assimilation—argue that learning English is the ultimate act of patriotism: that without the majority language one cannot understand or participate in the nation's democratic institutions. And some among the English-firsters add that English is necessary for economic success as well as ideological enlightenment. Such talk is common as well in the English-first debate today.

Furthermore, these three states have had, throughout their histories, large, single minority-language populations in addition to smaller numbers of speakers of other non-English languages. Despite individual measures mandating English as the language of instruction or the language of the laws, none of these states has passed an overriding official-language act, nor is it likely that they will at the present time, although official-English supporters have targeted Pennsylvania for future action. This is not to say that all states with similar population histories have done the same. California, with a significant number of Spanish and Asian-language speakers throughout its history, together with a long tradition of discrimination against these populations, recently passed an official-English law. And Hawaii, a state which, like New Mexico, had to wait for admission to the Union because that Union rejected its racial composition as un-American, now has two official languages, English and Hawaiian. Though the state's major second language is Japanese, Hawaiian was selected for legal protection because it is an endangered, indigenous language. While Spanish in the American Southwest was perceived as a local threat to English and to Americanization in the new states of the area, the language that in the eyes of the English-first nativists posed the greatest danger to the nation as a whole was German.

The Language Panic of World War I

The equation between language and nationality established in the eighteenth century by Locke and Michaelis, among others, was strengthened by nineteenth-century European nationalist movements and in particular by the work of such German-language philosophers as Johann Gottfried Herder ([1772] 1966), Johann Gottlieb Fichte ([1808] 1922) and Wilhelm von Humboldt. Fichte, concerned with resisting Napoleonic expansionism, argued that every linguistic group constituted a nation and should be self-governing. Von Humboldt, writing in 1837 of the superiority of the Indo-European languages over other linguistic groups, went further in defending the notion that language reflected national character and posited "an undeniable connection . . . between language structure and the success of all other kinds of intellectual activity" (1988, 44). Such assertions were characterized by contemporary philologists as racist and Eurocentric, a charge that von Humboldt, for one, could not successfully refute. Combined with the equation of English with liberty, this linguistic nationalism produced such statements as that of W. G. T. Shedd (1848, 658), an early editor of Coleridge: "Studying a well organized language . . . brings the mind of the student into communication with the whole mind of a nation . . . the whole genius and spirit of the people of whose mind it is the evolution." But unfortunately it also captured the popular imagination of the day, leading to such pernicious and absurd connections between language and ethnicity as the charge made in 1911 that Jews could not learn European languages "because of physical differences in the anatomy of their speech and hearing organs" (cited in Lieberson 1981, 4).

Ironically, however, this nation-language connection so effectively disseminated through German romantic language philosophy backfired as the Treaty of Versailles, breaking up the German Empire after World War I, attempted to redraw the map of Europe along linguistic lines at the expense of German (Guy 1989, 154). Furthermore, German itself, perceived to be the antidemocratic language of absolutism, was now seen to threaten American national unity. During and after World War I, negative feeling toward German, Polish, Czech, and the Scandinavian languages resurfaced, particularly in the Midwest (anti–German language feeling was common in England and France as well).

The United States entered World War I in April 1917. In June the federal government passed the Trading with the Enemy Act (50 U.S.C., Appendix). Section 19 of this act was designed to suppress or render transparent all foreign-language publication dealing with the conduct of the war or other war-related matters. It is reminiscent of the eighteenth-century suggestions for suppressing German in Pennsylvania discussed in chapter 3:

> It shall be unlawful for any person, firm, corporation, or association, to print, publish, or circulate, or cause to be printed, published, or circulated in any foreign language, any news item, editorial or other printed matter, respecting the Government of the United States, or of any nation engaged in the present war, its policies, international relations, the state or conduct of the war, or any matter relating thereto: *Provided*, That this section shall not apply to any print, newspaper, or publication where the publisher or distributor . . . has filed with the postmaster at the place of publication, in the form of an affidavit, a true and complete translation of the entire article containing such matter proposed to be published . . . in plain type in the English language.

Nonconforming printed matter was declared nonmailable, though the act permitted the president to issue permits freeing individual publishers from these restrictions. This regulation lapsed after the war, and an attempt in 1923 to reinstate a more sweeping version of the restriction, denying the use of the mails to any publication printed in a foreign language unless an English translation appeared in parallel columns, failed to gain support (HR 9727, 68th Congress, 1st session). The Great War affected language in the schools as well, finally accomplishing what earlier statutes had failed to do. In the fall of 1917 and the winter and spring of 1918, a language panic swept the country: German was specifically targeted as an enemy language to be rooted out.

Although in 1917 many public figures and educators sought to defend the study of German against a groundswell of popular opposition to the language, by 1918 the tide had turned and voices everywhere considered the use of German suspect. Reacting to charges that the German government was underwriting language instruction in American schools in order to prevent the assimilation of German-Americans and to further its war effort, and that German classes were hotbeds of subversion and espionage, school districts throughout the country promptly banned the teaching of German. On 25 May 1918 the *New York Times* reported that as many as twenty-five states had already removed German from their curricula.

Occasionally a voice was raised in defense of German language study, claiming that the language was necessary for anyone in the sciences, or that it was essential in order to unveil enemy plots, uncover strategy, and win the war. But even these rational arguments were dismissed, and the effort to dump German redoubled. Scribner's was urged to publish no German titles during the war. Sheet music dealers refused to handle German songs. At least one American Berlin was renamed Liberty. Even German foods were transmuted on restaurant menus: across the land, *German fried potatoes* became *American fries* and *sauerkraut* became *liberty cabbage*; some superpatriots even caught the *liberty measles* instead of the *German measles* (Mencken 1963, 258; *rubella*, the latinate medical term for the disease, was probably too foreign-sounding for the public taste).

The *New York Times* applauded a Board of Education plan to drop German from the New York City public schools as "sound hard common sense." Basing its opposition to German—a language it characterized as "suspect and taboo"—on educational as well as patriotic grounds, the *Times* asked, "Why neglect the one necessary tongue [English] in order to get a smattering of another?" It argued that students of German "don't, as a rule, know English sufficiently well, learn it amply, [or] use it in speaking and writing with correctness, let alone elegance." According to the *Times*, English would provide the "common bond" in a city "loud with strange languages and jargons." The abandonment of German is "a matter of polity, of patriotism, of Americanism," and the newspaper recommended that if a second language is needed at all, the schools should consider Spanish, which is more useful for business, or French, surely "more cosmopolitan and urbane" (25 May 1918, p. 12).

Across the United States between 1918 and 1920, local ordinances were passed forbidding the use of German. A Texas county defense council urged that German be forbidden. The state of Oregon went beyond federal restrictions on war-related minority-language publication, restraining the foreign-language press regardless of subject matter. The Oregon act made it unlawful "to print, publish, circulate, display, sell or offer for sale any newspaper and periodical in any language other than the English, unless the same contains a literal translation thereof in the English language of the same type and as conspicuously displayed" (Oregon 1920). The law, which remained in force for seven years, applied to pamphlets and circulars as well, and carried a penalty of up to six months in jail, a five-hundred-dollar fine, or both. Oregon passed another language-restrictive law in 1921 which required "that all records, reports and proceedings required to be kept by law shall be written in the English language," with the exception of druggists' or physicians' prescriptions.*

Writing on the connection between language and Americanization, Mahoney and Herlihy (1918, 3) argued that an inability to speak English posed "a threatening liability" in wartime: "The very first step in making a unified people back of our fighting line, a zealous industrial army to augment our fighting forces, is to teach the foreigner English." (We will look more closely at the

---

*Oregon 1920; an additional language exception was recently added to the Oregon statute, placing computers on a par with the classics: "machine language capable of being converted to the English language by a data processing device or computer" (*ELA* 1985, 178).

role of the schools in anglifying immigrants in the next chapter.)
Perhaps most drastic of all, and most indicative of public sentiment at the time, was the proclamation of Gov. William Lloyd
Harding of Iowa, issued in May 1918, forbidding the use of any
foreign language in the schools, in public, or on the telephone, a
more public instrument then than it is now. Flouting the doctrine
of separation of church and state, Harding even went so far as to
prescribe English as the official language of religion: "English
should and must be the only medium of instruction in public,
private, denominational and other similar schools. Conversation
in public places, on trains, and over the telephone should be in the
English language. Let those who cannot speak or understand the
English language conduct their religious worship in their home"
(New York Times, 18 June 1918, p. 12). Such attitudes had a chill-
ing effect on language use. According to James Crawford (1989,
23), as many as 18,000 people were charged in the Midwest during and immediately following World War I with violating the
English-only statutes.

A feeling of linguistic as well as political isolationism swept
the country after the war. In 1919 Iowa passed a law making
English the language of instruction for secular subjects in public
and private schools, though foreign languages were permitted
above the eighth grade (Iowa 1919, 219). In 1918 New York ordered non-English-speaking minors to attend school through the
fifth grade, permitting English classes in the workplace to fulfill
this requirement, and in 1919 the state allocated up to one hundred thousand dollars to "promote and extend educational facilities for the education of illiterates and of non-English speaking
persons" (New York 1918; 1919).

Other states were less concerned than New York with supporting a transition period for the acquisition of English. German
instruction was specifically banned in twenty-two states (Leibowitz 1971, 16). Early in 1919 the state of Indiana approved an
"emergency measure" requiring all school subjects to be taught
in English only, "provided, that the German language shall not be
taught in any of the elementary schools of this state." German
was also forbidden in Indiana's private and parochial schools. The
penalty for violating the English-only law was a fine of twenty-
five to one hundred dollars, up to six months in jail, or both, and

to underscore the severity with which the state regarded non-complying schools, "each separate day in which such act shall be violated shall constitute a separate offense" (Indiana 1919, 50–51). Apparently the Indiana General Assembly recognized the possibility that legislation singling out German for special treatment might be declared unconstitutional, for the legislature qualified the bill by noting that in case any section of the law was invalidated by the courts, the other sections would remain in effect.

During the nineteenth century, Ohio supported public English-German schools and in 1903 *required* German instruction in the public schools upon the demand of "75 freeholders resident in the district." In 1913 the state made such instruction optional and "auxiliary to the English language" (Leibowitz 1971, 16), and six years later it rejected German entirely by copying the Indiana law almost word for word, including the provision for unconstitutionality (Ohio 1919). The Ohio anti-German law was indeed specifically struck down by the United States Supreme Court decision in *Meyer v. Nebraska* in 1923 (see chapter 5).

Despite the eventual reversal of many English-only and all anti-German provisions, the English-first sentiment was not without its effect: although hamburgers and sauerkraut have resumed their place in American cuisine, the use of the German language declined drastically in the United States, and its place in the school curriculum would never be the same. But as we will see below, language shift has occurred on a large scale in the United States even without the repressive linguistic policies that accompanied World War I.

Language and the Law in Illinois

We have looked at minority-language situations in three American states and considered the general language anxiety caused by World War I. It will be instructive now to examine the minority-language issue in Illinois, a state which is both industrial and rural, and one with a complex history of minority-language speakers and attitudes that is perhaps more typical of the general American pattern of minority-language permissiveness within an implied or expressed official-English context. In

1923 Illinois passed one of the first official-English laws in the nation. The state has also dealt with the question of official English and the status of minority languages in its various state constitutions, where English is established as the language of government; in school laws designating English as the language of instruction but explicitly permitting the study of foreign languages, and most recently, bilingual education as well; and in the establishment of an English literacy requirement for voting.

Most other states have dealt with similar language issues, though for some the outcome has been more favorable in terms of minority-language status, while for others the result was more protective of English. On balance, while Illinois clearly has put English first, it has made room for minority languages as well. During the three periods in United States history when English-first movements have put pressure on the nation's legal and educational systems—1880 to the early 1890s, the period during and after World War I, and the present—Illinois has placed itself firmly in the middle of the road. The state has chosen English as its official language and its laws encourage transition to English rather than mother-tongue maintenance for minority-language speakers. However, official English in Illinois is statutory rather than constitutional and, more important, it is symbolic rather than restrictive: moves to suppress minority languages have been short-lived, and the state offers both official and informal support services to nonanglophones.

Although the Illinois official-language law was passed in 1923, the problem of language is addressed implicitly and explicitly throughout the legal history of the state. The fact that the Ordinance of 1787 (the Northwest Ordinance) as well as the constitutions and laws of Illinois are written in English gives that language at least semi-official status from the outset. Indeed, many states followed the pattern we have seen in Louisiana, inferring English as the nation's official language from the fact that it is the language of the United States Constitution. Nonetheless, from the outset, minority-language groups in Illinois asserted their rights as well: the French of Kaskaskia and Cahokia maintained separate courts in the 1780s. In 1794 the territorial laws were ordered translated into French so that francophone judges could enforce them, and a French school was set up for one month in

Cahokia. Shortly thereafter, the Cahokia French protested to Congress the abridgment both of their language rights and of their property rights, in particular, their right to keep slaves, slavery being prohibited by the Northwest Ordinance (Inquiry 1796, 151; Allinson 1907, 281).

The Illinois constitution of 1818 does not mention language, though article 2, section 17 reads, "The style of the laws of this state shall be, 'Be it enacted by the people of the state of Illinois represented in the General Assembly,'" a phrase which all but requires state laws to be drafted in English. As early as 1845 English was mandated as the official language of instruction in Illinois public schools, and the 1848 constitution gives the governor's oath of office in English.

Schedule 18 of the constitution of 1848, repeated without change in the 1870 constitution, requires that "all laws of the State of Illinois, and all official writings, and the Executive, Legislative and Judicial proceedings, shall be conducted, preserved and published in no other than the English language." This and similar requirements set by other states have been construed by the courts to establish English as the presumptive official language of the states.

While statutes may mandate or imply the drafting of laws in English, elsewhere the status of the official language has often been less clear. One area where the law in Illinois and other states has shifted to reflect changing attitudes toward English and minority languages is the publication of official notices. In many cases, such notices were originally printed in the minority-language press so as to reach concerned readers or, as was sometimes charged, to make the notice inaccessible to anglophones.

Although nativist movements like the Know Nothings subsided by the end of the Civil War, attempts to extend the legal sway of English did not. From the 1870s on, English-firsters pressed their cause at state constitutional conventions, in the schools, and in the courts. A series of lawsuits challenged the validity of the publication of official notices in a minority language, or in English in the minority-language press. Decisions in these cases are based on the legal doctrine that *publication* of laws must be done, as Blackstone maintains in his *Commentaries*, "in the most public and perspicuous manner; not like

Caligula, who . . . wrote his laws in a very small character, and hung them up upon high pillars, the more effectually to ensnare the people" (Blackstone 1803, 1: 46). Similarly, according to Henry Black's *Dictionary of Law* (1891, s.v.), *publication* means printing copies of a notice "in such a manner as to make their contents easily accessible to the public."

In the case of *Graham v. King* (50 Mo. 22 [1872]), an ordinance requiring advance publication of foreclosure notices was interpreted by the Missouri Supreme Court to require printing of such notices in English in an English-language newspaper. The Missouri case served as a precedent for later cases in Michigan and Illinois. Like their colleagues in other states, the Missouri court assumed the citizens of the state to be monolingual speakers of English or of another language, and made clear its opinion that only an English notice in an English-language newspaper satisfied the law's accessibility requirement: "An English advertisement in a German newspaper is bad. . . . Those among whom the [German] paper circulates would not be able to read it in the English language. And if it were published in German, then it would be a sealed book to the most of those who read and speak English."

In 1891 a New Jersey court in a similar ruling decided that merely printing an official notice did not constitute publishing it: "A notice contained in a German newspaper in a language other than English is not published but only printed" (*State v. Orange* 14 LRA 62, cited in Kloss 1940, 2: 935). The Michigan Supreme Court went a step further in a similar foreclosure case, ruling that while the legislature may explicitly provide for foreign language publication of official notices, in the absence of such explicit direction, English must be intended: "The English language is the recognized language of this country, and whenever the law refers to publication in newspapers it means those published in the language of the country" (*Attorney General v. Hutchinson*, 113 Mich. 245 [1897]).

On several occasions, Illinois legislators have indeed designated other languages in addition to English for official publications, though the English versions of such publications were always seen to have precedence in the case of disputed interpretation. However, responding to the English-first fever of the early 1890s, the Illinois Supreme Court invalidated laws explicitly permitting or requiring official publication in languages other than English.

In 1863 the city of Chicago gave its common council the discretionary power to publish ordinances, proceedings, and other public notices in a designated English-language newspaper as well as "in some newspaper printed in the German language," and in 1867 that municipal law was amended to *require* official publication both in an English-language paper and in the German-language newspaper having the largest daily circulation in the city. In 1891 William McCoy, in a class-action suit representing the city's taxpayers, challenged this practice. The Illinois Supreme Court ruled in McCoy's favor, arguing that when Chicago had become incorporated in 1875, it lost its home-rule powers and came under the jurisdiction of state law. The city ordinance of 1867 was therefore rendered invalid by schedule 18 of the 1870 state constitution, which required all official publication to be in the English language (*McCoy v. City of Chicago*, 136 Ill. 344 [1891]).

In 1916, at the start of the next wave of protective English legislation, the Illinois attorney general issued an opinion that the charters and names of domestic insurance companies were similarly required to be in English, "and that a proposed company having a name expressed in the German language cannot, therefore, be organized" under Illinois law (Illinois 1920, 304). The Illinois Supreme Court went further in 1916 and 1917, forbidding official English publications in the foreign-language press. In *Perkins v. Board of Commissioners of Cook County* (271 Ill. 449 [1916]), Dwight H. Perkins challenged the Forest Preserve Act of 1913 on the grounds that the ordinance was printed, albeit in English, in a Chicago German-language newspaper, the *Staats-Zeitung*, which as the complaint alleged was read only "by those of German nationality who adhere to the German language *in preference to* the language of this country" (emphasis added). The court agreed, ruling that such publication did not satisfy the constitutional requirement of schedule 18: "A notice or ordinance published in the English language in a newspaper printed in a foreign language cannot be said to be 'published,' in the sense in which that word is used in the constitution and laws of this

State." The forest preserve ordinance was rendered void, and its tax levy was enjoined.

In the related *People v. Day* (277 Ill. 543 [1917]), Mark L. Day refused to pay his real estate tax because the Cook County appropriation bill had been published in English in the *Staats-Zeitung* and nowhere else. The Illinois Supreme Court ruled that Day was not liable for that portion of his tax rendered void by improper publication of the appropriation, but that he was responsible for the payment of the rest of the assessment. Chicago city ordinances eventually came into line with such legal decisions and with the anti-German feeling that swept the country during and after World War I. Since 1922 the city's municipal code has specified publication of required notices in an English newspaper, provided that newspaper does not advocate the overthrow of the government by force or violence.

While Illinois has privileged the English language in the promulgation of laws and the publication of notices, it has also been tolerant of the state's minority languages, even during periods in American history when other states were taking a more repressive view of the language question. A proposal to publish five thousand copies of the 1848 constitution in German was overwhelmingly adopted, and committees were appointed by the constitutional convention to supervise publication in both German and Norwegian (with the translators being sworn to translate correctly). But not all minority languages received the same treatment: a proposal to print one thousand copies "in the Irish and French languages" was soundly defeated. The 1869 constitutional convention ordered separate copies of the new constitution in German and "Scandinavian," and while it rejected a move to print that document in French, it ordered copies of the English version to be supplied to foreign-language publishers in the hopes they would translate all or part of the constitution for their readers. And while the English-only requirement of schedule 18 of the 1870 constitution stipulates that the formal record of all court proceedings be in intelligible English, it does not limit the language of such court proceedings as "oral testimony, depositions, or documentary evidence." It further permits the court clerk to use a system of shorthand to record the minutes of such proceedings, though these must later be fleshed out in official

English—one judgment was vacated on appeal because the final record of the proceedings "was entered in a system of abbreviations which would be unintelligible to an English speaking person" (Illinois 1920, 305).

The Illinois legislature has frequently dealt with the legal position of English and minority languages in the schools, an issue that remains controversial today. As we have already noted, the 1845 School Law designated English as the language of instruction in Illinois schools. The official status of English was reaffirmed in later revisions of the school laws, which spelled out the right of schools to permit the teaching of other modern languages as well. According to the statute of 1845, "No school shall derive any benefit from the public or town fund unless the text books in said schools shall be in the English language, nor unless the common medium of communication in said schools shall be in the English language." Exempted from this requirement, however, were foreign languages being studied as such. A law passed in 1869 further clarified the right of instructors to use a modern language as the vehicle for instruction in that modern language, a pedagogical technique whose importance seems self-evident today but which was clearly something in need of legal shoring-up a century ago.

The legal specification of the right to teach foreign languages in state public schools was successfully defended in *Powell v. Board of Education* (97 Ill. 375 [1881]). In that case, a group of concerned citizens sued a St. Clair county public school district to enjoin the use of public moneys for German language instruction. The courts decided for the school board, and the Illinois Supreme Court upheld the judgment. The school in question offered one half-hour of German instruction per day in the first grade, and a maximum of one hour per day thereafter. Participation in the German lessons was voluntary, though 80 to 90 percent of the pupils "volunteered" for it. German instruction had been provided for some fifteen years, and the question had recently been approved at the polls as well. Reviewing the school laws, the Illinois Supreme Court concluded in its opinion that the teaching of modern languages in the state's public schools was legal, and that it did not diminish their character as *English* schools. Furthermore, the court ruled that since the teaching of modern languages had been common in the elementary branches for many years, it would take legislative rather than judicial action to forbid such instruction.

Perhaps in response to this finding, as well as to the move by the Catholic church in 1884 to expand its parochial school system into every parish in the country, with priests exhorting congregations that attendance at public school was a sin (Forbes and Lemos 1981, 105), in 1889 the Illinois legislature passed with little fanfare and virtually no opposition a compulsory education law which required English as the language of instruction in all public and parochial schools. It did not take long for the public to realize that the new act, called the Edwards Law after Richard Edwards, then state superintendent of public instruction, gave public school boards the authority to certify private schools as conforming to the English-only requirement. Quakers and many Protestant groups, including Swedish Lutherans, supported the English-only law. However, Catholics and German Lutherans opposed it, rejecting public regulation of the curriculum in their private schools. By 1890, there were 254 Catholic and 290 Lutheran schools in Illinois, many of them using German in whole or in part as the language of instruction (this account of the Edwards Law is summarized from Kučera 1955).

The Edwards Law triggered a nativist reaction, splitting the state along philosophical, ethnic, religious and party lines. English education was pitted against Catholic education. Opposition to the Edwards Law was viewed as an attack on public education, prompting violent anti-Catholic, anti-Democrat, and anti-German attacks in the press. In an editorial, the solidly Republican *Chicago Tribune* labeled as open enemies of the public schools the American Catholic clergy, "inforced by a number of bigoted Ultramontane sectaries . . . who are inspired by an inextinguishable hate of the American free school system. They want to break down the public schools and build up the parochial schools. They think no education is worth the having which does not consist chiefly of a catechism and is not administered exclusively under the control of priests. . . . They would grab a big slice of the taxes and have them used for the support of their dogmatic schools" (14 January 1890, p. 4). On the other hand, the *Tribune* identified as misguided friends of the schools those who every year called for more dollars for schools and higher pay for teachers.

In another editorial, the *Tribune* supported a claim that the Catholic church was "bent on securing the mastery of American youth" and it referred with pride to "the Protestant defenders of the public school system," agreeing that "Ballots [are] more potent than bullets" (24 February 1890, p. 4). In a pre-election edition, the newspaper published on its front page a number of reports of Sunday sermons in support of the Edwards Law, reports containing such phrases as "Our common schools are the first to feel the encroachments of Catholicism" and "How many members of Protestant churches do we find who are keepers of saloons and gambling hells?"

Making clear that it supported the use of the bible in the public schools, and urging its readers to vote for the "Little Red Schoolhouse," the *Tribune* also quoted one minister's tally that 229 of the 363 prisoners at the Joliet correctional facility who declared a religious preference were Catholic. Assuring his congregation, "I am not a bigot," this avowedly unbiased clergyman commented, "Surely this proportion does not seem to show that Catholic education has been a success" (3 November 1890, pp. 1–2).

The Edwards Law was closely associated with the Republican administration, and the law's passage had political repercussions for the GOP. Opposition to the law produced an unusual political alliance of German Lutherans, who normally voted Republican, and Catholics. Despite the campaign of hate and fear launched by the Republicans, the newly allied groups managed to defeat Edwards in his bid for reelection as school superintendent, replacing him with a Democrat who happened also to be a German American. In June 1891, discussing an unsuccessful attempt to remove the English-language requirement from the compulsory education law, the *Tribune* praised the state's Republicans for being reluctant to say "that an elementary education is sufficient with the American tongue left out, or forbidden to be taught to the American children of narrow-minded, un-American foreigners," and predicted that Illinois Democrats would support the complete exclusion of English from the schools if they thought it would get them votes (14 June 1891, p. 12).

Such characterizations did not appeal to voters. In 1892 Judge John P. Altgeld made the school language issue a central feature of his gubernatorial campaign, and the Democrats managed to end twenty years of Republican rule in the state. The Edwards Law was repealed in 1893, and a new compulsory attendance law was implemented without the English-language provision, though only for the time being.

The school language issue resurfaced in Illinois after World War I. In 1919 a bill to forbid the teaching of foreign languages in the elementary schools was introduced in Illinois, but it was tabled. In that same year, at the urging of Samuel Insull, chair of the State Council of Defense of Illinois, a group originally formed to coordinate the state's war efforts on the home front, the Illinois legislature revised the school code and English once again became required in public and parochial schools. In addition, at Insull's urging, a law was passed to facilitate the teaching of English to adults in the state in order to Americanize the foreign born and minimize work-related accidents.

Section 276a of the new Illinois School Code embodied the language of Insull's Defense Council. It is not surprising, then, that the legislation sounds a bit like wartime propaganda:

> Because the English language is the common as well as official language of our country [it was not, in fact, the de jure official language of the country], and because it is essential to good citizenship that each citizen shall have or speedily acquire, as his natural tongue, the language in which the laws of the land, the decree of the courts, and the proclamations and pronouncements of its officials are made, and shall easily and naturally think in the language in which the obligations of his citizenship are defined, the instruction in the elementary branches of education in all schools in Illinois shall be in the English language.

Addressing the Commercial Club of Chicago in 1919 on the wartime accomplishments of the State Council of Defense, Insull explained that his call for an English-only school law arose from purely patriotic motives, combined with the practical need to Americanize the foreign-born. For him, English-language schools formed the most important step in the Americanization process.

Insull argued that America could not function as a team if the members of the team spoke "a multitude of tongues," and he warned that multilingualism was a subversive activity: "A confusion of tongues is the simplest and most effective method for defeating a common purpose yet discovered; it was the method employed by Jehovah himself to accomplish that end" (Insull 1919b, 465).

Insull admitted that getting first-generation Americans to speak English was a difficult proposition. He shared the common suspicion of the loyalties of newly arrived immigrants: they could never become fully Americanized, he claimed, because they retained memories, however negative, of their homeland. Nor did Insull object to the teaching of foreign languages in the schools of Illinois, though he strongly objected to foreign-language schools: "It is these which most need to be Americanized, in behalf of a sound and enduring patriotism." Insull opposed the minority-language maintenance such schools attempted to provide: "There is no reason why we should go on maintaining and propagating the babel of languages through the second, and even the third and fourth, generations."

According to Insull, children could not be good citizens if they did not learn the basics of an elementary curriculum, "the three R's, common grammar and fundamental history," in English. By failing to provide an English education in the basics, "we deliberately make them poor Americans by allowing them to acquire their education in a foreign tongue" (465). Insull was willing to give up on the parents in an immigrant family—there were only two of them, after all, while there were generally four to ten children (his figures). He concluded, "We can't make a foreign-born citizen a good American by law. But we can make the schools of Illinois American by law, and thereby make it easier for those born here to be good Americans" (466).

In 1920, the same year that the Modern Language Association, meeting in Columbus, Ohio, urged Congress to support increased foreign language instruction now that the war had ended, Illinois tried to extend its English-only school law to the rest of the nation. Rep. Charles E. Fuller, of the Illinois 12th Congressional District, transmitted a petition from the Illinois Society of the Sons of the American Revolution to the U.S. House of Representatives "favoring the teaching only of the English language in elementary schools" (*Congressional Record*, 66th Congress, 1st Session, 23 March 1920). The House Committee on Education did not act on the measure.

While postwar legislators in Illinois affirmed the position of English as the one official language of government and education, they resisted the temptation to restrict minority-language rights. The Illinois constitutional convention of 1920–22, charged with the task of revising the constitution of 1870, dealt with the language issue in three major areas: literacy, the courts, and the schools. The delegates wrote into the new constitution an English literacy requirement for all appointed and elected officeholders, while rejecting a literacy test for voting. They affirmed English as the official language of the laws and public records of the state. And they rejected a constitutional requirement making English the language of instruction of the schools because—as we have just seen—legislation to that effect had already been passed in 1919.

The delegates to the constitutional convention overwhelmingly supported a requirement that public officeholders, whether appointed or elected, be able to speak, read, and write English. Opponents feared it might work as a racial and ethnic barrier, but the measure, which was regarded as both patriotic and practical, passed nonetheless. According to Sylvester J. Gee, the Republican delegate from Lawrenceville who spearheaded the English literacy drive, if an officeholder is not patriotic enough to learn English, "we do not owe him anything" (Illinois 1920–22, 995). Opposition to Gee's proposal was sporadic. Rodney Brandon, a delegate from Mooseheart County, felt the requirement was redundant. He asked the convention, "Is it true that we are so ignorant in the State of Illinois that we have to put in our Constitution a provision to prevent our people in this State from electing illiterate people to office?" More seriously, Brandon warned that literacy requirements were used in the South to prevent blacks from voting and holding office, and he feared similar misuse of a literacy requirement in Illinois (1260). Charles Hamill, from Cook County, objected that English was not necessary for offices such as road supervisor, and he expressed concern about an accurate measurement of literacy: "The question of whether a man can read or write the English language is one not easy to answer" (3713). The literacy requirement for officeholders was discussed on several occasions, and it ultimately passed the convention by a vote of 52 to 2.

Representative Gee and his supporters sought to make English literacy a requirement for voting as well, but this move proved much more controversial, and after some impassioned debate on both sides, it failed. Although most English-first advocates today strongly oppose bilingual ballots, many supporters of official English in the United States earlier in this century balked at requiring English for voting. For one thing, they recognized that testing literacy could be subjective and inaccurate, leaving considerable room for discrimination on the part of registrars. Although some states, like New York, had adopted such measures, literacy tests were associated with the denial of voting rights to blacks in southern states, and the U.S. Senate had quashed as racially discriminatory the Arizona Territory's English-only voting law as a condition for its admission to the Union in 1912.

The debate over English literacy for voting in Illinois did not single out one nonanglophone group (the state's German population was largely assimilated by that time), but instead targeted the newer immigrants who had come to the state before the war. Both supporters and opponents of the measure took patriotism as their theme. Sylvester Gee's motion met with considerable opposition from speakers who reminded the convention that a literacy requirement would disenfranchise many blacks and non-English-speaking patriots who had fought in the Civil War and the recently concluded Great War. George Lohmann, of Chicago, protested that many of his black constituents had not been well served by the schools. If the literacy requirement were passed, he warned, some forty thousand of Chicago's "colored voters" would reject the constitution. Unmoved, the paternalistic Gee denied that blacks had been discriminated against in Illinois schools: "In my county they sit in the same schools. I have a young man in my employment who is a bright colored boy. He has had the same opportunity as any white child, and he is able to read and write." As for the foreign born, Gee argued, "I do not ask anything of them that is not asked of American-born citizens, and I do not think it is asking too much that they be able to read and write the language of their country" (997).

Asked how a person could demonstrate literacy in English for the purposes of voting, Sylvester Gee replied, "I think to ask him to write his name," a requirement that seemed much less onerous than those proposed by other states (997). No delegate voiced the obvious objection that writing one's name is not necessarily a language-specific test of literacy. Instead, opponents focused on the unfairness of the test. Charles J. Michal, of Chicago, who pointed out that he himself had not been born in the United States, saw the English literacy requirement for voting as "an affront to the people who have not had an adequate opportunity to learn to write and read the English language, but who are nevertheless willing and desirous of becoming loyal citizens." Michal argued that prescribing education was despotic and inimical, something more appropriate to New England (where nativism had been strong in the mid-nineteenth century) than to an all-American midwestern state: "I think it is blue-bellied Yankeeism. I think it is not Americanism. I think it is hostile to the fundamental principle of our country, and I think the amendment ought to be voted down" (997–98). Joseph Fifer, of Bloomington, particularly objected to the unfair treatment of veterans that a literacy requirement implied: "To disfranchise certain men who in the darkest hour that this nation ever saw went out with their lives in their hands ready to do and die for our flag, would be an infernal disgrace" (998). This was apparently enough for Gee, who accepted a revision of his motion that dropped the issue of literacy altogether and focused on another vexed question, his recommendation to deny voting rights to conscientious objectors, a measure which also failed to win the convention's approval.

Lewis A. Jarman, a Republican delegate to the convention from Rushville, Illinois, put forward a motion to amend the Education Committee's report by requiring English as the language of instruction in all of the state's public and private schools. In a long speech defending his motion, Jarman claimed as his model a Nebraska law to the same effect and made no reference to the flap in Illinois over the Edwards Law in 1890, referring instead to the

English-only school law passed in that same year by the Wisconsin legislature in response to Gov. William D. Hoard's 1889 state of the state message, which called for "a reasonable amount of instruction in common English branches, especially . . . the ability to read and write the language of this country." Like the Edwards Law, though, Wisconsin's Bennett Law cost the governor the next election, and it too was quickly repealed (Kellogg 1918; Kučera 1955).

Jarman's motion clearly reflected the isolationism that swept the nation after World War I. Naming other states that had recently passed similar measures, Jarman contended that English-first laws were necessary to protect the nation "from the insidious wiles of foreign influence," a phrase that he borrowed from George Washington's warning against foreign entanglements in the well-known Farewell Address to the Troops. Jarman noted that Washington never imagined that Americans would have to protect the English language from such entanglements, adding, "Who indeed could conceive 'the insidious wiles' of modern Germany?" (1140).

Jarman made it clear that he would not ban German from the school curriculum, a move favored by many across the country. Nor was Jarman opposed to foreign-language instruction as such. Nonetheless, he did single out German as a problem language for American schools: "We have needed the alarm of war to awaken us to the significance of the fact that in some cities and communities of this country we have elementary schools where German is the only language spoken, except in that room where English is taught as a foreign language. . . . I think it is a reproach to any community of the United States, and a reflection upon its loyalty to American ideas, to have, not simply a public elementary school where German is taught, but to have German public elementary schools" (1140–41).

Jarman then set forth the now familiar one-nation, one-language doctrine, arguing the United States to be a special case because unlike Germany, where everyone shared the same ethnic heritage, "in this country national unity is not a matter of blood but of ideas." Thus language, for Jarman, would replace ethnicity as a primary socio-political force: "American ideas have been born in English and require English for their proper preservation and dissemination" (1140). Since in his opinion the goal of public education was national unity itself, any tolerance of minority languages would threaten the national fabric: "How shall we ever make these millions think America [sic] if we do not teach them to speak American?"

Citing the repeal of Wisconsin's English-only law in 1891, Jarman warned, "To make a public think German it is necessary to make it speak German. . . . If we permit the children and citizens to live, move and have their intellectual being in the language and literature of absolutism, it will be well nigh hopeless to attempt to preserve a pure democracy among them." Exciting ethnic stereotype further still, Jarman categorically asserted, "There has never been an absolutism among English-speaking peoples" (1141).

Jarman concluded his passionate speech by raising the specter of Babel and "the disintegrating tendencies of polyglot States" (1141). While he claimed to oppose an "America for Americans" exclusionist immigration policy, he rejected any notion of minority-language maintenance and drew applause from the convention with a final equation of English with liberty: "He is a public enemy who would in any way hinder [the schools] from teaching American ideas, cherishing American ideals, promoting American patriotism, and above all, producing American citizens, unhyphenated and uncompromising, a united democracy loving liberty, and thinking and speaking the language of liberty, our English undefiled" (1142).

The emotion stirred by Jarman's prepared remarks was quickly deflated when Frank S. Whitman of Belvidere reminded the delegates that the previous legislature had already reinstated English as the language of school instruction, and Jarman's amendment, which was no longer necessary, failed to pass. But it was clear to all that the sentiment of the delegates favored protecting English when such a move did not threaten to alienate voters. There was little discussion, for example, about carrying over from the previous constitutions schedule 18, requiring English as the official language of the state's executive, legislative, and judicial branches (4523). Breaking with precedent, however, the 1920–22 constitutional convention did not authorize the publication of the new constitution in any language other than English, and in 1923 Illinois passed its first official-language law.

Postwar official-language sentiment was colored not only by resistance to German and the languages of Asian as well as central and southern European immigrants. It was fueled, too, by the anti-British feeling of many Irish Americans, and by the tendency of many Americans and Europeans to refer to the language of the United States as American. Not since the 1790s had interest in a federal language been so intense. The journalist H. L. Mencken published his study *The American Language* in 1919; its immense popularity led to a second edition in 1921 and a third in 1923. Also in 1923 Rep. Washington Jay McCormick of Montana introduced a bill in the U.S. Congress to make American the nation's official tongue. McCormick's bill was not so much anti-German or anti–minority language as it was virulently America-first and anti-British. As proposed, the bill was sweeping in its scope: it would amend *all* congressional acts and government regulations, substituting *American* for *English* in references to language. McCormick hoped to "supplement the political emancipation of '76 by the mental emancipation of '23," and he advised American writers to "drop their top-coats, spats, and swagger-sticks, and assume occasionally their buckskin, moccasins, and tomahawks" (McCormick 1923). In an editorial, the *New York Times* took a jocular view of McCormick's proposal, suggesting it was prompted by news that London sightseeing buses had engaged special interpreters for Americans, or the need to supply English editions of American books with glossaries. The *Times* also found amusing the bill's implication that Congress would serve as a vehicle for standardizing the American language, though it guessed that turning Congress into a language academy could divert that body from its more harmful occupations. The editor concluded, "We must cut loose from allegiance to foreign grammar, and avoid as we would the plague all entangling linguistic alliances" (7 February 1923, p. 14).

McCormick's bill died in committee, but American was clearly in the air at the time, and similar bills appeared in a number of state legislatures: Minnesota (1923), North Dakota (1937), New Jersey (1944), and Massachusetts (1952). All but one failed. State Sen. Frank Ryan of Chicago sponsored a law making American—not English—the official language of Illinois. In 1919 the Illinois General Assembly had passed a resolution urging the

American representatives to the Versailles Peace Conference to support home rule for Ireland. Another resolution passed by the legislature at the same time urged the creation of a Jewish state in Palestine. Both statements reflected the sharpened ethnic interests of Illinois citizens, but in the eyes of Illinois lawmakers they had the added benefit of indirectly attacking the colonial policies of the British. Pro-Irish sentiment was spearheaded by Mayor William "Big Bill" Thompson of Chicago, who warned King George V to stay out of Chicago, and its result is clear in the wording of Ryan's official-language law, whose "whereases" attack those American Tories "who have never become reconciled to our republican institutions and have ever clung to the tradition of King and Empire." According to Ryan, such Anglophiles foster racism and defeat the attempts of American patriots "to weld the racial units into a solid American nation."

Ryan's law clearly appealed to the Irish electorate of the state, and although before passage it was toned down considerably, its original sentiment remained unaltered. As finally worded, the statute's Brit-bashing clauses were replaced by a paean to America as the world's welcoming haven for immigrants. The bill justified changing the name of the language for several reasons. It argued, for one thing, that newcomers to the United States considered its institutions and language to be American, not English. Furthermore, "the name of the language of a country has a powerful psychological influence upon the minds of the people in stimulating and preserving national solidarity." And finally, "the languages of other countries bear the name of the country where they are spoken."

The *Chicago Daily News* opposed Ryan's proposal, claiming that the phrase *American language* was originated by the then much-reviled Germans to show their dislike of the British. A similar view was voiced by the German-born clergyman Edward A. Steiner (1916b, 93), who faulted German American newspapers for insisting "that since the war, we have begun to speak something which is called *American*," though the term *American* in reference to language actually goes back to the America of the late eighteenth century (Mencken 1945, 143). Despite its passage, the Illinois law produced no sweeping changes in usage in the state, where English rather than American continued to be taught in the public schools. The Massachusetts official-English law, proposed unsuccessfully in 1952, would have remedied this oversight: besides declaring American the official language of the state, it would have prohibited the teaching of English in the schools, banning such terms as *English grammar* and *English language* from all textbooks, "so that all students within the commonwealth of Massachusetts shall know that they are studying the American language and are using the American language in their speech and writing" (*New Yorker* 28 [23 August 1952], p. 41).

In 1928 the Illinois Appeals Court observed that the state's official-American law did not conflict with the constitutional requirement that Illinois laws be published in English (*Leideck v. City of Chicago*, 248 Ill. App. 545 at 558). The case, which had been decided for the plaintiff, involved an injury claim, and on appeal the defense raised a number of issues, one of which was the assertion that the words *prima facie*, used in an instruction to the jury, were not English, consequently would not be understood, and thereby constituted an error in the trial. The Appeals Court disagreed, finding that *prima facie* was indeed English, had been English for some five hundred years according to the *Oxford English Dictionary*, and would not be misunderstood by a jury, whose members were by law required to understand the English language. (Neither the defense nor the court addressed the issue of whether the jury could understand *prima facie* as a technical legal term.) The court further ruled that while the legislature had changed *English* to *American* in establishing the state's official language, these languages were "in legal effect and intendment . . . the same thing." One obvious result of Ryan's law was to make Illinois' usage of American unique among the states, and the statute was quietly amended in 1969, as the official state language reverted once again to English (Public Act 76–1464).

Provisions for English as the language of instruction in Illinois schools and the adoption of a state official-language law did not prevent passage of a bilingual education law in Illinois in 1973. However, until 1988 the Illinois School Code technically prohibited bilingual education. Exempted from the 1919 state law requiring English as the language of instruction in the schools were "vacational schools where the pupils have already received the required instruction in English during the current school year." *Vacational* was a rare word even in its own day. Funk and Wagnalls's *Standard Dictionary,* the only dictionary that records it, calls the word colloquial. In the Illinois School Code, the word referred to schools held during vacation periods. A more appropriate term might have been vacation schools, either summer schools or weekend schools. The intent of the 1919 law was to require that English be the language of instruction, but it clearly exempted from that provision not public summer schools but supplementary parochial ones, what we would describe now as Sunday schools or vacation Bible schools.

When the School Code was overhauled in 1945, an error crept into this section of the code: the word *vacational* was incorrectly changed to *vocational.* Section 27-2 of the new code read, "Instruction in the elementary branches of education in all schools shall be in the English language except in vocational schools where pupils have already received the required instruction in English during the current school year." It is not clear how vacational became vocational. It may have been a typographical error or a revision on the part of some committee member who read the original "vacational" as a typo and sought to restore the original language. While minor, and unnoticed for forty-three years, the incorrect reference to "vocational" schools could have become a problem. Fortunately, section 27-2 of the School Code was revised again recently to permit the already existing bilingual education programs finally to conform to state law. In this last process of revision, which brought Illinois state law into line with federal rulings requiring special programs for students described in the regulations as "non-English-proficient" and "limited-English-proficient" (or NEP and LEP), the nonsense statement about vocational schools was dropped, although those involved in the revision of the law had no idea they were correcting an error in doing so. The section, which applies to public schools only, now reads, "Instruction in all public elementary and secondary schools of the State shall be in the English language except in second language programs and except in conjunction with programs which the school board may provide, with the approval of the State Board of Education pursuant to Article 14C, in a language other than English for children whose first language is other than English" (1988 Public Act 85-1389).

In Illinois, as in many other states, language has been both a symbolic and a practical issue. Illinois language laws have reflected public linguistic and ethnic prejudice, though as in most states its legislation has avoided the extremes of nativism and racism that conflict with federal constitutional protections. Illinois language law is also typical in that it has proved flexible enough to accommodate shifting attitudes or public policies toward language and education. In the next chapter, we will examine more closely how these attitudes and policies affected American schools in the twentieth century.

5 Americanization and the Schools

No principal, teacher or employee of the Public Schools
Department shall employ, patronize, aid or encourage the
Chinese in any way, but shall do all in their power to legally
promote their removal from this coast and to discourage
further immigration.
—*Unanimous resolution of the*
San Francisco School Board, 1886

Immigration to the United States increased dramatically after 1860, particularly between 1890 and 1910, and the majority of immigrants shifted from northern Europe and Great Britain to southern and eastern Europe and Asia. As a result, the nativism that had once appeared as the Native American party, or Know Nothings, and later as the more general anti-foreigner/anti-Catholic movements of the 1880s, resurfaced in a new and even more pervasive form as the Americanization movement of the early twentieth century. Unlike earlier nativisms, which tended to attract the radical fringe, the Americanization movement proved more centrist, involving intellectuals, educators, social workers, business leaders, and legislators, and many of its supporters favored education over repression (Hartmann 1948, 8). Reaction to the new immigration led to a significant amount of racism as well, though some of it had a genteel veneer of intellectualism and claimed grounding in such academic fields as anthropology, biology, and economics (Higham [1955] 1966, 155–56).

The Americanization movement produced conflicting theories of how to deal with the new immigrants and their supposed language handicaps. The remedies included outright exclusion, already decreed for the Chinese in 1882, and soon extended to the Japanese and Asian Indians, coupled with attempts to segregate those immigrants who were already in the country and prevent them indulging in such ordinary activities as fishing or owning dogs.* Between 1890 and 1920 entrance examinations, in English, were instituted for a variety of professions, like the law and civil service, and service-related jobs, like barbering; their intent was clearly to exclude aliens (Leibowitz 1976, 461). Also popular were calls for extending the period before naturalization to as much as twenty-one years, and deporting aliens who had not learned the language after five years, a measure that was supported by Theodore Roosevelt. Although his desire to prevent the United States from becoming a "polyglot boarding house" full of "hyphenated Americans" is often cited as proof of Roosevelt's uncompromising stand against immigration, Roosevelt did propose to naturalize Japanese immigrants. It was Woodrow Wilson, campaigning in California against this idea, who argued, "We cannot make a homogeneous population of a people who do not blend with the Caucasian race" (Leibowitz 1971, 29).

Although in 1917 seven states still allowed aliens to vote, after the war the mood of the country shifted more strongly toward strict control of immigration and of immigrants (Higham 1966, 214, 301). Just as Benjamin Franklin had not considered Germans to be "whites" in the eighteenth century, many native Americans—that is, assimilated immigrants from northern and western Europe—regarded the "new" southern and eastern Europeans as nonwhite. Higham reports that one Southern town excluded Italians from white schools, and for many years California maintained separate schools for Chinese children (169).

Language and the New Immigration

The Immigration Commission, or Dillingham Commission, as it was popularly known, was a joint House-Senate group created in 1907 and chaired by Sen. William P. Dillingham of Vermont. Its charge was to study the issues resulting from the new, massive immigration. In 1911 the commission issued a forty-volume report on its findings that attempted to

*See Jensen 1988 for a detailed account of Indian immigration and its restriction.

demonstrate the undesirability of the new immigrants and their general unfitness for American life. Language was but a minor issue for the commission, which concerned itself more with proving increased rates of criminality and mental illness among the new immigrants, though it did suggest that adults from such nontraditional areas of immigration as Herzegovina, Spain, Bulgaria, and Turkey were much less likely to acquire English than their predecessors. (In contrast, Calvin Veltman [1983, 10] finds no sound data on which to base the assumption that some groups assimilated more easily than others.)

Despite the commission's pessimism, its statistics showed that well over 95 percent of children born in the United States of foreign parents of all nationalities acquired English, and to no one's surprise, it confirmed that the longer immigrants lived in the U.S., the more likely they were to learn English (Immigration Commission 1911, 1:474–84), though it also documented that 40 percent of immigrants to the U.S. returned to their countries of origin within five years. Such a high percentage of nonpermanent residents clearly works in favor of minority-language retention (Molesky 1988, 46). As proof of the importance of adults acquiring English, the Dillingham Commission found that American-born children of non-English-speaking fathers were more likely to be behind in school than children of foreign-born fathers who had acquired English (13:85). Curiously, the commission did not consider the effect of mothers' language on children's educational progress, though elsewhere it noted that because of their social isolation, adult foreign-born women were somewhat less likely than adult men to learn English.

There were, of course, a good number of commentators who supported the "new" immigration and who considered the work of Americanization to be a challenge rather than a curse. Horace Kallen (1924) viewed the latest wave of immigrants as even more intent on Americanizing than those who had come before, and John Gavit (1922, 253), who debunked the "legend" of the new immigration, supported this claim with a reanalysis of the Immigration Commission's statistics, demonstrating, among other things, that "knowledge of the English language at the time of arrival is not a material factor in determining the rapidity with which the individual seeks citizenship," and that nonanglophone immigrants had a higher rate of naturalization than did immigrants from English-speaking countries.

In any case, though, Gavit agreed that a knowledge of spoken English should be required for citizenship, and he argued strongly for requiring the ability to read English as well (416). Kallen (1924, 147) also noted that, despite differing attitudes toward the immigrants and what to expect from them, one thing was clear to virtually everyone: "The foreigner should be required to learn English." In 1894 Rena Michaels Atchison, who viewed foreigners as paupers and criminals, called for a federal statute mandating compulsory education in the national language. (Although all the states required communities to offer free public schools, compulsory education was a recent and far from universal concept: in 1852 Massachusetts became the first state to require school attendance for minors; sixteen states did not adopt compulsory education laws until the early 1900s, six of these after 1914.)

World War I accentuated the perception that Americanization via English was essential, and both public and private organizations urged compulsory Americanization classes, though Frank V. Thompson, the superintendent of the Boston public schools, who supported his state's education requirement for all illiterates under twenty-one years of age, resisted the paradox that "to democratize our newer brethren we must resort to autocratic procedure." Thompson continued, "Laws prohibiting the use of a foreign language below the high school level not only violate all the canons of modern pedagogy but are also in a certain sense undemocratic, un-American" (1920, 15, 290).

Massachusetts had a compulsory education law for illiterates under twenty-one before 1890. In 1918 New York State passed a law requiring nonanglophones between the ages of sixteen and twenty-one to study English in school or in special classes on the job, though according to Thompson it was not well enforced (306); New York supplemented this with funds to establish adult education programs for those over twenty-one, who were beyond the reach of the state's compulsory education law. Utah required aliens up to age forty-five to learn English, though how effective this measure was is not clear. In 1919 the National Education Association called for compulsory Americanization classes (Kallen 1924, 147), though Thompson points out that many states instituting Americanization requirements (which usually meant English classes) for aliens did not actually fund such programs, and in some cases school districts were barred by law from using tax money to educate adults.

The *D.A.R. Manual for Citizenship*, first issued in 1920 in English and seventeen other languages, encouraged immigrants to learn English for practical reasons: it would help them to "work better, more easily, and more safely." English would bring them better jobs and the respect of their children, who "will think that they know more than you, their parents, if you do not learn to speak English." A knowledge of English would protect greenhorns, or "greeners," as newcomers were often called, against swindlers, and it would make them into good citizens. The DAR believed English was best learned in school, not on the street, and it naively advised its readers to choose their neighborhood carefully, which suggests the authors were little acquainted with the limited housing options open to immigrants: "Do not live in the crowded parts of a city, among those who speak a foreign language. Associate and make friends with those who speak English. Live among them. Learn their customs and the American way of living" (DAR [1920] 1934, 9–11).

Between 1919 and 1921 some twenty states passed Americanization statutes (Forbes and Lemos 1981, 155), and most American universities and normal schools began offering Americanization as a subject for prospective teachers to study (Higham 1966, 382n). The Ford Motor Company, the Pennsylvania Railroad, Hart, Schaffner, and Marx, International Harvester, and Kabo Corset, among others, taught English to employees on the job—Ford required attendance at English classes twice a week, after work (Higham, 244)—and unions backed the idea as well. The YMCA and local public schools introduced programs in adult education. The Los Angeles schools were among the first to undertake the project; their night-school graduates received citizenship papers in formal ceremonies, and the diplomas were accepted by the local courts as proof of English competence in naturalization hearings (Hartmann 1948, 80).

While learning English was the order of the day, not everyone agreed that it had to be done at the expense of one's native language. Herbert Adolphus Miller (1916, 38) expressed a common view that the maintenance of native languages "would tend to soften the abrupt transition from foreign to American ideas and ways of thought, and to obviate the breakdown in parental control and discipline often observed in immigrant families." Earl Barnes (1918, 172–73) insisted that immigrants learn English, though he supported a weak form of cultural pluralism. Acknowledging that English could never replace an immigrant's native language because of the "memory images" or "neuron patterns" already formed, Barnes added, "There would be a great loss in human thinking and feeling if all the world thought with the same patterns." He considered it foolish to throw out what was good of German culture just because the Germans were momentarily out of favor. John J. Mahoney (1920, 15) agreed, cautioning language teachers not to overreact to war hysteria: "Americanization does not imply that the immigrant must give up his cherished spiritual heritage. His language, his religion, his social customs he may retain, and yet become a good American. Americanization is a giving, not a taking away. The wise worker in Americanization will adhere to the policy of 'Hands off.'"

Nor was everyone agreed that the way to get newcomers to learn English was to require it. Frank V. Thompson (1920) argued that simply imposing language would not bring about Americanization. Edward A. Steiner (1914, 73), a German immigrant who became a clergyman and academic, felt that while the United States is "inhospitable to all foreign languages" (1916b, 94), forced language learning would assuredly backfire: "If there were a law compelling all immigrants to learn the English language, this country would be a linguistic battlefield in which every tongue from Sanskrit to Esperanto would struggle for supremacy and so destroy any hope of ever assimilating the 'stranger within our gates.' This subtle force of a common language creeps in everywhere, just because it is not driven" (1916a, 51).

Steiner's loyalties to the land of his birth clearly lay behind his warning that if official English was perceived by German Americans as yet another pro-British move by the United States, they would resist it (1916b, 106). At the same time he firmly believed in assimilation, and cautioned that if the Germans succeed in "making German co-equal with English in our public schools" (1916b, 103), then the same rights would be demanded for Czech, Hungarian, "Scandinavian," Finnish, and Yiddish, at the expense of national unity.

While many nativists still fear that the absence of an official-language law would lead inevitably to the building of a new Babel in the New World, Steiner took the opposite view. While he noted that in Canada, French and, to a lesser extent, Slavic languages remained a source of friction (1916b, 101), and cautioned that in the United States "a cleavage in the language now would mean to us a cleavage of the nation in its most vulnerable if not its most essential part" (102), Steiner warned that [—just as in the Bible—] Babel results not from a laissez-faire language policy but from official intervention: "If there had been governmental pressure brought to bear upon the immigrant's use of English we would have fallen heir to the confusion of Babel, and to the never ending language problems of many of the countries of Europe" (1916a, 51). Nathan Glazer (1966, 360) agreed with Steiner's assessment of linguistic laissez-faire: "America produced *without* laws that which other countries, desiring a culturally unified population, were not able to produce *with* laws." Both Fishman (1966) and Kloss (1966) come to this conclusion as well.

Like many an educated immigrant who adopted English as a vehicle of literary communication, Steiner resented what he perceived to be threats to the purity of his adopted tongue. He urged his readers to fight against the vulgarization of English "by our children, or by those whom they hear in the theater, the concert hall [he favored operas sung in English], and the schoolroom" (1916b, 106). Steiner complained as well of the prevalence of "coarse slang and vile oaths" and the inability of American college students "to speak a straight, dignified English sentence."* This rigidity was coupled with a certain blindness to the flexibility of English. Steiner insisted that while all immigrants quickly learned to spice their native tongues with anglicisms, the English language *never* borrowed from the immigrants. His contention that, with the exception of a few indigestible food terms,

*108; complaints about the quality of English seem perennial; see Baron 1982a.

"not one word [from an immigrant tongue] has obtruded itself permanently into our intellectual and emotional life" (100) is easily dismissed. (See, for example, Mencken 1919.)

Frances Kellor was a leading Americanization activist who at first embraced, but then drew back from, the required learning of English. As early as 1910 Kellor advocated compulsory schooling for nonanglophones and illiterates, together with the training of teachers in minority languages (Lape 1915). But ultimately her efforts were in the area of voluntary assimilation. Kellor supported the stocking of libraries with non-English materials to encourage native-language literacy (an idea that was controversial at the time—many library boards fearing a nativist backlash if they expended public funds on non-English materials—and one that is sometimes expressed by English-first supporters today as well).

Kellor's National Americanization Committee launched an "English Language First" drive to get immigrants to learn the language voluntarily and obtain their citizenship. Kellor balanced the English-first concerns for civics and for improved efficiency and safety in the workplace with the clear need for foreign languages in business and the desire to "safeguard American liberty more by encouraging free speech in all tongues than by limiting it to one." Fearing it as a potential tool for hatred and repression, Kellor emphasized that the decision on compulsory English must be made "on broader grounds than those inspired by fear, prejudice or resentment" (1920, 235–36).

The National Americanization Committee established a model project in Detroit, working with that city's Board of Commerce and local employers to encourage—or sometimes to coerce—employees to attend English classes. The Ford Motor Company's motion picture division made a movie depicting nonanglophones being turned away from jobs, and the foreign-language press and social agencies did what they could to steer immigrants into school. As a result of these efforts, night school attendance rose by more than 150 percent (Hartmann 1948, 129–30), though there were still many adults who were not served by the relatively small number of programs available: Thompson (1920, 59–60) notes that, despite its dramatic increase in attendance, the Detroit program reached only eleven thousand students, a mere 5 percent of that city's foreign-born adults. Today as well there are more nonanglophones seeking to acquire English than educational facilities can accommodate, an indication that assimilation and the learning of English remain vital to nonanglophones living in the United States.

Postwar Legislation

The question of compulsory English figures prominently in the debates over literacy requirements for voting and naturalization, which we have examined in chapters 2 and 5. It appears as well in the congressional debate over Americanization. In 1920 the U.S. Senate considered an Americanization bill sponsored by the Bureau of Education of the Department of the Interior. The bill would have provided $12.5 million to states requiring all native American illiterates under the age of twenty-one and all nonanglophone aliens under forty-five to become literate in English. Students would attend two hundred hours of English classes a year until they could pass a language examination to be set by the Secretary of the Interior. The Senate sponsor of the bill, William S. Kenyon of Iowa, insisted that the measure was not meant to insult or penalize immigrants, and that it would make native Americans more sensitive to the problems of the foreign-born. Kenyon admitted that learning English would "not make an American out of a person," though he considered it a necessary if not sufficient "step toward getting a nation of 110 million people to act and think without a foreign accent" (*Congressional Record* [1920] 59:1650). Kenyon contended that ignorance of English correlated with higher rates of factory and mine accidents, increased worker turnover, lower wages, poor productivity, and industrial unrest.

In arguing for adoption of the bill, Kenyon cited the 1918 annual report of Franklin K. Lane, secretary of the interior, who found that 10 percent of the residents of the United States could not read the laws of the land, and that a similar percentage of draftees during World War I were unable to read an order in English or write a letter home. (Others quote a 24 percent illiteracy rate among World War I draftees.) Lane argued that "all Americans must be taught to read and write and *think* in one language;

this is a primary condition to that growth which all nations expect of us and which we demand of ourselves" (Report of the Secretary of the Interior 1918, 16). Lane asked, with a rhetorical flourish,

> What should be said of a democracy which is challenged by the world to prove the superiority of its system of government over those discarded, and yet is compelled to reach many millions of its people through papers printed in some foreign language . . . [or] which permits tens of thousands of its native-born children to be taught American history in a foreign language—the Declaration of Independence and Lincoln's Gettysburg speech in German and other tongues? . . . [or] which permits men and women to work in masses where they seldom or never hear a word of English spoken? (Report 1918, 16)

Lane's recommendation was to make education a federal as well as a state concern. With all the other federal controls going into effect for highways, interstate commerce, and agriculture, Lane was optimistic that "surely without violation of our fundamental law we can find a way by which the Nation can know that all of its people are able to talk and read our own language" (17).

The Senate initially passed the Americanization proposal of the Interior Department over objections that it would discourage foreign business, that the government was overestimating the effect of a common language, and that imposition of the German language in Poland had only solidified Polish nationalism in opposition to the measure. However, the House rejected both the idea of federal intervention and the high price tag that accompanied it, and the federal government's role in educating nonanglophones was deferred for fifty years.

The United States Supreme Court did take a stand on the foreign-language restrictions resulting from the war. After World War I, sentiment against foreign languages was so strong that some states banned all foreign-language instruction at the elementary level. These laws had as their common target "the harmful effects of non-American ideas inculcated through the teaching of foreign languages" (*State of Iowa v. Bartels* 181 NW 508, later reversed), and it took a U.S. Supreme Court decision, *Meyer v. Nebraska*, in 1923 to overturn such laws in Nebraska, Iowa, Ohio, and elsewhere.

In 1919 the Nebraska legislature, in response to the recommendations of the war-oriented state Council of Defense, which had condemned state schools and the state university as "unpatriotic and seditious" (Thompson 1920, 296), passed an open meeting law, which is still in force, requiring that discussions of "political or nonpolitical subjects or questions of general interest . . . be conducted in the English language exclusively" (Nebraska 1919, chap. 234). According to Molesky (1988, 52), by 1919 some fifteen states had adopted similar English-only open meeting laws. Religious gatherings and lodges were exempted from Nebraska's English requirement, though one critic of the statute remarked wryly, "It is difficult to understand why a secret society or lodge should be favored over the legitimate meetings of more democratic citizens" (Luckey 1919, 118). In the same year, the Nebraska legislature tried unsuccessfully to abolish private schools (Thompson 1920, 130). In 1921 Nebraska did pass a comprehensive act making English the state's official language, prohibiting foreign-language education before the ninth grade, and protecting the use of English in all public gatherings. According to section 4 of Nebraska's Siman (English-only) Law, "It shall be unlawful for any organization, whether social, religious or commercial, to prohibit, forbid or discriminate against the use of the English language in any meeting, school or proceeding, and for any officer, director, member or person in authority in any organization to pass, promulgate, connive at, publish, enforce or attempt to enforce any such prohibition or discrimination." Violators were subject to fines ranging from twenty-five to one hundred dollars, and up to thirty days in jail.

Nebraska's law was strict and detailed, but not unique in this respect. South Dakota's statute marked an English education as a fundamental civic right, adding:

> It shall be unlawful for any person or persons to act, aid, assist, advise or be instrumental in abridging or attempting to abridge the privilege of any child to receive such [English] instruction by submitting therefor instruction in some foreign language either by shortening the course of

instruction in English in any school or by coercing, requiring or inducing any child to withdraw from a school in which instruction is given in English to attend a school in which instruction is given in any foreign language. (Cited in Flanders 1925, 21)

As we have seen, Illinois resisted the postwar suppression of foreign-language instruction. Connecticut and Vermont also refused to pass anti-foreign-language laws, and a bill targeting Japanese-language supplementary schools failed in Washington state. New Hampshire, which sought to accommodate its vocal French Catholic minority, adopted a compromise measure, with the approval of the state's Franco-American bishop, requiring instruction and administration in English but permitting foreign languages in devotional exercises and as subjects for elementary school instruction. Indeed, the National Catholic War Council declared in favor of English as the language of instruction in parochial schools so long as foreign languages were permitted in the curriculum, though many ethnic Catholics resented the English-first stance of the Irish-dominated American church hierarchy (Thompson 1920, 292–301; Lemaire 1966, 257).

Meyer v. Nebraska

In 1921 the French war hero Marshal Ferdinand Foch came to the United States on a triumphant visit, crisscrossing the country, accepting presents, collecting over a dozen honorary degrees from major universities, and speaking to adulatory crowds. The governor of Nebraska invited Foch to address the International Hero Congress in Omaha, but the *New York Times* pointed out that if he were to do so, the marshal, who spoke little English, would certainly be in violation of that state's English-only open-meeting law. The *Times* had eagerly supported bans on German at the start of the war but now considered Nebraska's pro-English measures, which had been passed in order to suppress the use of German in the state, unacceptable and unsophisticated because they were applied instead to a language of the Allies. In a derisive editorial the *Times* sniffed, "Possibly the Marshal, if he goes to Omaha, will be able to scrape up enough English to tell the Nebraskans what he thinks of their silly laws" (30 July 1921, p. 8). But Foch, although he traveled to South Dakota and Minnesota, did not make a formal visit to Omaha.

In addition to the open-meeting law, chapter 249 of the Nebraska Sessions Laws of 1919 prohibited the teaching of any foreign language before the completion of the eighth grade. Specifically, the applicable part of the statute reads, "No person, individually or as a teacher, shall in any private, denominational, parochial or public school, teach any subject to any person in any language other than the English language." Robert T. Meyer, a teacher in the Lutheran-run Zion Parochial School, was fined twenty-five dollars because, as the complaint read, "between the hour of 1 and 1:30 on May 25, 1920," he taught German to ten-year-old Raymond Papart, who had not yet passed the eighth grade. The Nebraska Supreme Court affirmed Meyer's conviction for "the direct and intentional teaching of the German language" (107 Neb. 657 [1922]).

Meyer, whose offense consisted of reading a German Bible story, claimed he was giving religious instruction in a parochial school outside normal school hours. In his support, his superiors argued that the school wanted students to learn enough German so that they could worship with their parents. Meyer further maintained that the anti-foreign-language statute wrongfully interfered with his right to choose and pursue a profession, as protected by the Fourteenth Amendment; that imparting knowledge in a foreign language was not inherently immoral or inimical to the public welfare; and that foreign-language instruction was not a legitimate subject for prohibitory legislation. The law, Meyer's appeal concluded, operated to deny him equal protection, and it denied parents the right to determine what their children would be taught.

The relevant portion of the Fourteenth Amendment reads, "No state . . . shall deprive any person of life, liberty, or property without due process of law," and had already been construed by the courts as guaranteeing the right to pursue a profession. The Nebraska Supreme Court disagreed, finding that control of the school curriculum was within the legitimate jurisdiction of the state. It decided that the Bible story reading was not a purely devotional exercise, but rather instruction in the German language as such, an activity proscribed by state law: "The fact that the study of the language is mingled with the study of a religious subject does not afford the teacher protection as against the penalty imposed by the statute."

In *Nebraska v. McKelvie* (108 Neb. 448, 187 N.W. 927 [1922], also reversed by the U.S. Supreme Court as a result of the *Meyer v. Nebraska* decision), the Nebraska Supreme Court had ruled that Latin, Greek, and Hebrew used exclusively for religious purposes were not covered by the state's instructional ban and could be taught outside normal school hours. However, in the *Meyer* case the state supreme court determined that the *McKelvie* decision did not apply, for unlike the "so-called ancient or dead languages . . . it does not appear that the German language is a part of the religion of this church." The state court further concluded that Meyer's school had purposely changed its afternoon hours to set aside time during the normal school day for German instruction in an attempt to circumvent Nebraska's English-only law. The court agreed with the state's argument describing "the baneful effects of permitting foreigners who had taken residence in this country, to rear and educate their children in the language of their native land." Such a situation, because it proved "inimical" to the public safety, inculcating in the children of immigrants "ideas and sentiments foreign to the best interests of this country," fell within the police powers of the state.

The Nebraska court dismissed the usefulness of foreign-language instruction for the young. It found that most parents, with the exception of some who were foreign-born, "have never deemed it of importance to teach their children foreign languages before such children have reached the eighth grade." It agreed as well that the teaching of a foreign language was harmful to the health of the young child: "The hours which a child is able to devote to study in the confinement of school are limited. It must have ample time for exercise or play. Its daily capacity for learning is comparatively small." Such an argument was consistent with the educational theory of the day, which held as late as the 1950s that bilingualism led to confusion and academic failure, and was harmful to the psychological well-being of the child. (According to Hakuta [1985, 27], the psychologist Florence Goodenough argued in 1926 that the use of a foreign language in the home was a leading cause of mental retardation.)

Justice Letton, who had written the opinion protecting Latin, Greek, and Hebrew in *Nebraska v. McKelvie*, dissented from the state court opinion. Not arguing from ethnicity or patriotism, but taking the view that language study was an essential part of a liberal education—a view not generally expressed at the time either by supporters or opponents of English-only laws, or by the court majority—Letton found that the state had interfered with the parents' right to teach their children "any science or art, or any language which contributes to a larger life, or to a higher and broader culture." He criticized the notion that language study was harmful to children, finding it the misguided result of "crowd psychology . . . a product of the passions engendered by the World War." Letton asserted that early childhood was the best time to learn a foreign or classical language and argued that the state had "no right to prevent parents from bestowing upon their children a full measure of education in addition to the state required branches." In his opinion, just as the state cannot prevent the study of music, art, or crafts, it cannot prohibit the study of foreign language unless that study interferes with the English education prescribed by state law.

The state and federal appeals courts, reacting both to Germany's role in World War I and to the problems the American Army had in dealing with draftees who could not understand English as the language of command, upheld Meyer's conviction, but that decision was reversed by the U.S. Supreme Court (262 US 390 [1923]). Writing the majority opinion for the court, Associate Justice James Clark McReynolds admitted that "the desire of the legislature to foster a homogenous people with American ideals, prepared readily to understand current discussions of civic matters, is easy to appreciate." McReynolds found that desire to have been quickened by "unfortunate experiences during the late war, and aversion toward every characteristic of truculent adversaries." He agreed that an informed citizenry needed to be literate in English, but he concluded that such an end could not be attained by unconstitutional means (McReynolds would later resist the innovations of the New Deal on similar constitutional grounds). In fact, the court affirmed that English could be required in schools: "The power of the state to compel attendance at some school and to make reasonable regulations for all schools, including a requirement that they shall give instructions in English, is not questioned." Moreover, McReynolds rejected the argument that the ban on foreign-language instruction was related to concern for the students' mental and physical health: "It is well known that proficiency in a foreign language seldom comes to one not instructed at an early age, and experience shows that this is not injurious to the health, morals, or understanding of the ordinary child." He maintained that "mere knowledge of the German language cannot reasonably be regarded as harmful" and that the Nebraska legislature had "attempted materially to interfere with the calling of modern language teachers, with the opportunities of pupils to acquire knowledge, and with the power of parents to control the education of their own."

McReynolds noted the intention of the Nebraska legislature "to promote civic development by inhibiting training and education of the immature in foreign tongues and ideals before they could learn English and acquire American ideals." He conceded the charge "that the foreign-born population is very large, that certain communities commonly use foreign words, follow foreign leaders, move in a foreign atmosphere, and that the children are thereby hindered from becoming citizens of the most useful type, and the public safety is imperiled." But he concluded that

> the protection of the Constitution extends to all,—to those who speak other languages as well as to those born with English on the tongue. Perhaps it would be highly advantageous if all had ready understanding of our ordinary speech, but this cannot be coerced by methods which conflict with the Constitution,—a desirable end cannot be promoted by prohibited means. . . . No emergency has arisen which renders knowledge by a child of some language other than English so clearly harmful as to justify its inhibition, with the consequent infringement of rights long freely enjoyed.

Dissenting from this opinion, Justice Oliver Wendell Holmes affirmed that the goal of having an English-speaking country was both desirable and legal; that youth was the best time to learn the *English* language; and that since there were parts of the state of Nebraska where a child could hear only Polish or French or German, it was not unreasonable to require that child to hear only English at school. Furthermore, Holmes maintained that an English-only requirement "is not an undue restriction of the liberty either of teacher or scholar. No one would doubt that a teacher might be forbidden to teach many things." While Holmes favored Nebraska's English-only "experiment," he did agree with the rest of the court in striking down the Ohio law specifically prohibiting the teaching of German below the eighth grade (*Pohl v. Ohio, Bohning v. Ohio, USSCR* 67:1051).

The decision in *Meyer v. Nebraska* was to some extent an empty victory for language teachers. World War I had forced the assimilation of German Americans, taking its toll on the study and use of German in the United States; no doubt the process of assimilation would have been completed without the war as well, though perhaps not quite so quickly. Kloss (1966; 1977) reports that in 1900 there were more than 600,000 students of German in American elementary schools; by the 1930s that number dropped to 70,000. Similarly, in 1915 some 324,000 students—close to 25 percent of the student population—studied German in American high schools (in contrast, only 8.8 percent were enrolled in French classes). By 1922 only 0.6 percent—fewer than 14,000 high school students—were taking German, while the percentage studying French had risen to 15.5 (Gilbert 1981, 263).

Because of changing immigration patterns and a change in the popular attitude toward Germany and its people, the status of German in the United States had shifted from immigrant mother tongue to that of a relatively unimportant supplemental or foreign language. After World War I, high school German enrollments climbed back only to about 2 percent. More and more private schools dropped German as the primary language of instruction, and German congregations generally shifted to English for their worship. This precipitous decline in the study of German, coupled with the high court's unequivocal stand on foreign-language teaching, meant that during World War II, American anti-German sentiment could no longer focus on language, and there were fewer attempts to suppress German in the schools or on the streets. On the contrary, official efforts during the Second World War supported special German instruction for intelligence gathering and the armed forces. Figures for German study dropped sharply again during and after World War II. In 1948, 43,000 students attended high school German classes, but that was only 0.8 percent of the student population, which suggests some anti-German backlash. Enrollments have since crept up once again to the interwar figure of 2 percent; postwar French study declined as well, to 4.7 percent in 1948, indicating a general loss of interest in foreign languages in American schools as the country once again turned inward, a loss of interest that neither the Sputnik crisis of the 1950s nor the balance of trade crisis of the 1980s has been able to reverse significantly.

Nonanglophone Children in School

The Supreme Court decision in *Meyer v. Nebraska* dealt with the rights of teachers to teach and of parents to control what their children learn. It did not confront the question of official English, which in fact seemed like a good idea to the court, nor did it deal with the question that remains as pressing today as it was in the 1920s: how to educate nonanglophone children in American public schools.

In 1903 fourteen states required elementary instruction in English. By 1923 that number had risen to thirty-four (Flanders 1925). In part this change represents the increased involvement of the states in educational matters: during this time, legislation was passed in a broad range of areas from mandatory physical education and fire drills to required instruction in the metric system (a constitutional provision in Utah for some years) and the humane treatment of household pets. However, as we have seen, language was a broad area of concern for legislators, and school laws on the subject would have been passed in any case.

Samuel Insull (see chapter 4) and others like him entrusted the task of Americanizing immigrants to the American public school system. It was the schools, after all, where immigrant children were first exposed to the ideals of their new homeland. It was assumed, for example, that while children might pick up English on the streets, it would not be good English, which could only be achieved through the intervention of formal education. The schools would expose children to everything from Americanism to the principles of hygiene. (It was assumed by the health authorities that working-class immigrants did not know how to bathe, take care of children, or prepare food; William H. Maxwell, superintendent of the New York City schools, claimed immigrant children even had to be *taught* how to play [*Education* 1913, 19].) And education in English was assumed to be the key to upward mobility in America. At least that is the picture that generations of educators, social workers, historians, and politicians have painted of the one institution charged with the task of melting foreigners down until they became unhyphenated Americans. However, in coupling English instruction with Americanization—or civics, as it also came to be known—school texts portrayed most minorities negatively, and while this may have caused many children to reject their roots, it did not encourage the positive self-image necessary for success, but contributed instead to what Richard Rodriguez (1982, 18) has called "the pain of public alienation."

Unfortunately, the schools were not well prepared to depunctuate their charges. They paid little attention to the special language needs of their immigrant children, and many children managed to learn English in spite of rather than because of the schools they attended (Higham 1966, 235–36). Several midwestern cities did maintain public German-English schools, and most reports suggest these were successful. For example, in 1889 the superintendent of Cincinnati's schools, John B. Peaslee, declared, "Those who devote one half of their school time to a foreign language learn fully as much as those who do not, and in some cases, as for instance composition, even more" (cited in Kloss 1940, 1:470). Although he accepted Cleveland's bilingual German-English schools without comment, the educator Herbert Adolphus Miller (1916, 75) complained that "the problem of teaching foreign children to speak English has never been regarded by the public schools as one of their serious problems." Miller recommended Americanizing speakers of languages besides German by adapting the methods of what he thought of as model English instruction programs in Puerto Rico and the Philippines, though as we shall see below, such teaching was relatively unsuccessful as well.

Frank V. Thompson lamented the fact that no special provisions were made for nonanglophone students and strongly objected to the common practice of placing non-English-speaking children in the lowest grades or in the "backward" or remedial classes. The so-called "steamer classes" instituted as early as 1901 by such cities as Boston, Cleveland, Rochester, and New York City were supposed to offer short periods of intensive English instruction to newly arrived children before mainstreaming them into the regular curriculum, but they accommodated only a small fraction of the eligible students and suffered from poor teacher preparation and inadequate methodology (Thompson 1920, 16–17, 118–19).

Non-English-speaking children were treated just like their anglophone comrades: they were all but ignored in the planning of lessons that presumed native-speaker language competence. A survey of state and city English-language curricula through the 1920s confirms a general silence on the question of teaching English to nonanglophone children, except for the occasional remark about the need to correct foreign accents and short lists of the types of pronunciation gaffes or errors in idiom different ethnic groups were likely to make. Although the California Immigration Commission (1920, 440, 459) opposed the English-only movement before, during, and after World War I, encouraging specialized research in teaching English as a Second Language (ESL) and applauding the appointment of an ESL instructor at the Los Angeles State Normal School to train teachers on Saturdays, the California Department of Education merely told its teachers to teach correct pronunciation to foreign pupils by means of "facial exercises [promoting] free and flexible lip, tongue, and jaw action" (California Department of Education 1932, 9). Massachusetts listed characteristic errors of pronunciation made by "foreign children," including the pronunciation of *length* with a short vowel (Massachusetts Board of Education 1916, 10). New York State would cure "dialectic difficulties" with "tip-tongue exercises" for Russians and Germans and "base tongue exercises" for those with Latin accents (1919, 9–10). And New York

City instructed its teachers that "the child of foreign parents has, in most cases, learned the language incorrectly from his associates and to this jargon he adds his foreign accent," which produced such pronunciation "errors" as *wuz* for *was*, *kewpon* for *coupon*, *Toosday* for *Tuesday*, *horse* for *hoarse*, *littel* or *litle* for *little*, and unaspirated initial *wh-* (for example, *witch* for *which*). The Board of Education condemned as well such atrocities as *couldjou* and *wanta*, forms that are still under attack in the New York City schools. The city recommended "vocal gymnastics and phonic drills" to correct these supposed anomalies, many of which are now considered fairly standard features of spoken English (1918, 2–3). As late as 1966 the linguist Harold Allen found the basic problem confronting ESL instruction in American schools to be "inadequately prepared teachers and inadequate materials," coupled with a distinct lack of recognition of ESL as an academic discipline in which research could be done or teachers trained (Allen 1966, Introduction).

In the face of teachers' passivity and the occasional hit-or-miss approach to nonanglophones in the classroom, Sarah T. Barrows (1922, 368–69) advocated a more active form of intervention. In her discussion of immigrant children in the kindergarten classroom, Barrows asserted that lack of English constituted a linguistic handicap, and she warned against the teachers' assumption that immersion was all that was necessary to inculcate English. Barrows observed an unwillingness of nonanglophone children to speak in the classroom, a situation that produced "an inertia, a habit of silence, which is hard to overcome. . . . In many schools the foreign-speaking child is allowed to come day after day and sit through the session, the teacher thinking that he will eventually begin to understand what he hears and will then naturally begin to speak."

What actually happened, according to Barrows, was that nonanglophone children understood less than teachers realized, and that their power to express themselves in English lagged even farther behind, particularly if they were exposed to English only in the classroom. Because such children invariably fell behind in subject matter too, she advocated "giving them a thorough foundation in English before requiring as much of them as is expected from children of American parents" (370). Barrows would not ban the child's use of a foreign language—in fact, she found bilingualism to be "a distinct advantage," a position that contradicted much of the language psychology of her day. But she would use the kindergarten class to reverse children's linguistic priorities, training them to regard English as their "mother tongue" and their "mother's tongue [as] the foreign language" (371).

Unfortunately, Barrows's concern with the problems of non-anglophones was exceptional. Colin Greer (1972) confirms that schools did not assimilate immigrant children well. More children failed in school than succeeded, and large numbers of them dropped out altogether. The Dillingham Commission found from 60 to 70 percent of children of foreign-born parents to be "retarded" in school (Immigration Commission 1911, 13:86). The figures Greer cites are similarly discouraging: in 1904, for example, 39 percent of New York City elementary pupils were as much as two years below grade level. Remedial classes were packed with immigrants from all ethnic groups, and for most students the promise of social mobility through education was an empty one. In 1910 New York City had a 30 percent high school dropout rate, which increased to 50 percent in the 1940s as the proportion of the teenage population attending high school increased. Greer claims that rather than promoting mobility, "the schools were more often agencies for maintaining social status pretty much as they found it." Even half of those immigrants from the most "favored" ethnic groups, the English and the Welsh, remained unskilled laborers (100). As Greer sees it, those immigrants who managed to succeed in bettering themselves in America did so because of the experience they brought with them from the old country and their ability to establish a middle class within their limited ethnic unit before entering the American bourgeoisie at large (84).

"Good English Makes Good Americans"

The public schools were dedicated to the inculcation of patriotism as well as English: by 1923 thirty-nine states required public schools to display the American flag (Flanders 1925, 10). The schools added to the already powerful equation of English with Americanism another powerful concept: that fluency in English was an indication of clear or logical thinking, which in turn was deemed necessary to the proper functioning of a democracy. In fact, while linguistic fluency certainly enhances comprehension, it may often disguise muddy logic or hide deceptive ideas, but the notion that good English was a sign not just of patriotism but of truth as well has proven so attractive in twentieth-century American classrooms that it has become all but impossible to dislodge. And good English could not be taught too early. Barrows (1922, 376) argued that kindergarten should be devoted to the acquisition of the language: "Our only hope for the future of the country lies in an enlightened patriotism, which can be attained only if our children are trained to clear and direct thinking, to clear and forcible expression of thought, and to a recognition of the responsibilities and duties which are theirs because they are an indispensable part of a great nation."

Translating this sentiment into classroom practice, schools across the United States launched good English drives as part of their Americanization efforts, and children earned points for linguistic espionage—perhaps not the most democratic of lessons—reporting the language errors of their classmates to their teachers. Good English campaigns from 1918 to the early 1920s consciously attacked the problem of what the schools considered the contamination of English by foreigners. They sought to ridicule and root out the errors of the non-native speaker. Supporting one such effort, a schoolteacher named Margaret Burnside wrote, "Isn't this a fitting time to make our language pure, to make it represent the highest, the noblest, the most beautiful in our thoughts, to make it American without a hyphen?" (1918, 658). And the campaigns produced such language loyalty oaths as the following "Pledge for Children" of the Chicago Woman's Club American Speech Committee:

I love the United States of America. I love my country's flag. I love my country's language. I promise:

1. That I will not dishonor my country's speech by leaving off the last syllables of words.

2. That I will say a good American "yes" and "no" in place of an Indian grunt "um-hum" and "nup-um" or a foreign "ya" or "yeh" and "nope."

3. That I will do my best to improve American speech by avoiding loud, rough tones, by enunciating distinctly, and by speaking pleasantly, clearly, and sincerely.

4. That I will learn to articulate correctly as many words as possible during the year. (Robbins 1918, 175)

These Good English campaigns had the practical advantage of being more democratic than English as a Second Language instruction—every child, not just the nonanglophone, could benefit from a unit on language improvement. As Robbins noted, even pupils in an exclusive private school, who have "never had their speech affected by foreign-born children . . . without exception try to talk as badly as they can" (1918, 167). Such programs were also easier to incorporate into the school syllabus, since they presumed a knowledge of correctness in English that teachers were supposed to have acquired as part of the teacher certification process, while no one really knew with any certainty how to teach English to nonanglophones. In the mid–1920s, there was almost no literature on ESL instruction for children, and very little had been written on ESL for adults, but books and pamphlets on correct English abounded.

To a great extent, the absence of a workable methodology meant that adult education in English, sentimentalized in such works as Leo Rosten's *The Education of H*y*m*a*n K*a*p*l*a*n* (1937), was actually not much better than that found in the elementary schools. What few adult facilities there were existed only in urban areas—Thompson (1920, 9) estimates that in 1910 only 1.3 percent of the foreign-born adult population attended night schools. And until the 1920s the sole qualifications a teacher needed to serve in the evening schools were the ability to speak English and the desire for overtime pay. Even later, when adult education programs were staffed by certified day school teachers, critics scoffed that methods used to teach children would fail with adults. Night school students often complained about the childishness of their lessons (Forbes and Lemos 1981, 159), a problem sadly confirmed by contemporary educators who found that night school materials and methods were seldom age- or subject-appropriate, ranging from the extremes of "Run, Spot, run" to abstract, incomprehensible lectures on tense and inflection (Lape 1915; Thompson 1920).

Parkhurst Whitney (1923, 13), who believed that "it's pretty hard to make an American out of a man, or woman, who can neither read nor speak, let alone think, American," criticized Americans for assuming "that the man or woman who doesn't know our language doesn't know anything." Whitney understood that the concept of native-tongue language loyalty must be taken into account in teaching English to immigrants, observing that "for a thousand years the racial minorities of Europe have protected their language against the encroachment of more powerful neighbors." Moreover, he found night schools to be ineffective in scope—they served only 10 percent of the nation's foreign born adults—and methodology, for which he quoted the complaints of a night school principal: "The prevailing method of teaching is uninteresting, and much of the stuff taught is worthless. . . . [The immigrant] is put in a child-sized seat, and disciplined as if he were a child, by some young teacher fresh from the normal school. He is set to reciting childish verses, and to learning dry rules of grammar. I have seen a teacher drill a class for a whole hour on the difference between 'this' and 'that.'"

Frank Thompson, who favored drilling children on correct pronunciation because they are pliant enough to lose their accents, objected to the overemphasis on phonics in adult classes, where accent reduction is a lost cause (179). He further warned that conventional methods of education, employing an autocratic instructor and passive students, are guaranteed to fail with adults (240; we have since learned that they do not succeed with children either). Inadequate facilities, lack of state funding, poor programs, an absence of standards for determining literacy, and the difficulties of attending school after work led to adult dropout rates of 50 to 80 percent (Miller 1916, 99; Thompson 1920, 68).

The whole concept of English as a Second Language was a new one in education in the period 1900–1920 (Howatt 1984, 212). What few language-learning experts there were at the time disagreed over the validity of the few methodologies that had been developed. Educators generally favored the newer, more "direct" methods of English instruction, which relied entirely on oral

English, coupled with pantomime where necessary, rather than the older, indirect method that focused on the translation of written language. Indirect instruction employed the student's native language to explain matters, and involved both paradigm practice and the memorization of vocabulary lists. According to Lillian P. Clark (1924, 2), the direct method, which is English-only, "associates objects and actions with the English symbols immediately, without the interpretation or translation of the English words into any other language." The Berlitz question-and-answer system, intended by its deviser to be teacher-proof, proved a popular direct method of instruction, as did François Gouin's attempt to mimic for second-language instruction the way in which children learn their native language. Both focused on the acquisition of practical conversational skills through dialogues involving everyday situations.

George Elmore Reaman (1921) sought to ground English instruction in "the essential core of language," recommending the study of sign language, ways in which foreigners make their wants known without English, and methods of teaching foreign languages. Peter Roberts, an educator working for the YMCA, wrote a more popular series of textbooks on teaching English to immigrant adults. Roberts opposed compulsory English for adults as un-American, noting that many immigrants had already been compelled to learn foreign tongues in Europe (1920, 89; in contrast to his distaste for "Prussianism" for adults, Roberts approved of compulsory English for children). Roberts adopted Gouin's method, designed to imitate natural mother-tongue acquisition but using subject matter appropriate for adult learners. Roberts's system, some thirty lessons divided among home, work, and "business life," promised to teach a base of seven hundred to one thousand words, which is, according to Roberts, "a larger stock than most men in the common walks of life use."* Roberts conceived of language learning as a logical (though unconscious) process, and he advocated a conversational, or aural/oral method, avoiding textbooks, spelling, or instruction in grammar. According to Roberts, "Grammar lessons in an

---

*(1912) 1918, 31; this is, of course, a serious underestimate of the basic native-speaker English vocabulary, which contains at least forty thousand words.

abstract form will drive away any body of men" (41), and he concentrated instead on building up associations of ideas and establishing logical connections between successive sentences.

The Roberts method sounds appealing, though in practice it strangles on a progression of simple sentences and simplistic ideas painfully broken down into component parts, and it is accompanied by the very drill Roberts claimed to avoid: "No lesson should be given the pupils without its corresponding grammar practice" (81), which includes pronoun paradigms and rings such sentential changes as:

I am getting warm.
You are getting warm.
He is getting warm.
We are getting warm.
You are getting warm.
They are getting warm. (69)

Present-tense dialogues may be repeated later in the future tense:

Tomorrow, the miner will go underground.
Tomorrow, the miner will take a match.
Tomorrow, the miner will strike a match.
Tomorrow, the match will be lighted. (83)

And although Roberts was criticized by his contemporaries for his optimistic stance on the new immigration, he advised teachers to "take account of race psychology" and to divide classes by sex (1920, 94–95). Moreover, he told his instructors that the Italians, Slavs, Hindus, Chinese and Japanese students they would encounter suffered from "a heritage of inefficiency and sloth" which would prove difficult to overcome ([1912] 1918, 100).

In 1920 P. P. Claxton, secretary of the interior and commissioner of education, reported that more than 95 percent of the American population could speak English. But he regarded the remaining 5 percent as a danger to the public peace, and for them Claxton recommended the Goldberger method of teaching English to adults (Goldberger 1920, 5). Although the Bureau of Education encouraged states to adopt laws similar to the New York statute which required everyone under twenty-one years of age to demonstrate a fifth-grade level of English literacy (Massachusetts had recently raised its requirement even higher, to a sixth-grade level), Henry Goldberger, a New York City public school principal and an ESL instructor at Columbia Teachers College, rejected the idea of compulsory English. The short pamphlet on ESL that he prepared for the Bureau of Education recommended English clubs rather than classes for adults to make the communication situation more realistic. The content of Goldberger's English lessons was pragmatic: "Teach to-day such English as the pupil can use at once" (11). This practical English includes "name, address, occupation, greetings, salutations, farewells, inquiries, showing gratitude, . . . age, weight, illness, good health, pain, hunger and thirst," as well as words about "buying, selling, repairing, cooking," technical terms on the job, household terms, and local and national holidays.

In grouping students Goldberger warned teachers to prevent the formation of "national cliques" which would delay the work of Americanization. Though he conceded that a teacher's knowledge of the students' language could be helpful, Goldberger, like Roberts, recommended the direct method of instruction, the employment of English to teach English. He rejected the synthetic, or one-word-at-a-time, method ("This is a hat, this is a book"), the declension of pronouns and the conjugation of verbs ("I walk, thou walkest, he walks, we walk, you walk, they walk"), and any other form of mechanical drill in favor of Gouin's analytic method favoring spoken language. Goldberger recommended the construction of "themes" of ten short sentences illustrating an action or goal—for example, opening a door or visiting a doctor—to be accompanied by a pantomime on the part of the instructor. He also advised a catechetical conversation, wherein the teacher asks questions and students provide simple answers ("With whom do you board? How many children have you?"). Students were encouraged to act out short dialogues about buying something, asking directions, opening a bank account, testifying in court (17–18). The forty-six-page booklet contains short monologues illustrating a day in the life of the immigrant: washing hands, making a fire in a stove, eating breakfast, going to work, eating lunch, shopping, eating supper, and going to bed. Like Roberts's examples, those of Goldberger suffer from syntactic atomization. Linguistic simplicity, carried to an extreme in the ESL classroom, is pedagogically deadly. (Similarly, researchers on reading methodology have found, to no one's surprise, that school reading texts for children are often ineffective because their language is so simplistic as to be utterly without interest.) The lack of drama the Goldberger dialogues create as they are acted out by instructor and students will drive away any body of men and women.

Ironically, a more modern, workable method of ESL instruction was available as early as 1899, with the publication of Henry Sweet's *Practical Study of Languages*, which rejected the osmotic process of the "direct" method in favor of graded lessons in phonology and the development of oral competency. Though it led to Otto Jespersen's *How to Teach a Foreign Language* (1904) and Harold Palmer's work on language teaching in England, it was ignored at the time by American schools, perhaps because of its British origins, and perhaps, as well, because it lacked an ideological grounding in Americanism (Allen 1973, 298; Howatt 1984, 213).

It would seem that such an ideological grounding for the ESL curriculum was more important than its actual effectiveness, a situation that has not changed today. For some critics of Americanization, like Henry Pratt Fairchild, learning English was not enough. For him, assimilation was spiritual and intellectual, not simply linguistic. The title of one of Fairchild's books—*The Melting-Pot Mistake* (1926)—reveals his negative attitude toward newcomers. A believer in the Nordic origins of the English, and therefore the American, race, who worried about pollution of the national "germ plasm" by aliens, Fairchild claimed that the schools, rather than serving as agents of Americanization, had become de-Americanized by "the insupportable burden of foreignness that has been laid upon them." He blamed both immigrant children and the "large proportion of the teachers [who] are only partly Americanized" as the chief causes in "the breakdown of the American public-school system" (234–35). While Fairchild's views seem extreme in retrospect, they do reflect a common fear that the teaching ranks might become polluted. The more moderate Steiner simply urged that "no teacher ought to be employed in our schools who does not speak English contagiously well" (1916b, 106).

While the scholars debated whether it was necessary for instructors to know the language of their students, school authorities turned Fairchild's advice into policy, moving to keep immigrants and bilinguals out of the teaching ranks by placing greater emphasis on accent in the testing and licensing of prospective teachers. Required speech courses were used to steer Chinese American elementary education majors away from teaching in California; those who did pass the speech test were frequently not permitted to teach Anglo children (Low 1982, 165–66; 178). In one extreme case, a 1925 Tennessee law required that all teachers from the university level on down to the kindergarten be citizens, and required those employed to teach white pupils to be native-born whites (Foreign Language Information Service 1940). As a result of these efforts to homogenize the language of the teaching corps, schoolteachers remained by and large monolingual English speakers untrained in any methodology to teach English to nonanglophones and unable to empathize with the nonanglophone student. Those teachers who did read up on ESL theory often opted for an eclectic approach, using a bit of everything, both direct and indirect. As recently as the 1950s, little special preparation was required for teachers of what New York City called "English to the foreign born," and even today one of the biggest complaints about both ESL and bilingual education is the inadequate methods training of classroom teachers. Indeed, one "methodology" that is still current goes so far as to claim that ESL training is unnecessary for teaching children or adults. A version of what is now called immersion, or the sink-or-swim approach to English, it suggests that nonanglophones merely need the chance to listen to a native speaker in order to pick up English. After all, it is argued, children are adaptable when it comes to language learning. So high an authority on language education as the United States Supreme Court affirmed this in *Meyer v. Nebraska*, stating that childhood is the best time to acquire a second tongue.

The immersion method is popular in both day and evening schools because it is traditional—the first attempts at ESL in American schools early in this century used a monolingual English approach, provided little in the way of translation on the part of teachers (though bilingual students often translated for their classmates), and introduced grammar through the rote practice of paradigms and sentence patterns (Howatt 1984, 213). Immersion is also popular with the schools because it is both cheap and administratively convenient. Immersion can be accomplished without separate classes for children or specialist instructors for either children or adults. One San Francisco newspaper columnist, a vocal supporter of English-first, recently suggested that since immigrants do not need to learn perfect English, untrained volunteers would make the most suitable English teachers: unlike professional instructors, volunteers would not "get hung up on grammar rules and stuff like that" and they would cost less than regular teachers to boot (Wright 1986).

While inadequate instruction is only one of many factors contributing to the high dropout rates of adults from English classes earlier in this century, it is likely that the high dropout rate among immigrant children reported by Greer must be attributed in large part to the failure of the schools to provide nonanglophones with ESL or bilingual education of any sort. For children with little or no English, immersion virtually guarantees that they will fall behind in skills development and content areas as they either struggle to keep up with what is said, or withdraw into a world of their own. The psychologist Kenji Hakuta (1985, 225) deflates the myth that children are sponges waiting to soak up language: "Children are not the instantaneous second-language learners painted in our folklore, and . . . it may take them even longer to learn the kinds of language necessary to perform well in school."

However, Paulston (1981, 476) finds that language acquisition, or the lack thereof, is a function of complex social factors, and the school's role in the process is therefore a limited one, even under the best of circumstances. In view of this, the fact that many children did acquire English—probably on the streets and schoolyards, and on the job, rather than in the classrooms through formal lessons and interaction with instructors in overcrowded urban classrooms—would seem to be more a tribute to their own intelligence and initiative than it is to the educational system that virtually ignored their presence.

Crime and Punishment

One standard method of inculcating English-first in American schools has been to suppress the students' native tongue, punishing them for using the wrong language. The method may be as old as language instruction itself. By the seventeenth century, according to the Newbolt Report on English in the British school system (1921), schools in Great Britain were so thoroughly committed to a classics curriculum with Latin and Greek as the languages of instruction that the use of English on school grounds was proscribed: "It is a usual custom in schools to appoint *Custodes* ['spies'] or *Asini* ['dunces'] to observe and catch them who speak English in each form." Those so caught could transfer the opprobrium of the dunce cap by catching another student using the vernacular (John Brinsley, *Ludus Literarius* [1627], cited in Newbolt 1921, 37–38; the report adds that the practice was still common at Eton in the late nineteenth century).

Similarly, nineteenth-century French schools, under orders to spread the national language to that half of France which was still not francophone, took to the task aggressively, using the same methods and punishments to enforce French that the eighteenth-century Jesuits had used to make their charges speak Latin (Weber 1976, 457). In the 1890s children caught using Breton were "put on dry bread and water or sent to clean out the school latrine," or they were made to wear a "token of shame," which Jesuits had formerly used to enforce Latin on French-speaking students (313). The French army picked up where the schools left off, on one occasion canceling all leaves in a Quimper barracks when some soldiers were heard speaking Breton (83*n*).

Tove Skutnabb-Kangas (1984, 309–10) labels as violent the requirement that some minority-language speakers—for example Lapps in Norway, Finns in Sweden, Kurds in Turkey, and Native Americans in the United States—attend centralized assimilation schools that isolate children from their families and exterminate their native culture and language. (In contrast, majority-language boarding schools reinforce home traditions.) She further describes Finnish and Welsh children punished for using their home languages by being made to carry heavy loads or wear collars that restrain head movement. (In 1846 Welsh was allowed in classrooms only as a vehicle for teaching English; it was banned completely between 1871 and 1939, since which time it has been permitted again [Wardhaugh 1987, 84].)

American schools were equally zealous to convert everyone to English. When the United States took the Philippines from Spain in 1898, it imposed English in the schools, together with the practise of suspending students or lowering their grades for using a non-English language (Ruppenthal 1919, 660; Smolicz 1986, 99). A similar English-only policy applied for a time in Puerto Rico, which was acquired through conquest at the same time, though Spanish was eventually reinstated there as the language of primary school instruction. From 1859 on, the city of San Francisco forced its Chinese residents to attend segregated Chinese-only schools, where the Chinese language was forbidden. A Chinese American teacher reports of her own experience attending one of these schools in the 1940s: "Most of the teachers penalized us for speaking our home language. If they caught us speaking Chinese to each other, even during our recess time, we were penalized—our privilege taken away" (Low 1982, 172).

Native American schools run by the Bureau of Indian Affairs had for many years the goal of "breaking up the use of Indian dialects, and the substitution therefor of the English language" (Morgan n.d., 13). In 1887 the BIA announced: "Instruction of Indians in the vernacular is not only of no use to them but is detrimental to the cause of education and civilization and will not be permitted in any Indian school. . . . The impracticability, if not impossibility of civilizing Indians of this country in any other tongue but our own would seem obvious" (cited in Forbes and Lemos 1981, 139)."

It was the policy of the BIA to employ only English-speaking teachers who were charged with the task of assimilating Indian children into white society. As one tactic of assimilation, Native American children were punished—they were beaten or had their mouths washed out with soap—if they lapsed into Navajo or Hopi or Cherokee at the boarding schools many of them were forced to attend by a government which at times withheld food from parents who wanted to keep their children at home (Castellanos 1983, 30; *Report on Indian Education* 1976, 7; *English*

Language Constitutional Amendments 1989, 96). In 1928 the Merriam Report shifted the BIA focus away from deracination, encouraging the support of tribal languages (Allen 1973, 313), but English remained the language of instruction and punishments continued (Crawford 1989, 26). The 1951 Bureau of Indian Affairs manual stressed the importance of English in the schools but suggested the beginning of a reversal of its long-held English-only policy: because "language expression is essential to the development of thought, the use of native languages by Indian children may not be forbidden." Nonetheless, the BIA was slow in implementing bilingual education (*Report* 1976, 122). Punishment for using Indian languages was common in the Canadian Yukon as well.

Until the late 1960s many schools in the American Southwest, which was originally settled by Hispanics and forcibly annexed to the United States, forbade the use of Spanish. Punishments included writing several pages of "I must not speak Spanish in school" and standing on "the 'black square' for an hour or so," as well as fines, suspension, "Spanish detention," paddling, and even expulsion (Carter and Segura 1979, 184–88).

This policy of active minority-language suppression does not encourage linguistic assimilation, and probably was never meant to. It did not turn young English gentlemen into fluent speakers of Latin and Greek, though it taught many of them to respect and fear the magisterial languages and ultimately to reject them. In the last quarter of the nineteenth century, after some one hundred years of French-only school laws, French remained a foreign language for half that country's citizens and 25 percent of them spoke no French at all (Weber 1976, 67–70). Although the percentage has improved, regional variation and local languages remain strong in many parts of France.

Linguistic Colonialism in Puerto Rico

The United States did no better in its attempts to anglify its non-English-speaking possessions. Puerto Rico was occupied by American forces in 1898 during the Spanish-American War and became a possession of the United States. In 1900 the Organic Act passed by the U.S. Congress conferred

American citizenship to all born on the island. In 1899 Victor S. Clark, the interim director of Puerto Rican schools, recommended that English replace Spanish as the language of instruction. Defending his action, Clark, who was initially blind to local realities, claimed to find no language loyalty among Puerto Rico's Hispanics. Confronted with an island illiteracy rate of 90 percent and a variety of Spanish that he considered a patois with "little value as an intellectual medium," Clark maintained that it would be just as easy to teach the Puerto Ricans English as it would be to set up schools teaching standard Castilian Spanish (Osuna 1949, 342).

However, this and subsequent American attempts to anglify Puerto Rico show that school language policy cannot be effectively driven by political or ideological desires. Clark was quickly forced to admit his mistake, acknowledging that Spanish had "a tenacious hold upon popular sympathy" (342). He then advocated teaching both Spanish and English, in order to preserve Spanish on the island. This initial policy of bilingualism was supported as well by Martin Brumbaugh, commissioner of education for Puerto Rico (1900–1903). Brumbaugh's successors, however, sought to place the island's schools on an English-only basis as quickly as possible, and in 1903 English became the official language of instruction for all subjects (except Spanish) and at all levels, though the shift to all-English classrooms was carried out gradually, as staff could be trained to teach English (Osuna 344–45).

Attempts to substitute English for Spanish at the elementary level in Puerto Rican schools proved to have limited success, in part because "no scientific approach to the teaching of English had been yet devised" (347). The English of the teaching staff was often weak, particularly in rural areas. Reporting on the complete failure to instill English in the Puerto Rican population after seventeen years of bilingual schooling, José Padín (1916, 16), general superintendent of the Puerto Rican schools, commented:

> While it is true that our eighth-grade pupils are able to understand simple oral and written English, there is overwhelming evidence to show that they are totally deficient in English composition; that they do not have a grasp on the structure of the language; that they are singularly weak in

the fundamental characteristics of English speech; and that, in general, their knowledge of English or, rather, their lack of knowledge, is an altogether inadequate return for the amount of time and effort devoted to the acquisition of the language.

To remedy the situation, Padín recommended emphasizing spoken and written English instead of English reading. Because the Puerto Rican eighth graders tested in Padín's survey inflected adjectives and made the sorts of errors in idiom, noun plurals, pronoun forms, and verb tenses that were typical of non-native speakers, he recommended the use of textbooks emphasizing correction of the linguistic errors made not by mainland children, but by second-language learners. And Padín advised using Spanish as a medium to explain English to the students (23–24; the use of Spanish to teach English was proscribed at the time, no doubt because the English-only method was so strongly advocated for teaching adult learners on the mainland).

Padín's work led to the adoption in 1917 of Spanish as the language of instruction in the first four grades in Puerto Rican schools. English was introduced as a special subject and became the general language of instruction in grade six. However, even this plan proved ineffective, partly because many teachers did not know enough English to carry it out, and partly due to the high early dropout rate: few children, particularly in the countryside, stayed in school beyond the third grade. Nor did the transitional plan meet with the approval of mainland American politicians, who were convinced that the only way to Americanize Puerto Rico was through the medium of English, and the sooner, the better. They repeatedly scolded island authorities for their failure to oust the Spanish "patois" and spread what the British once called the American patois.

While a 1926 study conducted by Columbia University recommended removing English entirely from the early grades, a 1928 study by Victor Clark, sponsored by the Brookings Institution, urged the retention of English in the elementary curriculum to prevent that language from becoming the exclusive property of the privileged classes. There was an ideological as well as a social aim in Clark's proposal, revealing his continuing prejudice against Puerto Rican language and culture: "English is the chief source, practically the only source, of democratic ideas in Puerto Rico" (Osuna 1949, 363).

In 1937 President Franklin Roosevelt expressed his disappointment that after nearly forty years of American rule, the people of Puerto Rico had little or no knowledge of "the language of our nation." Instructing Dr. José M. Gallardo, his newly appointed commissioner of education for Puerto Rico, that English must be taught on the island "with vigor, purposefulness and devotion, and with the understanding that English is the official language of our country," the president echoed the common notion that English was essential for understanding the American way: "Only through the acquisition of this language will Puerto Rican Americans secure a better understanding of American ideals and principles" (Roosevelt 1941). But even Gallardo, with a presidential mandate to convert the natives, found it necessary to stress Spanish as the language of instruction, with English as a specific subject in the first six grades, a policy that provoked displeasure in Washington (Osuna 1949, 381–83).

During hearings of the U.S. Senate Subcommittee on Territories and Insular Affairs held in San Juan in 1943, senators complained in a manner reminiscent of earlier hearings on New Mexico statehood that they could not make themselves understood on the island. Secretary of the Interior Harold Ickes, referring to the Senate committee hearings, expressed his disappointment over the failure of efforts to promote English in Puerto Rico. Ickes insisted that "practical bilingualism is desirable and can be achieved" (Osuna 391), a statement which is easier for a politician than an educator to make.

Language experts were predictably pessimistic about converting Puerto Rico to English. Using the ever-present example of Quebec, Gallardo pointed out that bilingualism could only be achieved in a bilingual environment, whereas in Puerto Rico students were exposed to English only in school (Osuna 385–86). Algernon Coleman, a professor of French at the University of Chicago, surveyed the state of English education in Puerto Rico in 1939 and found no progress during the years of American rule, partly because English instruction was not based on any sound educational theory and partly because of "the small number of opportunities that most Porto Ricans have for speaking English in any continuous fashion as a genuine vehicle of intercourse with others" (Osuna 392–94). Coleman rejected the likelihood of bilingualism, suggesting instead that English be promoted as a supplementary language. Unfortunately, Coleman noted, teachers aiming at realizable goals are criticized as anti-American "by persons who look upon the teaching of English from other than an educational point of view" (395).

Language in Puerto Rico has always been more a political issue than an educational one, tied up with issues of statehood or independence, cultural pluralism and Americanization. With no clear solution to the political problem in sight, observers are tempted to describe the language problem as hopeless. Even as late as 1961, we find continuing echoes of Victor Clark's initial misjudgment of linguistic conditions in Puerto Rico: Joseph Matluck complains that because of competition from English, standard Spanish in Puerto Rico has few norms, nor do Puerto Ricans feel they need them; consequently, "there is no linguistic consciousness whatsoever in the schools, without which it is impossible to fight the pressure of English and the progressive deterioration of Spanish syntax on the Island" (cited in Poplack 1982, 4).

Principles of Exclusion

The policy of English-first failed in Puerto Rico, nor does an exclusive official-language policy seem likely to succeed in mainland classrooms. The ill treatment of one group of non-anglophones by the San Francisco schools led to an upheaval that has polarized the nation on the question of students' right of access to the majority language, English, and their right or desire to maintain their minority language as well. Victor Low (1982, 25) traces the state of California's systematic attempts to deny its Chinese population the benefits of education. San Francisco School Superintendent John Pelton was ignored when he called for bilingual education for Chinese students as early as 1867. Pelton also favored teaching Chinese to Americans for the purposes of establishing trade with the East, but his recommendations were rejected for more than a century. When their right to schooling was finally acknowledged in court (*Tape v. Hurley*, 66 Cal. Reports 473 [1885]), the Chinese children of San Francisco were segregated in their own institutions and not allowed to attend neighborhood schools. Not until 1929 did the city's Chinese schools shift from de jure segregation to a system of de facto segregation based on neighborhood population patterns.

While it denied Chinese schoolchildren the full benefits of an education, San Francisco also did what it could to discourage the Chinese graduates of its schools from returning as teachers or administrators. They were systematically failed in the college speech classes necessary for teacher certification on the grounds that their supposed Chinese accents evidenced a generally inadequate command of English. One result of this segregationist and discriminatory treatment has been self-fulfilling: the existence of a class of Chinese-American students in San Francisco schools with limited English-speaking ability. (Conklin and Lourie 1983, 38, report that the Chinese in general are strongly language-retentive, estimating that in 1970 some three-fourths of Boston's Chinese population spoke little or no English; while this phenomenon may be cultural in part, it is no doubt affected by the frequent, externally imposed isolation of Chinese Americans from the mainstream of society.)

In the 1970s the failure of the San Francisco schools to provide an English education to its Chinese pupils reached the attention of the United States Supreme Court. *Lau v. Nichols* (414 US Reports 563 [1974]) was a class action suit brought by the guardian of Kinney Kinmon Lau on behalf of the more than eighteen hundred non-English-speaking Chinese American students of the San Francisco Unified School District, alleging violation of the students' rights under the Fourteenth Amendment. The U.S. government filed an amicus curiae brief in favor of the plaintiff. Despite California's policy to insure that all students master English and to require such mastery for high school graduation, these students were not receiving any supplemental English instruction. In essence, though they were attending school, they were being given no education at all. The United States Supreme Court agreed. In its opinion supporting Lau, the court observed: "Students who do not understand English are effectively foreclosed from any meaningful education. . . . We know that those who do not understand English are certain to find their classroom experience wholly incomprehensible and in no way meaningful."

According to Reynaldo F. Macías (1979), since language rights are not fundamental rights according to the U.S. Constitution, and the class of non-English speakers is considered too vague by the courts, in order for legal action to be effective, it must link language discrimination to the loss of a fundamental right that the courts do recognize. The courts have been more ready to act on discrimination in voting or in the criminal justice system. They have also accepted cases involving discrimination on the basis of national or racial origin. As a result, many language discrimination cases are filed under the equal protection guarantee of the Fourteenth Amendment.

Lau v. Nichols, like *Meyer v. Nebraska*, was argued as an abridgement of equal protection, but as it had done in 1923, the Supreme Court again sidestepped the constitutional issue of protection for official or minority languages. Instead, it decided for Lau on the basis of section 601 of the Civil Rights Act of 1964 (42 USC sec. 2000d). In 1970 the Department of Health, Education and Welfare, which held that ignoring the needs of non-English-speaking groups was a form of national-origin discrimination, had ordered school districts receiving federal funds to rectify the language deficiencies of students speaking little or no English. In the *Lau* decision, the court found that the provisions of this law had not been upheld: "It seems obvious that the Chinese-speaking minority receive fewer benefits than the English-speaking majority from respondents' school system which denies them a meaningful opportunity to participate in the educational program—all earmarks of the discrimination banned by the regulations."

Finding discrimination, the court ordered the San Francisco school district to change its ways. However, the petitioners did not ask for, nor did the court prescribe, any specific remedies for San Francisco schools to adopt, though the court listed as two possible options either the teaching of English to these Chinese students, or direct instruction in Chinese, while allowing that other acceptable solutions might also be possible. As such, the court created no language rights for the plaintiffs (Macías 1979,

92). The court did require the San Francisco school district to come up with a plan to integrate its non-English-speaking students into its schools, and the result has been the so-called Lau remedies, most of them centering on some sort of transitional bilingual-education program. In addition, the doctrine that inattention to the educational needs of nonanglophones constitutes discrimination on the basis of national origin is now part of federal law (20 U.S.C.A. 1703[f]), applying to all districts, not just those receiving federal funds (Macías 1979, 92–93).

Since 1974 many school districts have entered into agreements with the federal government and applied for federal funds to implement such programs for speakers of Chinese, Spanish, and other minority languages. The court has warned that while it is permissible in bilingual programs to isolate non-English-speaking students in separate classes, such programs should not be used as a means of permanent segregation, and students must be continually evaluated to determine when they are ready to be mainstreamed with the rest of the school population.

However, few bilingual programs have been adequately funded or staffed by trained teachers. Students are often placed in such programs inappropriately (for example, on the basis of having a Hispanic-sounding last name, rather than on linguistic ability), and student progress is often inadequately monitored. Bilingual programs have acquired the stigma of remedial education, though they are certainly not remedial in theory, and they are often regarded as controversial even among educators. Confusion over the purposes and implementation of bilingual education has clearly added fuel to the present official-English drive as well: many people, including some minority-language activists, suspect bilingual programs of being minority-language maintenance rather than transitional ESL efforts.

Ironically, the arguments in favor of bilingual education gain support from arguments favoring vernacular over classical education. In the face of an educational tradition dominated by Latin and Greek, English had to fight to establish itself as the language of instruction in British and American schools. John Locke ([1693] 1705) advocated an English education for those students destined for trade, as opposed to higher callings, and Benjamin

Franklin established an English School in Philadelphia, also designed to be practical or vocational in nature. Noah Webster (1790, 7) distinctly favored an English education over a classical one: "If children are to acquire ideas, it is certainly easier to obtain them in a language which they understand, than in a foreign tongue." Just as today's teachers have found that many children whose dominant language is not English are often academically incompetent in two languages, both English and their native tongue, Webster also recognized that academic competence in one's first language must be firmly established before going on to a second language: "We often see young persons . . . puzzling their heads with French, when they can hardly write two sentences of good English" (7).

Today's monolingual English schools, like those of 1890 or 1940, present a stern, impenetrable barrier for the nonanglophone, resulting in continued low achievement and high dropout rates. Even otherwise enlightened schools prefer to avoid language issues if at all possible. They continue to deal with the language problem by ignoring it. Thus a local, private preschool in Urbana, Illinois, catering to the children of university faculty and international graduate students, accepts no more than four non-English-speaking children per class and requires these nonanglophone children to speak only English during school hours. Of course, the public schools do observe federal guidelines, but although ESL or bilingual programs exist in the schools, I have seen nonanglophone children mainstreamed and ignored here as well.

While they have had over a century to deal with the presence of non-English speakers in anglophone classrooms, American schools are not entirely to blame in failing to deal adequately with non-English-speaking pupils. Language teaching methodologies were virtually nonexistent in American schools until the early twentieth century, and although they have made rapid strides, particularly since World War II, no single method of teaching English as a second language has emerged triumphant. Moreover, psychologists until recently believed that immigrant and other non-English speakers were mentally inferior to homegrown, anglophone Americans, and that bilinguals—in particular, first-generation Americans speaking a native language and learning English as well—suffered intellectual handicaps from having to think in two languages. Since students tend to achieve at levels anticipated in advance by their instructors—a phenomenon known as the Pygmalion effect—teachers who expected immigrant children to perform poorly in their classes more often than not found their predictions fulfilled. And more often than not, the victim was not only blamed, but punished as well: the dropout rates of nonanglophone schoolchildren have always been unacceptably high.

For those who stayed on, American schools further inhibited assimilation by either ignoring nonanglophone students, sending them for speech therapy or remediation, or placing them into the inaptly named vocational tracks—long the dumping ground for students judged unable to handle intellectual tasks—or even worse, into classes for the educationally handicapped. That bilingual classes have become such dumping grounds as well may be signaled by reports of their failure. Calvin Veltman (1983, 380–81) reports that bilingual education programs reduce achievements of both English-mother-tongue and minority-mother-tongue children. He adds that if "the goal of MLE [minority-language education] programs is to equalize educational opportunity by permitting minority-language children to begin their formal education in a more familiar language, the data indicate that the opposite is in fact the result." Sandra McKay (1988, 341; 347) reports a 50 to 100 percent dropout rate in elementary school language submersion programs; she further indicates that 26 percent of bilingual programs for first graders are in fact English-only.

It is painful to realize that American public schools refused to cater to the needs of nonanglophone children until recently, when court rulings and federal legislation forced them to deal with the issue, and it is discouraging to observe that even after the need for formal language instruction has become clear to educationists, many schools continue to resent and resist providing their clients—the students—with what those clients need and want, an education. However, we cannot expect the schools to solve the language problem singlehandedly. It is also a painful irony that when the schools ignored the existence of non-anglophone students, they were universally credited with Americanizing generations of immigrants, while now, as schools finally struggle with the formal teaching of English to non-English speakers, they are bitterly attacked for failing no matter what method they try or how genuine their intention to succeed.

6 The Future of English

The implicit premise in American law is that English is the official language of the United States.
—*Arnold Leibowitz*

Although there are still a large number of minority-language speakers coming into the country, the English language continues to function as the language of the laws, the courts, the schools, and the business community of the United States. This is confirmed by legal experts as well as by the most recent census data (1980), which reveal that despite an increase in the Hispanic population, English is probably as strong in the United States as it has ever been. Fifteen percent of Americans speak a minority language or live in a household where one is spoken. But not all of them are immigrants. Sixty percent of minority-language speakers are native-born, and two-thirds of the minority-language population is concentrated in eight states. Nonetheless, an extremely large number of minority-language speakers use English as well. Eighty-two percent of those who speak a language other than English at home report they speak English well or very well. Indeed, English is spoken by more than 97 percent of the people in the nation, a fact which is often ignored by supporters of official-English legislation (Waggoner 1988, 69). Furthermore, the United States remains largely a monolingual, English-speaking nation: 90 percent of persons five to seventeen years old and close to 89 percent of persons eighteen and over speak only English. Researchers have found nothing to indicate that these figures will change significantly in the long run, which is good news to supporters of official-English, but bad news to those who would like to increase the nation's second-language competence.

In addition, English continues strong as the international language of technology, trade and diplomacy, and language watchers insist that, barring nuclear war or natural catastrophe, English is in no danger of losing its international status in the foreseeable future. The linguist David Crystal (1987, 358–59) reports that more than 316 million people speak English as a first language and another 300 million use it as a second language. English is an official or semi-official language in more than sixty countries. And it is a primary vehicle for storing and transmitting information: 75 percent of the world's mail and 80 percent of its computer data are written in English.

Not everyone regards this dominance of English with complacency. The linguist Randolph Quirk reports that while the use of English continues to increase in specialized, technical registers, these are used by relatively small numbers of people. On the whole, Quirk sees a decline in the spread of English and an increase in the use of indigenous languages for government and education in such areas as West Africa and the Philippines. Quirk reports further that "the weight of responsibility placed on English as a medium for internal communication in such countries as India or Malaysia or Kenya is far less than it was a generation ago" (1990, 81). Stanley Lieberson (1981) suggests that a shift in world trade could upset the English linguistic hegemony, and other researchers suspect that the acquisition of English as a second language around the world may have leveled off. Richard W. Bailey (1990, 85) observes that international population trends continue to shift the balance of linguistic power away from English. He adds: "Even the major centers of the anglophone world (Britain, Canada, the United States, and Australia) are becoming more and more diverse in languages and language varieties. These demographic facts have implications for the future of English and for the kinds of languages we will use in the future."

Considering the fate of earlier international languages (Kahane and Kahane 1979), it may be wise to reserve judgment about the future of English, but it is not yet possible to ring its death knell at home or abroad. After all, the power of a language depends on more than just raw numbers of speakers, and no one language is waiting in the wings to take over the leadership role. (It is of course possible to imagine a world without one dominant international language.) English continues strong despite an unfavorable balance of trade for anglophone nations, while successful manufacturers like the Japanese must either adopt the language of their trading partners or use English (Wardhaugh 1987, 11), a situation which can lead to the sort of complaint voiced by the Japanese writer Nishio Kanji: "It should be regarded as normal for us to sit in a Paris hotel and place our orders in Japanese, just as foreigners use English in Japan" (quoted in Buruma 1989, 454). Nor is it clear that a shift in the world's balance of languages would affect the numbers of English speakers within anglophone countries.

Nonetheless, while the position of English remains strong, there is persistent anxiety among Americans that their language is on the wane at home, in terms of both the quality of English that is used and the number of Americans who use it. That this anxiety has remained relatively unchanged over the past two or more centuries suggests that concern about the status of English is both a natural phenomenon and one that may be unwarranted. Even so, attempts to protect English continue strong, as do moves to suppress the public use of other languages in the United States. Ohio and Alabama are the two latest states to propose English-only legislation: the Ohio legislature is considering an English-only bill similar to the one approved in Arizona in 1988, and a constitutional amendment making English the official language of Alabama will appear on the ballot in June, 1990 (*EPIC Events* 2 [May–August 1989]). As it has been in the past, such state and local nativism tends to be blocked at the federal level. A Pomona, California ordinance requiring that 50 percent of all signs and advertising copy be written in the English alphabet—a statute targeting the area's Asian community—was recently struck down by a federal district court judge. And in 1989 the United States Senate rejected several attempts to give preference in the immigration law revision to immigrants who speak English.

Managing Plurilingualism

So important are questions of language and so endemic is linguistic competition that Louis-Jean Calvet (1987, 43) maintains that the history of the world is made up of attempts to manage plurilingualism. Official-language legislation throughout the world is triggered by a variety of causes, social, political, and ideological. While advocates of English-only in the United States tend to be identified as conservatives (in fact, not all of them are), official-language legislation in the international arena has never been clearly a left- or right-wing issue. The intent of such legislation frequently goes beyond the symbolically patriotic as it strives to modernize, standardize, or otherwise buttress a language perceived to be primitive, threatened, or in decline; to break the hold of a classical or colonial language over a modern or native vernacular vying to replace it; or to unify speakers of a variety of tongues under the umbrella of one or more official languages in the service of a newly unified national state. Such linguistic unification is frequently perceived as a necessary precursor of industrialization. (There is no proof that this must be so, however, though commonality of language certainly facilitates education, a necessary component of modernization.)

Official-language legislation is generally imposed to deal with a complex linguistic situation, where languages or dialects are competing for recognition. It is a common means of forcing cultural unity on newly independent states—but according to Le Page (1964, 17), in striving for harmony such legislation can produce discord as well: "Very large numbers of people in the world today are having laws and other social arrangements made for them in languages which they do not understand," and as Wardhaugh (1987, 168) reminds us, these language policy decisions are being made by politicians, not linguists. Arnold Leibowitz (1976, 450) notes further that designation of an official language is almost always coupled with restrictions on the use of other languages or with discriminating legislation in other areas, and these are likely to produce resentment and, eventually, a backlash.

Generally speaking, linguistic friction and violence occur around the globe not where language rights are protected, but where they have been suppressed. Beer and Jacob (1985, 3) argue that conflict emerges when language difference represents disparate status and unequal access to economic, social, or political success, particularly in areas of rapid development with an emerging, upwardly mobile middle class. Some nations with fairly clear geographic divisions among their language groups, such as Switzerland, Belgium, Italy, and Yugoslavia, tend to designate official unilingual and bilingual regions in order to remain, or try to remain, stable political units in the face of linguistic and cultural difference. Switzerland, for example, has four national languages: German, French, Italian, and Romansh. Although only the first three are designated official languages, the Swiss constitution instructs the government to safeguard the nation's linguistic diversity, and children are educated in the dominant language of the local canton. Part of Belgium is designated as Flemish-speaking, part as French, though each region has pockets where speakers of the non-majority regional language predominate. Brussels, the capital city, which is located in the Flemish region, is officially bilingual, though it is surrounded by pockets of French-dominant settlement. Beer (1985, 229) attributes Belgian national conflict to the fact that the rapid development of the Flanders economy was not immediately accompanied by increased social and political rights for the previously subordinate group of Flemish speakers.

Supporters of official English in the United States are fond of pointing to Canada as well as Belgium as two important Western democracies where language conflict remains unresolved, causing social friction and unnecessary duplication of government services. India, with several official, national, and regional languages, is sometimes cited as well as a failed polyglot nation. Seldom mentioned in the English-only propaganda is the Soviet Union, where opposition to official Russian and the assertion of minority-language rights has been making news lately.

As E. Glyn Lewis (1972) describes it, Russia under the tsars practiced forced assimilation and the suppression of minority languages, and the initial goal of the Communists after the Revolution was to unify and modernize the diverse nation by means of universal Russian. While it is the current goal of authorities in the Soviet Union to spread Russian as the lingua franca in all areas of the USSR, regional and local languages with as few as five hundred speakers are officially recognized as well. Despite this central support both for official Russian and for many minority languages—the one blatant exception being Yiddish, the language of some two million Soviet Jews, which is officially proscribed (Lewis 1972, 268)—cultural and linguistic conflicts continue to surface in Azerbaijan, Estonia, Georgia, Lithuania,

Moldavia, and elsewhere within the vast Soviet sphere. Gregory Guy (1989) maintains that this discontent has arisen not because of the official Soviet language policy, but from the abrogation of the language rights of one minority by another, for example, the restrictions on Armenian imposed in Azerbaijan. However, a broader perspective reveals a widespread reassertion of local ethnicity—including language rights—at the expense of official Russian and national russification. Thus in 1989 the consideration of laws in Estonia and Moldavia requiring knowledge of the local language in certain circumstances caused Russian-speaking emigrants to the region to complain of reverse language discrimination.

Surprisingly enough, France—perhaps the most linguistically chauvinist of nations—has no official-language legislation. Unlike Britain, France did not spread its language among its colonies outside of educating a small francophone native governing class. Nor does France establish French in its current statutes, though several laws deal with the use of minority languages and the Bas-Lauriol law of 1976 aims to protect French from foreign borrowings (Héraud 1982, 244). Calvet (1987, 72) reminds us that although French may have been the universal language of eighteenth-century Europe, it was not even the majority language in France. Furthermore, despite two centuries of efforts to spread the Parisian or standard variety of French throughout metropolitan France by means of a national system of education, civil service, and military conscription, the French remain persistent in their loyalty to local dialects and regional languages, and France, though irreversibly French with a linguistic self-consciousness to rival that of any nation, remains at the same time a linguistically diverse land.

While many countries do designate an official language— 64 of 161 national constitutions do so (Blaustein and Epstein 1986)—there has been increasing legal recognition on the international scene of minority-language rights as well. Reynaldo Macías describes two basic kinds of language rights covered by modern international law: freedom from discrimination on the basis of language, and the right to use one's language in the activities of communal life. The League of Nations guaranteed minority-language rights, including the right to mother-tongue

schooling. The United Nations charter protects against the denial of mother-tongue rights and defends the opportunity to learn
the majority language (Macías 1979, 86–89). In 1953 UNESCO took
the position that the use of the mother tongue in early education
was essential, though mother-tongue teaching materials remain
scarce for many languages throughout the world. The Helsinki
accord of 1975, of which the United States is a signatory, contains
a clause protecting national minorities and regional cultures. As
Landry (1983, 370) maintains, even if immigrant languages are
not included within the scope of the Helsinki agreement, it
should protect Chinese, Japanese, Spanish, French, and the Native American languages of the United States, at the very least.

Some nations are clearly moving in the direction of recogniz-
ing minority-language rights. After a long period of government
suppression of such minority tongues as Catalan—the language
of Spain's industrial heartland—and Basque, the Spanish constitution of 1978 establishes Castilian as Spain's official language
while also protecting unnamed national or local languages. Similarly, the Italian constitution officially protects indigenous linguistic minorities, though only some of that country's minorities actually receive such protection, while others remain
ignored or persecuted (Héraud 1982, 252–53).

If the effectiveness of language-tolerant regimes is uncertain,
officially monolingual states do not resolve the question of language minorities with much success either. Turkey pretends
that its large Kurdish minority does not exist. The Kurdish language has been forbidden in Turkey since the linguistic modernization efforts of 1923. The very word *Kurd* was banished from
the Turkish vocabulary, and in an attempt to render them linguistically invisible, the Kurds were renamed *Mountain Turks*
(Beer and Jacob 1985, 3; Skutnabb-Kangas 1984, 74). Nonetheless, the Kurds, who are persecuted in Iraq as well as Turkey,
remain a significant unassimilated ethnic population, and a serious problem for these two countries. The Turks, in turn, present a language problem for other European nations. In Bulgaria,
for example, ethnic Turks were required until recently to take
Bulgarian names; they forfeited a month's salary if they spoke
Turkish in public.

Beer and Jacob (1985, 1) report that only 4 percent of political states are "nation-states," that is, states comprising a single ethnic group, and according to Héraud (1982, 252), only a small number of such truly monolingual states as Iceland or Portugal have "adequate linguistic regimens." Wardhaugh (1987, 23) lists in addition a number of countries where more than 90 percent of the population speak "the sole official language." These include Austria, Bangladesh, the Dominican Republic, East and West Germany, Japan, North and South Korea, and Tunisia. Wardhaugh is uncertain about adding the United States, the United Kingdom, China, and France to the list as well. Taking a similar position, Tove Skutnabb-Kangas (1984, 174) claims that with more than twenty million non-English or limited-English speakers, the United States can hardly be called an English-speaking country. Despite such objections, though, it is clear that the United States and the other nations on Wardhaugh's list of "questionable" states do have a consensus as to the nature of their official language and do not have the linguistic diversity or competition found in Ghana, Haiti, India, Indonesia, Nigeria, Senegal, Tanzania, and Uganda, where according to Wardhaugh the official language is used by less than half the population.

Many countries handle the language problems of local minorities differently from those of immigrants. While England may be linguistically diverse from an internal point of view, to the outside world it presents an English-only front. The United Kingdom balked at the European Community's recommendation that the children of guest-workers be educated in their home language, insisting instead that the focus should be on introducing immigrants to the host country language (Martin-Jones 1984, 430; Wardhaugh 1987, 237). Although Skutnabb-Kangas (1984, 67, 287; 291–92) reports that Sweden in 1983 dutifully provided immigrants with 240 hours annually of Swedish instruction on the job, a figure soon to be raised to 600 hours, she finds bilingual education in Germany and Denmark both discriminatory and exclusionist in practice, though not in aim, with many guest-workers' children dropping out or not attending school at all.

Furthermore, statistics show that guest-workers are not returning home from European host countries, but are remaining as permanent residents. According to Wardhaugh, because of this phenomenon, once-unilingual Germany is now becoming an immigrant country (1987, 240). In any case, the United Kingdom and other nations of Europe will have to confront the issue yet again, for when the members of the community open their borders in 1992 they are supposed to extend linguistic as well as employment and migration rights to all the citizens of the European Community. Conflict has already surfaced over the exclusion of Gaelic, Luxemburgian, Basque, and Catalan from *Lingua*, which is a plan to facilitate foreign-language study in member states (Monahan 1989, A32). Eurolanguage policy may ultimately prove more difficult to iron out than many of the other economic and political compromises involved in creating the E.C.

Official English

Language policy, or the lack of it, has developed in the United States in much the same way it has in England, through indirection and reaction to local circumstances. It has often been pointed out that this lack of planning has led to almost universal adoption of the national language in the United States, while countries with more specifically defined language programs have failed in their efforts to spread their official language. In tracing American resistance to the establishment of a federal language policy to British roots, Shirley Brice Heath (1978) argues that since the triumph of English over French in fourteenth-century England, there has been no attempt to establish the language as official in the British Isles. Actually, while England has not designated a state language, first Latin, then French, and finally English functioned as the official language of the English courts, schools and government through a combination of traditional practice, conquest, and government decree. When the Anglo-Saxons came to England in the fifth century, they spread their language at the expense of the local Celtic tongues, which eventually disappeared. Furthermore, since the fifteenth century, England has either imposed or promoted an English-only policy within its borders as well as in Scotland, Wales, and Ireland, thus effecting the apparently irreversible suppression of Gaelic, destroying Cornish and Manx, and doing serious damage to Welsh. Unlike France, which treated its language as private property, imperial England officially encouraged the spread of English in its colonies, and it continues to support English instruction abroad through the British Council and the overseas service of the BBC. Such language policies, combined with the international influence of England, and later, the United States, have contributed to the dominance of English on the world scene today (Calvet 1987; Wardhaugh 1987).

English was a colonial language imposed in North America, as it was in parts of Asia and Africa, by a conquering power. But in the United States, as in English Canada, Australia, and New Zealand, native non-English-speaking populations were not uniformly converted to English, as they had been in the British Isles, but were instead marginalized—though a sizable portion of the surviving natives did ultimately adopt the colonial language (and in Australia today there is a new and ambitious official policy of preserving home languages while extending competence in English). English initially became dominant in these regions through the immigration and subsequent population growth of anglophones from the British Isles. Once naturalized, the English colonies in these regions began to assimilate newly immigrant speakers of other languages by means of the well-understood but tacit assumption that English functioned as an official language as well as a convenient lingua franca.

In Canada the situation was slightly different in that both English and French were colonial languages that had become dominant in separate regions of what later became, through British conquest in the eighteenth century, the Canadian federation, and the French Canadians have only recently begun to win back language rights that were long denied them under British rule. French Canadians have little interest in protecting the rights of other minority-language speakers. Rather, they insist that immigrants to Québec learn French and resist funding to assist non-French minority-language users, for example the Ukrainians or Asians of English Canada, an attitude which exacerbates language tensions in the country (Wardhaugh 1987, 262). Experiments in bilingual education have been successful in francophone Canada because the English-speaking middle class there still regards French as a culturally prestigious language. However, there are indications that nonanglophone immigrants to French Canada would prefer to learn English rather than French, and it remains to be seen whether attempts to assimilate these populations to French are equally successful.

Like Canada, the United States is not simply a nation of immigrants, it is a nation of Native Americans and annexed or conquered peoples as well: the Hawaiians, the French of Maine and Louisiana, the Dutch of New York, the Swedish of New Jersey and Delaware, and the Hispanics of the Southwest and Puerto Rico (not to mention black African slaves who were in some cases initially denied access to English altogether in an effort to prevent rebellion). Despite these similarities, there are some differences in the linguistic situations of the United States and Canada. While Canada maintained a clear French-English split, most noticeable in the controversies over the status of French and English in the province of Quebec, the United States pitted English against not one, but a variety of minority-language groups.

Speakers of what was until recently the largest minority language in the United States, German, who were concentrated in Pennsylvania and the Midwest, succumbed to the process of assimilation triggered by urbanization, nativism, and World War I, as well as to the linguistic dilution produced by the new immigration that took place between the Civil War and World War I. German is now in third place as a minority language spoken in the United States, following Spanish and Italian (and closely followed by French). The American Southwest did not become the "Québec" of the United States because from the outset it was sparsely populated by its Hispanic settlers, and because Hispanic immigration was largely cut off after the Mexican War. Although the original Hispanic families of the Southwest showed a high degree of language retention, particularly in the rural areas where they remained, they were quickly outnumbered by Anglos once the latter began entering the area in force after annexation in 1848. (Mexican immigration did not resume in large numbers until the labor shortages of the two world wars, by which time English had gained an unerodable advantage.) Quebec, on the other hand, retained a majority French population who could be expected to react negatively, and with vigor, to the repression of their language in the national and the provincial arena.

Furthermore, unlike French, it is clear that Spanish was not a prestige language in the Old or New Worlds during the eighteenth and nineteenth centuries. Consequently, there was little effort to encourage it as a useful refinement for anglophone children to learn in American schools. There are now four times as many self-reported Spanish speakers in the United States as German ones, but unlike the Québecois, they are far from a unified population. They come from the Southwest itself, and from Mexico, Puerto Rico, and Cuba, as well as from a variety of Spanish-speaking countries. They are not necessarily compatible in terms of politics, culture, or dialect. And they are concentrated in cities all over the country, not just in Florida and the Southwest (1980 census figures show about 80 percent of Hispanics living in urban areas).

Calvin Veltman (1983) finds that despite a high rate of Spanish-language retention, a high proportion of young Hispanics speak only or primarily English. While statistics are lacking to determine the rate of anglicization for minority-language speakers before World War II, Veltman's analysis provides strong support to his claim that Hispanics anglicize at approximately the same rate as other groups have done (214).

None of this augurs well for long-term Spanish-language maintenance of the kind the French Canadians have been trying to achieve. Nor is there an indication that Hispanic Americans support linguistic separatism of the Canadian variety. Instead, the separatism seems to be coming from the English-only side. While proponents of an English Language Amendment argue that their legislation will prevent divisiveness along ethnic lines in the United States, members of language minorities regard official-English legislation as an attempt to marginalize them, to separate them further from the American mainstream, an argument repeatedly made during hearings on the English Language Amendment in 1988.

English Language Amendment Hearings

On 11 May 1988 the House Subcommittee on Civil and Constitutional Rights of the Committee on the Judiciary, chaired by Rep. Don Edwards of California, held hearings on four English Language Amendment proposals introduced in the 100th

Congress. While the hearings lasted under three hours—oral testimony was limited to members of Congress—they generated some four hundred pages of testimony and supporting documents reiterating the two primary positions we have seen accompanying such discussions for the past two centuries: an insistence that English is the glue holding an ethnically diverse America together, and a fear that official-language legislation masks racial discrimination and specifically targets one ethnic group—in this case, Hispanic Americans. Claims that English is the key to an understanding of American ideals are balanced against warnings that voters will be disenfranchised and the public safety endangered by restrictions on government use of languages other than English.

Rep. Norman Shumway of California (*English Language Constitutional Amendments* [hereafter, *ELCA*] 1989, 33), a sponsor of one of the ELA resolutions, began his testimony before the subcommittee by speaking in Japanese in order to demonstrate his openness to language study and to illustrate the necessity for a single language of government. Shumway warned of a drift toward a bilingual society that only an official-English law can halt, while Rep. Stephen Solarz of New York (*ELCA* 64) countered with census data showing 98 percent of Americans speak English well or very well. Rep. Patricia Schroeder of Colorado (11) expressed the fear that under an English Language Amendment, her state and many other places in the country would have to change their names. (Schroeder's fears may be read as rhetorical, although, as we saw earlier, Walt Whitman favored changing Spanish and French place names, and some localities shed German place names during World War I.)

Rep. William S. Broomfield of Michigan (46) reprised the stand of the Dillingham Immigration Commission, insisting that today's immigrants are different from the earlier immigrants from Eastern Europe and Italy, while Solarz (64) noted that there are fewer non-English-speakers in the United States today than there were in 1900 or 1920. Rep. Gerald D. Kleczka of Wisconsin added that the proportion of foreign-born in the country has declined from 14 percent in 1920 to only 7 percent today (80).

Broomfield (46) voiced the complaint so frequently expressed over the centuries that immigrants can now live in the United States without learning English and objected that the federal government abets "this dangerous condition." On the other hand, the minority-language statistician Dorothy Waggoner (122) reported in written testimony her conservative estimate that only a little more than two million American residents speak no English at all, and Solarz (64), who insisted that the threats to English are imaginary, reminded the subcommittee that the children of all the immigrants in his Brooklyn constituency learn English.

Rep. Norman Mineta of California stressed the divisiveness of the English Language Amendment. Mineta told the subcommittee that the ELA

> will put up barriers, not tear barriers down, for those seeking to improve their proficiency in English. It will set up a class of "outsiders"—unable to communicate with their government, and their government unable to communicate with them—all based on language skills. . . . As an American of Asian ancestry, I know too well how some people to this day still consider those who are not in the "mainstream" as being somehow less than fully American. In fact, people still compliment me, with genuine surprise, on how well I speak English. (15–17)

Representative Solarz added that during World War II, government publications in Yiddish and sixteen other minority languages helped to unify the nation, not divide it (64–65), and Sen. John McCain of Arizona reported that many of his Hispanic and Native American constituents perceived the ELA as "a direct assault on their ability to preserve their culture and heritage" (78). The divisiveness of official-English legislation was apparent as well in reactions to a move by Chicago alderman William Henry to require applicants for retail grocers to demonstrate proficiency in the English language. Henry claimed his proposal was a response to complaints of black residents against Arab and Asian merchants, and that it would soothe racial tensions in the city, while representatives of the ethnic groups viewed the measure as both discriminatory and inflammatory (Ethnic groups 1989).

Keeping English First

The 1988 ELA hearings in the 100th Congress were adjourned indefinitely, and no further action has been taken to establish Federal English. Whether action will be forthcoming remains to be seen: some observers insist the ELA is a dead issue, while others are certain that an age so clearly protective of the American flag and the pledge of allegiance will surely do something to install English in its rightful place. A constitutional English Language Amendment stands a chance of success because, as Milroy and Milroy (1985, 3) observe, linguistic discrimination remains publicly acceptable in the United States, while other forms of discrimination do not. If history repeats itself, however, the ELA will not pass, and though states may continue to implement local versions of official English, federal practice will continue to keep them in check.

In the United States, Shirley Brice Heath argues, the founders eschewed an official-language policy out of a sense that it would violate "democratic ideals . . . [and] the realities of language change" (1978, 80). This alone, in her opinion, should convince present leaders that no English Language Amendment is called for. As we have seen, the nation's initial language situation was somewhat more complex than that which Heath describes. The founders were certain that national and linguistic unity went hand in hand and never conceived of the United States as permanently multilingual. They may even have resisted designating an official language because they could not decide on an appropriate name for it, whether American, English, or Federal. Of course North Americans did not have a monopoly on the notion that language and nation were both unique and inextricably bound in the Old World or the New. The feeling was common as well in Latin America. To cite one example, Antonio Caro, founder of the Columbian Academy in 1874, proclaimed that "language is the mother country!" (Guitarte and Quintero 1968, 567).

As we have seen, some American founders feared the effects on the mother country of minority-language populations of German, French, Swedish and Dutch speakers, while others used minority-language advertising as a way of attracting settlers to the underpopulated nation. But this reluctance to privilege English does not mean that on the occasions when official American policy has tolerated or promoted minority languages, it did so out of any sympathy for cultural pluralism. From the start, virtually everyone in the United States, anglophone or not, recognized explicitly or implicitly that English was to be the language of government, courts, and culture. And while nativist movements have occasionally made Americans hyperconscious of the nonanglophones among them, the awareness of linguistic difference has never been far from the surface.

Practically speaking, Americans have had to recognize, sometimes officially, sometimes unofficially, the presence of large numbers of non-English speakers on American soil, granting them certain linguistic and cultural rights while at the same time integrating them into the mainstream of American society. The presence of non-English-speaking populations has often promoted official tolerance in the interests of producing an informed citizenry, maintaining efficient communication, and assuring public safety. Nonetheless, English has always been the de facto standard in the United States as a whole, and public policy has dealt with bilingualism as a temporary, transitional facet of assimilation, just as English-firsters would have wanted it, and just as those nonanglophones who come to the United States intending to stay view the situation as well.

While English is and will undoubtedly remain first in the United States, there are two basic problems inherent in designating an official language for the country. For one thing, the designation will do little to accelerate the learning of English. Even now, with no federal official-English laws, the educational system cannot keep up with the adult demand for English classes. Both supporters and opponents of an American English Language Amendment stress the need to do something about the long waiting lists of nonanglophones seeking to learn English (*ELCA* 1989). In addition, despite the existence since the eighteenth century of public and private language-maintenance programs, the children of nonanglophone permanent residents of the United States continue to abandon their parents' native tongues in favor of English.

For another thing, although designating English as an official language will probably do little to accelerate the already rapid adoption of English by nonanglophones, neither will it be able to blot out minority languages in the United States. Declaring a national language has not always proved effective in this regard for other nations. With some notable exceptions (the suppression of Erse in Ireland and Native American languages in the Western Hemisphere, neither of which encouraged national unity or assimilation), severely repressive measures taken against minority-language populations in other countries have often failed to exterminate local languages and dialects. It is not likely that any mild-mannered American fiat like the English Language Amendment will accelerate language loss, or that the federal courts, with their long tradition of resisting excessive curbs on minority languages, will permit it to do so. Even more to the point, language has never been the crux of violent confrontation in American society, and with more than 97 percent of the American population speaking English it is not likely that language per se will become a sustained confrontational issue in the future.

Reluctant to appear too nativist, supporters of the ELA, like their predecessors in the official-English movement, allege the practical advantages of learning English. It has long been argued that, politics aside, a knowledge of English is essential for economic success in the United States. English is clearly useful, possibly necessary, but certainly not sufficient for achieving such success. And it is not clear that official legislation can enforce the learning of English. Most states required English as the language of instruction for many years, though significant numbers of students passed through the schools without acquiring a sufficient command of standard English. Indeed, this was the situation that led to the *Lau* decision and the attempt to remedy the situation through bilingual education programs. Furthermore, no matter what official-English supporters maintain, depending on the English language as the great democratic equalizer and guarantor of achievement is bound to lead to disappointment. More often than not, advancement in one's profession or social position cannot be directly tied to linguistic proficiency.

Though it has long been one of our most publicized national goals, fluency in English alone does not produce success, even for majority-language speakers of Anglo-Saxon ancestry. The language situation is even more frustrating for minority-language speakers. For them, language—the most visible sign of their ethnicity—is often used as an excuse to hide deeper levels of discrimination. As Joshua Fishman (1988, 131) has put it, as bluntly as the idiom of the social scientist will allow, "Mastery of English is almost as inoperative with respect to Hispanic social mobility as it is with respect to Black social mobility."

Fluency in English is universally advanced as a sine qua non for assimilation, yet the abandonment of a minority language in favor of English has seldom convinced American society at large to welcome into its midst former speakers of other tongues, while switching to English is all but certain to produce feelings of anxiety, guilt, or alienation in those experiencing language loss. Even third-generation, native English-speaking descendants of nonanglophones have not always found entrance into the egalitarian mainstream smooth going because the undercurrent of ethnic prejudice remains.

Supporters of the English Language Amendment commonly oppose bilingual education, hoping their law will force American schools to return to the teaching of English (this in spite of the fact that all federally funded bilingual programs are transitional in nature, and that English has never been abandoned by the public schools). The United States is often thought of as a nation of immigrants who eagerly tossed their ethnic identity into the melting pot in order to reap the benefits of Americanism. But assimilation was never easy, and such official mechanisms of assimilation as the schools did not always accomplish their task. As we saw in chapter 5, a convincing case can be made that English was learned in many cases despite rather than because of the efforts of the public schools.

More troublesome, at the moment, is the problem of deciding just how the schools should handle the problem of educating nonanglophone children. As Abigail Thernstrom (1980, 622) points out, while the Supreme Court's *Brown v. Board of Education* ruled that "separate but equal" educational facilities gave children a sense of inferiority and inevitably built discrimination into the education process, the *Lau v. Nichols* decision asserts just the opposite, arguing that the desegregation and mainstreaming of children with limited or nonexistent English proficiency effectively denies them any education at all.

The issues are even more cloudy because bilingual education is poorly understood and unevenly implemented by educational authorities. Programs called bilingual often do not merit the name. In this regard Chuong Hoang Chung (1988, 286–87) complains that Vietnamese students are placed in Spanish or Filipino bilingual programs, or that Asian students from various language backgrounds—Chinese, Vietnamese, Lao, Samoan—are placed together in one class so that the language of instruction has to be English.

Questions of language variety also plague bilingual programs. Some years ago Joshua Fishman remarked in a lecture that Puerto Rican parents in New York City objected when teachers in a Spanish-English bilingual program used Puerto Rican Spanish. If their children were going to learn Spanish in school, the parents wanted it to be a classical, literary variety of Spanish, not what they considered the unacceptable Puerto Rican street dialect. Their insistence put the children in the difficult position of having to master two foreign tongues in school: not just English, but Castilian Spanish as well.

Resistance to using the language students bring with them to school as the initial language of instruction is widespread. William Beer (1985, 230–31) is one of many observers who fear that bilingual education will produce students who are illiterate in two languages. Specifically, Beer sees Hispanics coming out of bilingual programs who cannot use English well enough to assimilate but "whose Spanish remains at the level of uneducated vernacular." Skutnabb-Kangas (1984, 249) posits that this "double semilingualism" may be true at the level of vocabulary rather than that of syntax, though it is more likely that this phenomenon is a creature of the differing prestige of linguistic varieties. In other words, when E. D. Hirsch (1987) claims that bilingual students are "literate in no language," he does not mean that students are unable to use either of two languages, but rather that they have not mastered the *standard* form of either of those languages. While the readiness with which charges of illiteracy are brought forth reveals the linguistic politics of education, it also ignores the true learning that can and does go on in a classroom when teachers and students communicate in the same language variety, standard or not.

Transition to English has been a major goal of the American school system since the early part of this century. Although the schools may do the job poorly, or not at all, it is not likely that they will be allowed either by the courts or by the American public to abandon the effort altogether. If school districts, citing an English Language Amendment, decided to go out of the business of educating nonanglophone children, they would certainly face charges of national-origin discrimination. *Lau v. Nichols* was decided on the basis of federal statute rather than constitutional law because the Supreme Court avoids constitutional decisions unless absolutely necessary. If such a suit were brought again after passage of an English Language Amendment, though, even a conservatively constituted Supreme Court would have difficulty allowing schools to ignore a significant percentage of their students.

Given that American schools must accept students no matter what language they bring with them, what is most controversial is the method to be used for inculcating English in nonanglophone children. G. Richard Tucker (*ELCA* 1989, 146) warns that while immersion may be successful in teaching French to middle-class, highly motivated Canadian anglophones, it is not the best method for teaching unmotivated, potential dropouts in the United States. On the other hand, while well-designed bilingual programs have a proven track record of success (see Crawford 1989), American educators cannot generally field effective bilingual classes because of the expense and the difficulty in finding suitably trained speakers of the languages involved to teach in the programs. Moreover, they face resistance arising from the popular misconception of such programs as language-maintenance efforts rather than as transitions to English. It is clear that the schools must be encouraged or in some cases required to explore solutions to the language education problem, and it is likely that their chances for success will be increased if they are not constrained either by official-English laws or by methodologies imposed by jurists *or* politicians rather than educators.

Not Only English

There are other reasons as well not to designate an official language for the United States. In the absence of convincing evidence that language diversity is threatening the hegemony of English in the country, affecting its ability to function as the language of government and society, or producing any potential disruption of the Union, it is best to avoid such legislation because of the negative effects it will produce. Privileging one language leads necessarily to implied or expressed proscriptions against other languages. This denial of minority-language rights produces resentment and causes a divisiveness which, as evidence from Canada and Belgium shows, may persist long after such rights have been restored, and in doing so it can actually slow assimilation rather than speed it up. American minority-language speakers perceive official-language legislation as an attempt to discriminate against them—the record shows that official English at the state and local level has often been discriminatory—and no amount of argument will convince them otherwise.

Furthermore, it is not English but minority languages in the United States which face extinction. John Weightman (1988) agrees with the claim made by a number of researchers that "to remain healthy, a language needs a solid core of monolingual speakers, who act as an indisputable point of reference for bilinguals." But conditions in the United States have made it impossible to maintain such a core of monolingual minority-language-speakers over a number of generations, and there is no reason to believe things have changed in this respect. It is true that some Americans have reacted in fear to the "new" immigrants of the present day, just as established Americans reacted to the "new" immigrants earlier in this century, but all statistics show a high percentage of Hispanic and Asian children adopting English.

The passage of an English Language Amendment may privilege the English language, but it remains to be seen whether such an amendment can be used to facilitate discrimination on the basis of national origin or to abridge free speech. We do not have to search far in the legal record to see that language restriction laws have been implemented as obvious tools of discrimination, and they have been thrown out by the federal courts to the extent that they violate constitutional protections.

Although an ELA will not speed the acquisition of English by nonanglophones, opponents of the amendment fear that it could abridge rights currently guaranteed by the Constitution. When federal laws conflict, the most recent is given precedence. In a case of conflict between Fifth or Fourteenth Amendment protection from discrimination and an English Language Amendment establishing and protecting the official language, the ELA could take precedence, though possibly only in narrow questions of language per se. But narrow questions of language can have wide ramifications.

Arnold Leibowitz (1982, 17) warns, for example, that constitutional appeals in language cases have not succeeded, while those based on the civil rights acts, like the *Lau* decision, usually do. Thus in *Carmona v. Sheffield* (325 FSupp 1341 [1971]), which was argued on constitutional grounds, the Federal District Court wrote that requiring government to make translation services available to everyone would cause chaos: "If adopted in as cosmopolitan a society as ours, enriched as it has been by the immigration of persons from many lands with their distinctive linguistic and cultural heritages, it would virtually cause the processes of government to grind to a halt. The conduct of official business, including the proceedings and enactments of Congress, the Courts, and administration agencies, would become all but impossible" (cited in Leibowitz 1982, 17).

It is of course anyone's guess what sort of implementing legislation Congress would draft subsequent to the passage of an English Language Amendment, or how future courts would interpret such an amendment. We cannot safely say what an ELA would change. But there is also some concern about whether an official-language amendment could succeed in its basic aim of making English any more official than it is already. Pointing to the failure of the Irish government to further Gaelic despite offering bounties for its use, and the success of Swahili as a national language in Tanzania despite that nation's inability to field an official-language campaign, the linguist Ralph Fasold told the Subcommittee on Civil and Constitutional Rights, "Official efforts in support of a particular language have a miniscule impact compared to the natural social forces at large in a society" (*ELCA* 1989, 141). Again, the American historical record supports this contention: no nation has been able to achieve through legislation the kind of linguistic uniformity that the United States has achieved through "natural social forces" and with minimal official intervention.

But what is even more important to consider in evaluating the usefulness of either official-English legislation or laws to protect minority-language rights, court orders and constitutional amendments cannot teach English to nonanglophones or make them retain their minority language, nor can they make English speakers learn other languages. Even teachers have trouble doing that. If there is a language crisis in the United States, it is not because there is no official language—English is the American official language—nor is it because too many Americans use "foreign" languages or nonstandard varieties of English. Rather, it is because large numbers of Americans do not learn to read or write well enough in any language or language variety to make that language work for them.

With or without the passage of official-language laws, English will still be first in the United States. As Leibowitz (1969, 50) has said, "The premise in American law is that English is the official language of the United States." Moreover, regardless of the law and regardless of how desirable it may be, the language situation in the United States is not likely to change radically from what it has been in the past or what it is right now. Nonanglophones will continue to meet with resentment from many English speakers. In extreme cases, they will come up against discriminatory laws or regulations that will block their progress or thwart their ambition. Some of them will fight these laws, and in some cases they will have limited success. But in most cases, nonanglophones will continue to learn English, sometimes imperfectly, at least for early generations of immigrants or for those otherwise isolated from the standard English mainstream. They may in turn either resent their native speech as culturally backward or economically limiting, or generally un-American. And ultimately they may either resent or regard with some nostalgia the loss of their own native tongue, going so far as to try to preserve it among their children through after-school instruction programs.

Anglophone Americans too will continue for the most part to resist learning other languages either in school or after school (the more extremely naive of them arguing that if English was good enough for the Bible, it is surely good enough for them), or they will learn foreign languages imperfectly. Language laws will certainly remain on the books, and new ones will come from time to time. But it will be changing social forces rather than simple legislation that will ultimately change the language situation in the United States. It is not likely that laws, either alone or combined with appeals to practicality or to patriotism, can do much to make the United States any more or any less monolingual than it already is. Nor is it clear that they should.

Appendix:
State Official-
English Laws
(as of mid-1990)

No legislation

Law passed

Law pending

Law recently rejected

"English-plus" law
(advocating knowledge of
English plus one other language)

Note: Many states that do not have "official-language" statutes may have specific statutes requiring English for certain situations, e.g., school instruction, state and local legislation, judicial and other official or public records, official notices, public signs, and so forth.

Bibliography

Legal Cases Cited

Attorney General v. Hutchinson 113 Mich. 245 (1897).
Farrington v. Tokushige 273 U.S. 284 (1927)
Graham v. King 50 Mo. 22 (1872).
Lau v. Nichols 414 U.S. Reports 563 (1974).
Leideck v. City of Chicago, 248 Ill. App. 545 (1928).
McCoy v. City of Chicago, 136 Ill. 344 (1891).
Meyer v. Nebraska 262 U.S. 390 (1923).
Perkins v. Board of Commissioners of Cook County 271 Ill. 449 (1916).
People v. Day 277 Ill. 543 (1917).
Powell v. Board of Education 97 Ill. 375 (1881).

Other Works Cited

Adams, John. 1856. *Life and works*. Boston.
Adams, John Quincy. 1875. *Memoirs of John Quincy Adams*. Ed. Charles Francis Adams. Philadelphia: J. B. Lippincott.
Allen, Harold B. 1966. *TENES: A survey of the teaching of English to non-English speakers in the United States*. Champaign, Ill.: National Council of Teachers of English.
————. 1973. English as a second language. In *Current trends in linguistics*, vol. 10, ed. Thomas A. Sebeok, 295–320. The Hague: Mouton.
Allinson, May. 1907. The government of Illinois, 1790–1799. *Transactions of the Illinois State Historical Society* 12: 277–92.
An answer to an invidious pamphlet, intituled, "A brief state of the Province of Pennsylvania." 1755. London.
Atchison, Rena Michaels. 1894. *Un-American immigration: Its present effects and future perils: A study from the census of 1890*. Chicago: Charles H. Kerr.
Bailey, Richard W. 1990. English at its twilight. In *The state of the language*, ed. Christopher Ricks and Leonard Michaels, 83–94. Berkeley: Univ. of California Press.
Baldensperger, Fernand. 1917. Une prédiction inédite sur l'avenir de la langue des Etats-Unis (Roland de la Platière, 1789). *Modern Philology* 15: 91–92.
Bancroft, Hubert Howe. 1889. *Works*, vol. 9. San Francisco: History Co.
Barnes, Earl. 1918. Spoken English as a factor in Americanization. *National Education Association Addresses and Proceedings* 56: 171–73.

Baron, Dennis E. 1981. Planning the American language: Federal English. *Language Problems and Language Planning* 5: 239–50.

———. 1982a. *Grammar and good taste: Reforming the American Language.* New Haven: Yale Univ. Press.

———. 1982b. *Going native: The regeneration of Saxon English.* Publication of the American Dialect Society 69. University, Ala.: Univ. of Alabama Press.

———. 1986. *Grammar and gender.* New Haven: Yale Univ. Press.

———. 1987. Federal English. *Brandeis Review* 6 (Spring): 18–21.

———. 1988. The English Language Amendment: Backgrounds and prospects. ERIC Document. Washington, D.C.: ERIC Clearinghouse on Languages and Linguistics, Center for Applied Linguistics.

———. 1989a. Going out of style? *English Today* 17 (January): 6–11.

———. 1989b. *Declining grammar and other essays on the English vocabulary.* Urbana, Ill.: National Council of Teachers of English.

Barrows, Sarah T. 1922. The foreign child and his speech handicap. *Education Review* 64: 367–76.

Bartel, Klaus J. 1976. German and the Germans at the time of the American Revolution. *Modern Language Journal* 60: 96–100.

Beer, William R., and James E. Jacob, eds. 1985. *Language policy and national unity.* Totowa, N.J.: Rowman and Allanheld.

Bennett, David H. 1988. *The party of fear: From nativist movements to the New Right in American history.* Chapel Hill: Univ. of North Carolina Press.

Black, Henry Campbell. 1891. *A dictionary of law.* St. Paul, Minn.: West Publishing Co.

Blackstone, William. [1765] 1803. *Commentaries on the laws of England.* Ed. St. George Tucker. Philadelphia.

Blaustein, Albert P., and Dana Blaustein Epstein. 1986. *Resolving language conflicts: A study of the world's constitutions.* Washington, D.C.: U.S. English.

Brissot de Warville, Jacques Pierre. 1791. *Nouveau voyage aux Etats-Unis de l'Amérique septentrionale.* Paris. 3 vols.

Bristed, Charles Astor. 1855. The English language in America. In *Cambridge essays, contributed by members of the University,* 57–78. London.

Brown, Everett Somerville. 1920. *The constitutional history of the Louisiana purchase, 1803–1812.* Berkeley: Univ. of California Press.

Burnside, Margaret. 1918. A good English drive. *English Journal* 7: 655–58.

Buruma, Ian. 1989 Behind the garden wall. *Times Literary Supplement* 28 April–4 May, 454, 458.

Califa, Antonio J. 1989. English-only laws would mean loss of rights. *Civil Liberties* 365 (January): 8.

California, State of. 1879. *Debates and proceedings of the constitutional convention*. Sacramento.

California Commission on Immigration and Housing. 1917. *A discussion of methods of teaching English to adult foreigners*. Sacramento: California State Printing Office.

―――. 1920. The immigrant and the state. In Philip Davis, *Immigration and Americanization: Selected readings*, 440–74. Boston: Ginn.

California Department of Education. 1932. *A guide for teachers of beginning non-English children*. Department of Education Bulletin no. 8.

Calvet, Louis-Jean. 1974. *Linguistique et colonialisme: Petit traité de glottophagie*. Paris: Payot.

―――. 1987. *La guerre des langues et les politiques linguistiques*. Paris: Payot.

Cardell, William S. 1822. *American Academy of Language and Belles Lettres Circular no. 3*. New York.

―――. 1825. *Essays on language*. New York.

Castellanos, Diego. 1983. *The best of two worlds: Bilingual-bicultural education in the U.S.* Trenton, N.J.: New Jersey State Department of Education.

Channing, Walter. 1815. Essay on American language and literature. *North American Review* 1: 307–14.

Chastellux, Marquis de. 1787. *Travels in North America*. London.

Christian, Jane Macnab, and Chester C. Christian, Jr. 1966. Spanish language and culture in the Southwest. In *Language loyalty in the United States: The maintenance and perpetuation of non-English mother tongues by American ethnic and religious groups*, ed. Joshua Fishman, 280–317. The Hague: Mouton.

Chung, Chuong Hoang. 1988. The language situation of Vietnamese Americans. In McKay and Wong, 276–92.

Clark, Lillian P. 1924. *Teaching our language to beginners*. Washington, D.C.: Government Printing Office.

―――. 1934. *Federal textbook of citizenship training*. Washington, D.C.: Government Printing Office.

Conklin, Nancy Faires, and Margaret A. Lourie. 1983. *A host of tongues*. New York: The Free Press.

Cooper, James Fenimore. 1838. *The American democrat*. Cooperstown, N.Y.

Crawford, James. 1989. *Bilingual education: History, politics, theory, and practice*. Trenton, N.J.: Crane Publishing.

Crystal, David. 1987. *The Cambridge encyclopedia of language*. Cambridge: Cambridge Univ. Press.

Dale, Charles V. 1985. Legal analysis of S. J. Res. 167 and H. J. Res 169 proposing an amendment to the U.S. Constitution to make English the official language of the United States. In *The English Language Amendment*, 32–35, 89–95.

Daughters of the American Revolution. [1920] 1934. *D.A.R. manual for citizenship*. Washington, D.C.: DAR.

Davis, Emma C. 1906. The teaching of English in the primary grades of the Cleveland public schools. National Society for the Scientific Study of Education Fifth Yearbook, part. 1: 66–75.

Education of the Immigrant. 1913. U.S. Bureau of Education Bulletin no. 51, pp. 1–52.

The English language amendment: Hearing before the subcommittee on the Constitution of the Committee on the Judiciary, U.S. Senate. 1985. Washington, D.C.: Government Printing Office.

English language constitutional amendments: Hearing before the subcommittee on Civil and Constitutional Rights of the Committee on the Judiciary, House of Representatives (May 11, 1988), serial no. 120. 1989. Washington, D.C.: Government Printing Office.

"English-only" rule prompts bias complaint. 1988. *Chronicle of Higher Education*, 20 July, p. A3.

Ethnic groups rip English rule for grocers. 1989. *The Champaign-Urbana News-Gazette*, 7 December, p. A8.

Fairchild, Henry Pratt. 1926. *The melting-pot mistake*. Boston: Little, Brown.

Faust, Albert Bernhardt. 1909. *The German element in the United States*. Boston: Houghton Mifflin.

Feer, Robert A. 1952. Official use of the German language in Pennsylvania. *Pennsylvania Magazine of History and Biography* 76: 394–405.

Ferguson, Charles A., and Shirley B. Heath, eds. 1981. *Language in the USA*. Cambridge: Cambridge Univ. Press.

Fichte, Johann Gottlieb. [1808] 1922. *Addresses to the German nation*. Trans. R. F. Jones and G. H. Turnbull. Chicago: Open Court Publishing Co.

Fishman, Joshua. 1988. "English only": Its ghosts, myths, and dangers. *International Journal of the Sociology of Language* 74: 125–40.

Fishman, Joshua, Michael H. Gertner, Esther G. Lowy, William G. Milan, et al. 1985. *The rise and fall of the ethnic revival: Perspectives on language and ethnicity*. Berlin: Mouton.

Fishman, Joshua, Vladimir C. Nahirny, John E. Hofman, Robert G. Hayden, et al. 1966. *Language loyalty in the United States: The maintenance and perpetuation of non-English mother tongues by American ethnic and religious groups*. The Hague: Mouton.

Fishman, Joshua A., and Vladimir C. Nahirny. 1966. The ethnic group school and mother tongue maintenance. In Fishman 1966, 92–126.

Flanders, Jesse Knowlton. 1925. *Legislative control of the elementary curriculum*. New York: Bureau of Publications, Teachers College, Columbia University.

Forbes, Susan S., and Peter Lemos. 1981. A history of American language policy. In Select Commission on Immigration and Refugee Policy, 97th Congress, 1st Session. *Staff report on U.S. immigration policy and the national interest*. Appendix A: 9–194. Committee Print.

Foreign Language Information Service. 1940. *Legal disabilities of aliens*. New York: FLIS.

Franklin, Benjamin. 1959–. *The papers of Benjamin Franklin*. Ed. Leonard W. Labaree. New Haven: Yale Univ. Press.

Franklin, George Frank. 1906. *The legislative history of naturalization in the United States: From the Revolutionary War to 1861*. Chicago: Univ. of Chicago Press.

Free, William J. 1968. *The Columbian Magazine and American literary nationalism*. The Hague: Mouton.

Gavit, John Palmer. 1922. *Americans by choice*. New York: Harper and Bros.

German emigration to America. 1820. *North American Review* 11: 1–19.

Gilbert, Glenn C. 1981. French and German: A comparative study. In Ferguson and Heath, 257–72.

Glazer, Nathan. 1966. The process and problems of language-maintenance: An integrative review. In Fishman 1966, 358–68 .

Goldberger, Henry H. 1920. Teaching English to the foreign born. U.S. Bureau of Education Bulletin no. 80. Washington, D.C.: Government Printing Office.

Gonzalez, Roseann Duenas, Victoria F. Vasquez, and John Bichsel. 1989. Language rights and Mexican Americans: Much ado about nothing. In *English language constitutional amendments*, 181–204.

Grant, Steven A. 1978. Language policy in the United States. *ADFL Bulletin* 9.4 (May): 1–12.

Greenblatt, Stephen J. 1976. Learning to curse: Aspects of linguistic colonialism in the sixteenth century. In *First images of America: The impact of the New World on the Old*, ed. Fredi Chiapelli, Michael J. B. Allen, and Robert L. Benson, vol. 2, 561–80. Berkeley: Univ. of California Press.

Greer, Colin. 1972. *The great school legend: A revisionist interpretation of American public school education*. New York: Basic Books.

Guitarte, Guillermo L., and Rafael Torres Quintero. 1968. Linguistic correctness and the role of the academies. In *Current Trends in Linguistics*, ed. Thomas A. Sebeok, vol. 4, 562–604. The Hague: Mouton.

Guy, Gregory R. 1989. International perspectives on linguistic diversity and language rights. In *English language constitutional amendments*, 153–58.

Hartford, Beverly, Albert Valdman, and Charles R. Foster, eds. 1982. *Issues in international bilingual education: The role of the vernacular.* New York: Plenum Press.

Hartmann, Edward G. 1948. *The movement to Americanize the immigrant.* New York: Columbia Univ. Press.

Heath, Shirley Brice. 1977. A national language academy? Debate in the new nation. *Linguistics* 189: 9–43.

———. 1981. English in our language heritage. In Ferguson and Heath, 6–20.

———. 1985. Language policies: Patterns of retention and maintenance. In *Mexican-Americans in comparative perspective*, ed. Weber Connor, 259–82. Washington, D.C.: The Urban Institute Press.

Heath, Shirley Brice, and Frederick Mandabach. 1978. Language status decisions and the law in the United States. In *Progress in language planning: International perspectives*, ed. Juan Cobarrubias and Joshua Fishman, 173–206. Berlin: Mouton.

Héraud, Guy. 1982. The status of languages in Europe. In Hartford, Valdman, and Foster, 241–63.

Herder, Johann Gottfried. [1772] 1966. *On the origin of language.* Trans. Alexander Gode. New York: Ungar.

Higham, John. 1966. *Strangers in the land: Patterns of American nativism: 1860–1925.* 2d ed. New York: Athenaeum.

Hirsch, E. D. 1987. *Cultural literacy: What every American needs to know.* Boston: Houghton Mifflin.

Howatt, Anthony P. R. 1984. *A history of English language teaching.* Oxford: Oxford Univ. Press.

Humboldt, Wilhelm von. [1836] 1988. *On language: The diversity of human language-structure and its influence on the mental development of mankind.* Trans. Peter Heath. Cambridge: Cambridge Univ. Press.

Hutchins, Rev. Joseph. [1787] 1806. Sermon preached in the Lutheran Church, on the opening of Franklin College, in the Borough of Lancaster, Pennsylvania, July 17, 1787. Philadelphia. [Shaw Shoemaker 10602]

Illinois, State of. 1920. *Constitution of the State of Illinois, Annotated.* Springfield: Legislative Reference Bureau.

———. 1920–1922. *Proceedings of the Constitutional Convention of the State of Illinois.* 5 vols. Springfield: Illinois State Journal Co.

Immigration Commission. 1911. *Report of the Immigration Commission.* Washington, D.C.: Government Printing Office.

Indiana, State of. 1919. *Laws of the State of Indiana.* Indianapolis: William R. Burford.

Inquiry into the official conduct of a judge of the Supreme Court of the Northwest Territory. 1796. *American State Papers.* 1834. Ser. 10, vol. 1., no. 89, pp. 151–52. Washington, D.C.

Insull, Samuel. 1919a. *Final report of the State Council of Defense of Illinois, 1917–1918–1919.* N.p.: State of Illinois.

———. 1919b. Speech to the Commercial Club of Chicago (Jan. 18). In *Illinois in the World War,* ed. Marguerite E. Jenison, vol. 6, 456–66. Springfield: Illinois State Historical Society, 1923.

Iowa, State of. 1919. *Acts and joint resolutions passed at the regular session of the thirty-eighth General Assembly of the state of Iowa.* Des Moines: State of Iowa.

Jacob, James E., and David C. Gordon. 1985. Language policy in France. In Beer and Jacob, 106–33.

James, Henry. 1906–1907. The speech of American women. *Harper's Bazar* 40: 979–82, 1103–06; 41: 17–21, 113–17.

Jefferson, Thomas. 1903. *Writings.* New York: G. P. Putnam's Sons.

Jensen, Joan. 1988. *Passage from India: Asian Indian immigrants in North America.* New Haven: Yale Univ. Press.

Judd, Elliot L. 1987. The English Language Amendment: A case study on language and politics. *TESOL Quarterly* 21: 113–35.

Kahane, Henry, and Renée Kahane. 1979. Decline and survival of Western prestige languages. *Language* 55: 183–98.

Kallen, Horace. 1924. *Culture and democracy in the United States.* New York: Boni and Liveright.

Kalm, Peter [Pehr]. [1937] 1966. *The America of 1750: Peter Kalm's travels in North America; the English version of 1770.* Rev. and ed. Adolph B. Benson. New York: Dover.

Kellogg, Louise Phelps. 1918. The Bennett Law in Wisconsin. *Wisconsin Magazine of History* 2: 3–25.

Kellor, Frances. 1920. *Immigration and the future.* New York: George H. Doran.

Kloss, Heinz. 1940. *Das Volksgruppenrecht in den Vereinigten Staaten von Amerika.* Essen: Essener Verlaganstalt. Vol. 1. (1942: vol 2.)

———. 1966. *Excerpts from the national minority laws of the United States of America.* Occasional Papers of Research Translations no. 16. Honolulu: East-West Center.

———. 1971. The language rights of immigrant groups. *International Migration Review* 5: 250–68.

_____. 1977. *The American bilingual tradition*. Rowley, Mass.: Newbury House.

Kohler, Max J. 1921. New test for voters. *New York Times* 23 October, sec. 7, pp. 2, 4.

Kučera, Daniel W. 1955. *Church-state relationships in education in Illinois*. Catholic University of America Educational Research Monographs 19, part 1. Washington, D.C.: Catholic Univ. of America Press.

Landry, Walter J. 1983. Future Lau regulations: Conflict between language rights and racial nondiscrimination. In *Theory, technology, and public policy on bilingual education*, ed. Raymond V. Padilla, 365–76. Rosslyn, Va.: National Clearinghouse for Bilingual Education.

Lape, Esther E. 1915. The "English First" movement in Detroit. *The Immigrants in America Review* 1.3 (September): 46–50.

Laws published in the German language. 1834. *American state papers*. Class X. Miscellaneous. Vol. 1. Washington, D.C.

Leibowitz, Arnold. 1969. English literacy: Legal sanction for discrimination. *Notre Dame Lawyer* 45: 7–67.

_____. 1971. *Educational policy and political acceptance: The imposition of English as the language of instruction in American schools.* ERIC Document 047 321. Arlington, Va.: ERIC Clearinghouse for Linguistics, Center for Applied Linguistics.

_____. 1976. Language and the law: The exercise of political power through official designation of language. In *Language and politics*, ed. William M. O'Barr and Jean F. O'Barr, 449–66. The Hague: Mouton.

_____. 1982. *Federal recognition of the rights of minority language groups*. Rosslyn, Va.: National Clearinghouse for Bilingual Education.

_____. 1984. The official character of the English language in the United States. *Aztlan* 15: 25–70.

Lemaire, Hervé B. 1966. Franco-American efforts in behalf of the French language in New England. In Fishman 1966, 253–79.

Le Page, R. B. 1964. *The national language question: Linguistic problems of newly independent states*. London: Oxford Univ. Press.

Levy, Jack. 1982. Policy implications/complications arising from native language attrition in U.S. ethnolinguistic minority groups. In *The loss of language skills*, ed. Richard D. Lambert and Barbara F. Freed, 191–201. Rowley, Mass: Newbury House.

Lewis, E. Glyn. 1972. *Multilingualism in the Soviet Union: Aspects of language policy and its implementation*. The Hague: Mouton.

Lieberson, Stanley. 1981. *Language diversity and language contact*. Stanford: Stanford Univ. Press.

Lindsay, Vachel. 1928. The real American language. *The American Mercury* 13: 257–65.

Literacy test wins in wild convention. 1915. *New York Times* 26 August, p. 5, col. 1.

Locke, John. [1690] 1694. *An essay concerning humane understanding.* 2d ed. London.

————. [1693] 1705. *Some thoughts concerning education.* 5th ed. London.

Louisiana, State of. [1814] 1844. *Journal des délibérations de la convention d'Orléans.* Jackson.

————. 1845. *Proceedings and debates of the convention of Louisiana.* New Orleans.

————. 1845. *Journal of the proceedings of the convention of Louisiana.* New Orleans.

————. 1861. *Official journal of the proceedings of the convention of the state of Louisiana.* New Orleans.

————. 1864. *Official journal of the proceedings of the convention for the revision and amendment of the constitution of the state of Louisiana.* New Orleans.

————. 1864. *Debates in the convention for the revision and amendment of the constitution of the state of Louisiana.* New Orleans.

Low, Victor. 1982. *The unimpressible race: A century of educational struggle by the Chinese in San Francisco.* San Francisco: East/West Publishing Co.

Luckey, G. W. A. 1919. Important changes in the Nebraska School Law. *Educational Review* 58 (September): 109–19.

Macías, Reynaldo F. 1979. Language choice and human rights in the United States. In *Language in public life,* ed. James Alatis and G. R. Tucker, 86–101. Georgetown University Round Table on Languages and Linguistics. Washington, D.C.: Georgetown Univ. Press.

Mackey, William F. 1983. U.S. language status policy and the Canadian experience. In *Progress in language planning: International perspectives,* ed. Juan Cobarrubias and Joshua Fishman, 173–206. Berlin: Mouton.

Mahoney, John J., and Charles M. Herlihy. 1918. *First steps in Americanization: A handbook for teachers.* Boston: Houghton Mifflin.

————. 1920. *Training teachers for Americanization.* U.S. Bureau of Education Bulletin no. 12. Washington, D.C.: Government Printing Office.

Mahoney, John J., and Charles M. Herlihy. 1918. *First steps in Americanization: a handbook for teachers.* Boston: Houghton Mifflin.

Marshall, David F. 1986. The question of an official language: Language rights and the English Language Amendment. *International Journal of the Sociology of Language* 60: 7–75.

_____. 1989. Federal language rights in the United States: A summary. In *English language constitutional amendments*, pp. 159–80.

Massachusetts Board of Education. 1916. *A course of study in English expression (1–6)*. Boston: Bulletin of the Board of Education no. 18.

McCormick, Washington Jay. 1923. Language by legislation. *The Nation* 116 (11 April), p. 408.

McKay, Sandra. 1988. Weighing educational alternatives. In McKay and Wong, 338–66.

McKay, Sandra Lee, and Sau-ling Cynthia Wong. 1988. *Language diversity: Problem or resource?* New York: Newbury House.

Martin-Jones, Marilyn. 1984. The newer minorities: Literacy and educational issues. In *Language in the British Isles*, ed. Peter Trudgill, 425–48. Cambridge: Cambridge Univ. Press.

Michaelis, Johann David. [1759] 1769. *A dissertation on the influence of opinions on language and of language on opinions*. London.

Miller, Herbert Adolphus. 1916. *The school and the immigrant*. Cleveland: The Survey Committee of the Cleveland Foundation.

Milroy, James, and Lesley Milroy. 1985. *Authority in language: Investigating language prescription and standardisation*. London: Routledge and Kegan Paul.

Molesky, Jean. 1988. Understanding the American linguistic mosaic: A historical overview of language maintenance and language shift. In McKay and Wong, 29–68.

Monahan, Jane. 1989. Plan for foreign-language teaching approved by European Community. *The Chronicle of Higher Education* 5 July, pp. A29, 32.

Morgan, Thomas J. N.d. *Indian Education* N.p.

Native American Association. 1838. Memorial to Congress. U.S. Serials 325, no. 98.

Nebraska, State of. 1919. *Sessions Laws*. Lincoln.

_____. 1921. *Sessions Laws*. Lincoln.

New Mexico, State of. 1910. *Proceedings of the constitutional convention of the proposed state of New Mexico*. Albuquerque: Press of the Morning Journal.

_____. 1911. *Annotated constitution and enabling act of the state of New Mexico*. Santa Fe: Arthur G. Whittier.

_____. 1912, 1915, 1917, 1941. *Laws of the State of New Mexico*. Albuquerque: Albright and Anderson.

New York City Department of Education. 1918. *Foreign accent: A supplement to the syllabus in English*. New York.

New York State. 1916. *Revised record of the constitutional convention of the State of New York, April sixth to September tenth, 1915*. Albany: J. B. Lyon.

————. 1918, 1919. *Laws of the State of New York.* Albany: J. B. Lyon.

————. 1919. *Oral English.* Albany: Univ. of the State of New York.

Newbolt, Henry. 1921. *The teaching of English in England.* London: HMSO.

Newman, Edwin. 1974. *Strictly speaking: Will America be the death of English?* Indianapolis: Bobbs-Merrill.

Ohio, State of. 1919. *Legislative acts passed and joint resolutions adopted by the eighty-third General Assembly.* Springfield: Springfield Publishing Co.

Oregon, State of. 1920, 1921. *The general laws.* Salem: State Printing Department.

Osuna, Juan José. 1949. *A history of education in Puerto Rico.* Rio Piedras, P.R.: Editorial de la Universidad de Puerto Rico.

Padín, José. 1916. *The problem of teaching English to the people of Porto Rico.* San Juan, P.R.: Porto Rico Department of Education Bulletin no. 1.

Paulston, Christina Bratt. 1981. Bilingualism and education. In Ferguson and Heath, pp. 469–85.

————. 1986. Linguistic consequences of ethnicity and nationalism in multi-lingual settings. In Spolsky, 117–52.

Pennsylvania. 1837. *Proceedings and debates of the convention of the commonwealth of Pennsylvania to propose amendments to the constitution.* Harrisburg.

Poplack, Shana. 1982. Bilingualism and the vernacular. In *Issues in international bilingual education: The role of the vernacular,* ed. Beverly Hartford, Albert Valdman, and Charles R. Foster, 1–23. New York: Plenum Press.

Quirk, Randolph. 1990. Further thoughts: Sound barriers—ten years on. In *The state of the language,* ed. Christopher Ricks and Leonard Michaels, pp. 79–82. Berkeley: Univ. of California Press.

Read, Allen Walker. 1933. British recognition of American speech in the eighteenth century. *Dialect Notes* 6: 313–34.

Reaman, George Elmore. 1921. The new citizen: Modern language instruction: A method of teaching English to foreigners. Ph.D. diss., Cornell Univ.

Report of the Secretary of the Interior (Franklin K. Lane). 1918. *Reports of the Department of the Interior for the fiscal year ended June 30, 1918.* Vol. 1. Washington, D.C.: Government Printing Office.

Report on Indian Education. 1976. Washington, D.C.: Government Printing Office.

Robbins, Katharine Knowles. 1918. The work of the American speech committee of the Chicago Woman's Club, and notes upon its school survey. *English Journal* 7: 163–76.

Roberts, Peter. [1912] 1918. *English for coming Americans: teacher's manual*. New York: Association Press.

———. 1920. *The problem of Americanization*. New York: Macmillan.

Rodriguez, Richard. 1982. *Hunger of memory: The education of Richard Rodriguez*. Boston: David R. Godine.

Roosevelt, Franklin D. 1941. On the importance of teaching the English language in Puerto Rico. Speech delivered on 17 April 1937. *The public papers of Franklin D. Roosevelt*. Vol. 6, pp. 160–161. New York: Random House.

Ruppenthal, J. C. 1919. The legal status of the English language in the American school system. *School and Society* 10: 658–66.

Rush, Benjamin. 1787. Strictures on the pedantic phraseology of the medical faculty, with plain botanical observations on several American plants. *The Columbian Magazine* 1: 805–08.

———. 1951. *Letters of Benjamin Rush*. Ed. L. H. Butterfield. Princeton: Princeton Univ. Press and the American Philosophical Society.

Shanahan, Daniel. 1989. We need a nationwide effort to encourage, enhance, and expand our students' proficiency in languages. *Chronicle of Higher Education* 21 May, p. A40.

Shedd, W. G. T. 1848. The relation of language to thought. *Biblia Sacra* 5: 650–63.

Simon, John. 1980. *Paradigms lost*. New York: Clarkson N. Potter.

Simon, Paul. 1980. *The tongue-tied American: Confronting the foreign language crisis*. New York: Continuum.

Simpson, David. 1986. *The politics of American English, 1776–1850*. New York: Oxford Univ. Press.

Skutnabb-Kangas, Tove. 1984. *Bilingualism or not: The education of minorities*. Clevedon, England: Multilingual Matters.

Smith, Horace Wemyss. 1879. *Life and correspondence of the Rev. William Smith, D.D.* Philadelphia. 2 vols.

Smith, William. 1755. *A brief state of the province of Pennsylvania*. London.

———. 1756. *A brief view of the conduct of Pennsylvania, for the year 1755*. London.

Smolicz, J. J. 1986. National language policy in the Philippines. In Spolsky, 96–116.

Spolsky, Bernard, ed. 1986. *Language and education in multilingual settings*. San Diego: College-Hill Press.

Steiner, Edward A. 1914. *From alien to citizen*. New York: Fleming H. Revell.

———. 1916a. *The confession of a hyphenated American*. New York: Fleming H. Revell.

————. 1916b. *Nationalizing America*. New York: Fleming H. Revell.

Stowe, Calvin Ellis. 1838. *Report on elementary public instruction in Europe*. Harrisburg, Pa.

Thernstrom, Abigail. 1980. Language: Issues and legislation. In *Harvard encyclopedia of American ethnic groups*, ed. Stephen Thernstrom, 619–29. Cambridge: Harvard Univ. Press.

Thompson, Frank V. 1920. *Schooling the immigrant*. New York: Harper and Bros.

Thompson, Richard T. 1982. Implications of language attrition research for national language policy. In Richard D. Lambert and Barbara F. Freed, eds., *The loss of language skills*, 202–06. Rowley, Mass.: Newbury House.

Tibbetts, Arnold, and Charlene Tibbetts. 1978. *What's happening to American English?* New York: Charles Scribner's.

de Tocqueville, Alexis. [1835] 1945. *Democracy in America*. New York: Alfred A. Knopf. 2 vols.

Twitchell, Ralph Emerson. 1912. *The leading facts of New Mexican history*. Cedar Rapids, Iowa: The Torch Press.

United States Congress. 1849. *Annals of the Congress of the United States*. Washington, D.C.

United States House of Representatives. 1826. *Journal of the House of Representatives*. Washington, D.C.

————. 1850. *Journal of the 1849 Convention*. U.S. Serials 581, House misc. doc. 39.

————. 1876. New Mexico. U.S. Serials 1710, House rpt. 503, part 2.

————. 1888. Admission of Dakota, Montana, Washington, and New Mexico into the Union. U.S. Serials 2601, House rpt. 1025.

————. 1892. Admission of New Mexico. U.S. Serials 3044, House rpt. 736.

————. 1911. Report on the Constitutions of New Mexico and Arizona. U.S. Serials 6078, House rpt. 33.

————. [1794–95] 1977. *The journal of the House of Representatives*. 3d Congress, 1st and 2d Sessions; vols. 6–7. Rpt. Wilmington, Del.: Michael Glazier.

United States Senate. 1869. A request from New Mexico for raises for official translators. U.S. Serials 1361, Sen. misc. doc. 28.

————. 1902. *Hearings before the subcommittee of the Committee on Territories on HB 12543*. U.S. Serials 4420, Sen. doc. 36.

————. 1902. *Report of the Committee on Territories on the new statehood bill*. U.S. Serials 4410, Senate rpt. 2206.

————. 1910. Report on an act enabling the people of New Mexico and

Arizona to form a constitution and state government. U.S. Serials 5583, Sen. rpt. 454.

Veltman, Calvin. 1983. *Language shift in the United States*. Berlin: Mouton, Walter de Gruyter.

Von Hagen, Victor Wolfgang. 1976. *The Germanic people in America*. Norman: Univ. of Oklahoma Press.

Waggoner, Dorothy. 1988. Language minorities in the United States in the 1980s: The evidence from the 1980 census. In McKay and Wong, 69–108.

Wardhaugh, Ronald. 1987. *Languages in competition: Dominance, diversity, and decline*. Oxford: Blackwell.

Weber, Eugen. 1976. *Peasants into Frenchmen: The modernization of rural France, 1870–1914*. Stanford: Stanford Univ. Press.

Weber, Samuel Edwin. 1905. *The charity school movement in colonial Pennsylvania*. Philadelphia: William J. Campbell.

Webster, Noah. 1783. *Grammatical Institute of the English Language*. Hartford.

———. 1789. *Dissertations on the English language*. Boston.

———. 1790. On the education of youth in America. In *A collection of essays and fugitiv writings*. Boston.

———. 1831. Letter to Rebecca Greenleaf Webster, 16 February. In *Letters of Noah Webster*, ed. Harry R. Warfel, p. 426. New York: Library Publishers.

Weightman, John. 1988 Francophony in trouble. *Times Literary Supplement* 1–7 April, 355.

Whitman, Walt. 1856. America's mightiest inheritance. *Life Illustrated* 1, n.s. no. 24 (12 April): 185–86.

———. 1904. *An American primer*. Ed. Horace Traubel. Boston: Small, Maynard.

Whitney, Parkhurst. 1923. They want to know what their children are saying. *Colliers* 72 (14 July): 13, 21.

Wilkins, John. 1668. *An essay towards a real character and a philosophical language*. London.

Wright, Guy. 1986. Let's teach English. *San Francisco Chronicle* 23 November. In McKay and Wong 1988, 362–63.

Index

217